Data Processing

T F FRY ACMA, MBIM, MIDPM, FRSA
Formerly Head of Department of Business & Secretarial Studies
Cassio College, Watford, England

Butterworths
London · Boston
Durban · Singapore · Sydney · Toronto · Wellington

All rights reserved. No part of this publication may be reproduced or transmitted in any form or by any means, including photocopying and recording, without the written permission of the copyright holder, applications for which should be addressed to the Publishers. Such written permission must also be obtained before any part of this publication is stored in a retrieval system of any nature.

This book is sold subject to the Standard Conditions of Sale of Net Books and may not be re-sold in the UK below the net price given by the Publishers in their current price list.

First published, 1983

© T F Fry, 1983

British Library Cataloguing in Publication Data

Fry, T. F.
  Data processing.
  1. Business—Data processing
  I. Title
  001.6′02465   HF5548.2

  ISBN 0-408-01171-8

Library of Congress Cataloging in Publication Data

Fry, T. F. (Thomas Frederick)
  Data processing.

  Includes index.
  1. Electronic data processing.   2. Electronic digital
    computers.
  I. Title.
  QA76.F78   1984   001.64   83-13296

  ISBN 0-408-01171-8

Typeset by Phoenix Photosetting, Chatham
Printed in England by Page Bros Ltd., Norwich, Norfolk

Contents

PART	1 DATA PROCESSING PRINCIPLES	1
Chapter 1	INTRODUCING DATA	3
Chapter 2	DATA: SOME CHARACTERISTICS	15
Chapter 3	DATA PROCESSING SYSTEMS	27
Chapter 4	DATA PROCESSING METHODS	43

PART	2 DATA PROCESSING PRACTICE	49
Chapter 5	INTRODUCING COMPUTERS	51
Chapter 6	REPRESENTING DATA IN A COMPUTER	63
Chapter 7	DATA INPUT	73
Chapter 8	OUTPUT	91
Chapter 9	COMPUTER STORAGE	101
Chapter 10	PROCESSING BY COMPUTER	132
Chapter 11	PROCESSING MODES	140

PART	3 SYSTEMS AND SOFTWARE	153
Chapter 12	THE COMPUTER DATA PROCESSING SYSTEM	155
Chapter 13	CHECKS AND CONTROLS	175
Chapter 14	COMPUTER LANGUAGES AND PROGRAMS	185
Chapter 15	PROGRAM ELEMENTS AND STRUCTURES: DEVELOPING A PROGRAM	200
Chapter 16	ORGANIZATION OF A DATA PROCESSING DEPARTMENT	213
Chapter 17	EXAMPLES	230

INDEX 247

PART 1
Data processing principles

Chapter 1
Introducing data

In 1754 a craftsman, M. Carpenter, made a dining table. He worked alone in a shed attached to his cottage, using timber he had cut from a tree felled some three years previously and left to weather in his garden. He sold the table to a local farmer living in the outskirts of his village and then made two written entries to record the sale—by adding the name of the farmer to the list of tables he had sold that year and by recording that he had received 15s. 9d. from the farmer in payment.

In 1983 a farmer visited his nearest town and from a furniture shop in the High Street purchased a table for use in his dining room. He paid for it by using a bank credit card. The total number of written entries relating in one way or another to the manufacture and sale of this table amounted to 295. These included entries recording the felling and processing of the timber in a plantation and sawmill in Canada; import and export documentation; entries relating to the manufacture of the table in a factory in the north of England, to its sale and delivery to a wholesale distributor in the Midlands and to its subsequent sale and delivery to the High Street shop from which it was purchased by its final owner. A further series of entries was made over the following few months as payment was made by instalments through the bank credit system.

Perhaps this simple illustration will help to highlight a few points:

(1) The dramatic increase in the volume of records generated as industrial and commercial activities have developed over the years, becoming, in the process, very much more complex.

(2) The need to devise formal routines, procedures and systems as a framework within which this mass of records can be effectively recorded and dealt with.

(3) That it has become impractical to cope with all these records by solely manual means and that recourse has been had to a range of mathematical and machine aids.

(4) The dependence of society generally in all its varied areas of

4 Introducing data

activity upon the information provided through these records for the effective performance of all of the activities and relationships with which we are involved today.

Recognising these points, this book has the following aims in view: to examine how and why these records originate, and how they can be organised and marshalled to provide the information essential to the successful running of the activities to which they relate; also to identify patterns through which this can be accomplished and to review techniques for ensuring the continued accuracy of the records being handled; furthermore, to discuss how mechanical and other aids of one type or another can be used to help in these processes.

Before enlarging on these points, it would, perhaps, be best to note and explain some of the terms we shall be using throughout this book.

Data

'Data' is the term given to all the facts and figures that are generated by and that record an event, an activity or a situation. As isolated facts and figures they may not be meaningful in themselves, but they can be marshalled and processed in various specific ways in order to give them a useful meaning.

Now, the simplest of our activities can produce facts—items of data—relating to it. If, for instance, we walk down to our local shop, two of the data items generated could well be: (1) the distance we have walked, (2) the time taken to walk this distance. As isolated items of data these may mean very little to us, but if we wanted information on the total distance walked during a week in order to see whether we had met a predetermined target for our quota of exercise over the period, then by adding item (1) to data collected from other walks we had taken we would finish up with information that would enable us to make a judgement on the effectiveness of our exercise programme and, indeed, could well influence our future actions by, perhaps, leading us to a decision to take a longer walk tomorrow. Also, should we be aiming to achieve a given walking speed in miles per hour, then by relating these two items of data we could compute the speed at which we had walked and so produce information to compare with our target.

To apply this argument to a commercial situation, if we were concerned in making the table mentioned earlier, we might well finish up with the following items of data:

(1) Eight 2 m lengths of timber were used, each 30 cm × 3 cm, and four 1 m lengths, each 12 cm square.
(2) The cost of the timber is £2.75 and £3.50 per metre, respectively.
(3) A. Carpenter worked for seven hours making the table.
(4) A. Carpenter was paid at a rate of £2.25 per hour.

Each of these data items as it stands means very little. To convert them into useful information it becomes necessary to subject them to various processes—for example, to associate the quantity of each type of timber used with its unit price and then to carry out a calculation by multiplying to find the cost of the timber used. The application of these processes to data is called *data processing*.

Data processing

Data processing embraces the techniques of sorting, relating, interpreting and computing items of data in order to provide meaningful and useful information. For example, the above data items when suitably processed would provide the information that the direct material cost of the table was £44.00, that the direct labour cost was £15.75 and that the total direct costs of making the table were therefore £59.75.

However, it will be evident that to arrive at these figures the data must be processed according to predefined procedures and rules arranged in a specific order. It would, for instance, be pointless to add the number of lengths of timber to the number of hours worked—the answer would be a nonsense. We first have to relate the length of a piece of timber to the number of pieces used and then compute the total quantity for each type of timber; this, in turn, must be related to the metre cost; and so on. In other words, we must work to a series of defined logical steps designed to give the result we are looking for.

Data processing system

The term 'data processing system' relates to an assembly of these steps in logical order, defining the instructions and procedures that must be applied to the data items at each stage so as to obtain the useful and meaningful information the system is designed to produce. Essential features in such a specification would be the identification of data items that have to be associated with each other, the specification of calculations that have to be made, and showing how the resultant computations should be marshalled together and how the final results should be presented.

Information

Perhaps, at this stage, it would be best to look at information from two points of view. On the one hand, information can be said to be the product of a data processing system. As we saw above, by processing items of data generated by an activity according to defined rules, useful information can be obtained. On the other hand, information can also be regarded as an essential requirement to the pursuance of an activity. Doubtless, before the table we have been discussing was produced, it was necessary to provide some information regarding its design and structure—probably in the form of a technical specification. We can see in all of this a cyclical process (Fig. 1.1): an activity generates data; data items are subjected to defined rules and procedures known as data processing; data processing produces useful information; and this information, in turn, controls, influences or determines the activity.

Another rather arbitrary distinction we can make at this stage between two categories of information is as follows:

Operating information consists of information needed for and produced by the day-to-day running of a business. For example, information produced from data relating to the table mentioned above could take the form of an invoice to be sent to the purchaser of the table.

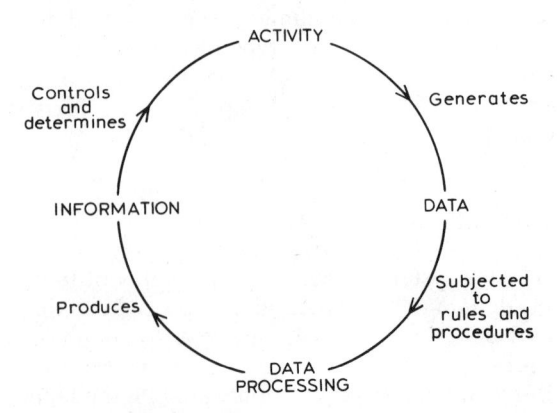

Fig. 1.1. The cyclical process

Management information is the information accruing from a data processing system and made available to management upon which decisions can be based relating to the overall conduct of the business. It may, for instance, include the total value of all the tables sold over a period of time, to enable profitability to be assessed and decisions arrived at to guide manufacturing activity.

At this point we can enlarge a little on the four points made earlier in this chapter, the first of which was connected with the volume of data.

Data: where from?

It will be evident that as the range and complexity of the activities with which mankind is involved have increased, so the volume and complexity of data generated by these activities have similarly increased. Some of the main areas in which, over the years, a dramatic escalation has taken place are now listed.

Personal data. In early years little or no recorded data existed on individuals. Identities were a matter of only local concern, with names often associated with the trade people pursued. By and large, trading activities were limited to the exchange of goods on a barter basis. As society developed, an ever-increasing range and volume of data relating to people, their possessions and their activities became necessary. An early example of this was the compilation 900 years ago of the Domesday Book, containing data resulting from a nationwide survey of land ownership. From the first rudimentary data held on people—formal names and addresses, birth and death dates, etc.—record keeping has progressed until today the list of the aspects of our lives on which data records are held is almost endless: income tax records, health records, employment records, motor tax records, insurance records, to name but a few.

Business and trading data. We have already noted that the earliest form of trading—barter—generated little or no recorded data. However, each subsequent development in industrial, trading and business activity brought in its wake more and more records. The introduction of currency led to the keeping of data on commodity values expressed in currency, as well as records of the flow of currency in and out of a business. Credit trading further expanded the range of data records, with the need to keep account of debtors and creditors, and eventually comprehensive bookkeeping systems appeared. As businesses grew in size and complexity, the importance of effective management skills became apparent, and with information the basic tool for exercising these skills, the generation and processing of data on all aspects of business activity became essential.

Technical and scientific data. Starting off with the need to record accurate measurements of physical properties (sizes, weights, volumes, etc.), invention and innovation in these areas has progressed at an ever-accelerating rate. Not only has this resulted in a dramatic increase in the range and, therefore, the choice of available products and processes, but also it has carried with it the need for increasingly complex specification. For example, the volume of data relating to a penny-farthing cycle of 80 years ago bears no comparison with that generated in the design and manufacture of an aircraft jet engine today.

Legislative data. Again, the past century or two has seen a vast increase in the volume of data called for by both central and local government from both individuals and businesses. Some well-known categories are census records, voting register records, income tax records, police records, etc.

All in all, when we compare today's businesses with those of only 100–200 years ago, we find an almost phenomenal increase in the amount of data that is generated and has to be stored and processed both for internal administration and to meet external demands.

Data: types of record

If we take an overall look at the records with which a business will be concerned, it is possible to break them down into a number of fairly well-defined categories (Fig. 1.2) as follows:

(1) Those flowing into the organisation from external sources, such as purchase invoices, delivery notes and cash receipts.
(2) Records generated by the day-by-day internal activities of the business—for example, the amount of material used on a specific job, the number of hours taken to accomplish a given task or the cost of heating an office.
(3) Permanent or semi-permanent records needed for reference

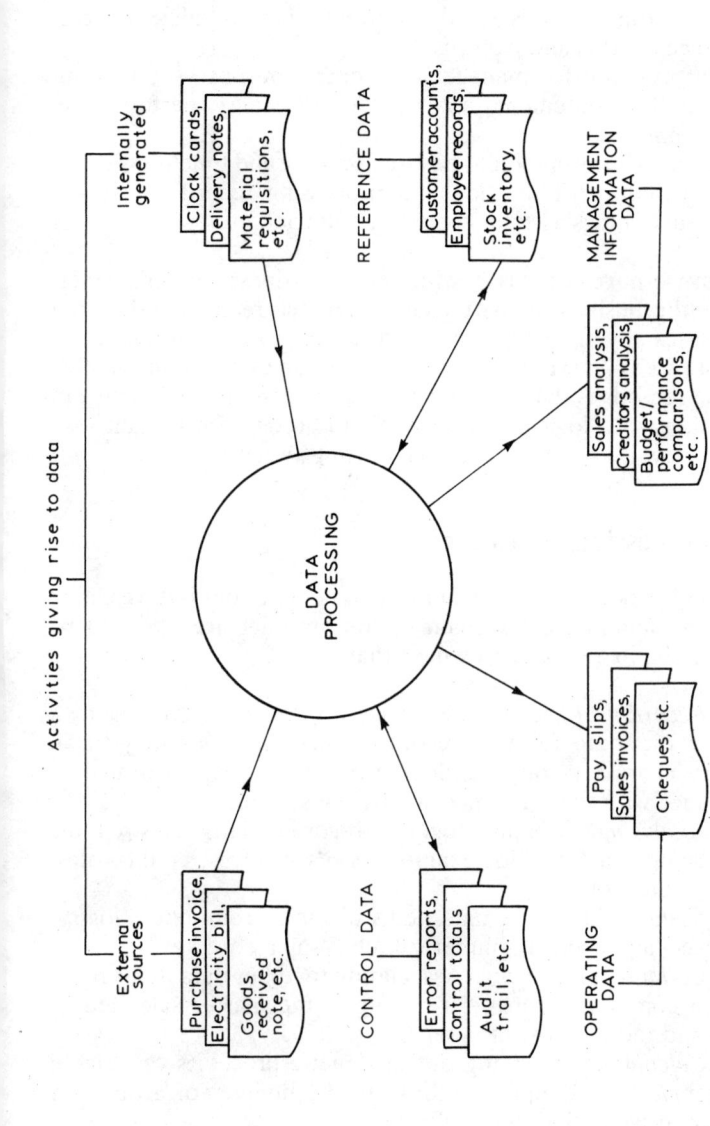

Fig. 1.2. Types of data

purposes, of which customer accounts, employee records and price lists are examples.

(4) Operating records for distribution, such as sales invoices, remittance advices and payslips.

(5) Information for management control purposes—for example, cash flow statement, analysis of total sales, performance/budget comparisons.

(6) Control information to ensure accuracy and timeliness of the whole procedure of keeping and processing records. This will include such things as error reports, audit trial, etc.

Thus, we have records flowing into a business, records generated by the business activity itself, reference records and output records (usually known as reports) resulting from an interaction of the first three. As we have seen, the mechanics of the interaction of these records is data processing and the assembly of the list of instructions in a logical format that will accomplish the aims we have in view is known as a *data processing system*.

Data processing operations

We shall be looking at these in more detail later on, but we can at this point summarise the main operations that are likely to be encountered in a data processing situation.

(a) *Recording*. The process of *writing* the data relating to a situation on some form of recording medium. This may be in ordinary characters or in coded form. It will be performed in accordance with the rules specified by the system.

(b) *Analysing*. Grouping together recorded data items relating to the same function—for example, sales invoices, credit notes, delivery notes, etc.

(c) *Sorting*. Arranging data items within a group into a logical sequence—alphabetical, numerical, etc.—by record key.

(d) *Collating or merging*. Associating together data items relating to a common record—for example, the master sales ledger record and the sales invoices relating to it.

(e) *Calculating*. Carrying out arithmetic processes on related data items—for example, multiplying the number of articles by their unit price to find the total value.

(f) *Comparing*. Testing one data item against another in order to determine a course of action—for example, comparing actual stock with minimum stock level to decide whether to reorder.

(g) *Matching.* The process of checking that the identifying elements in related data items are identical.

(h) *Verifying.* Checking to verify the accuracy of recorded data, calculations, etc.

(i) *Filing.* Storing data records for future reference in a logical or known sequence so that they can be readily located.

(j) *Retrieval.* The process of selecting and extracting data records from file that are required for use in the processing routine.

(k) *Updating.* The process of keeping master data records up to date by the application of movement data items.

(l) *Rearranging.* Assembling data records in the order and the pattern required for any particular purpose such as output reports.

(m) *Communicating.* The process of preparing output records in a manner that will be understandable to the user.

(n) *File maintenance.* The deletion of records no longer required and the insertion of new.

Data recording and processing in practice

How these types of data record (1–6 above) and these basic data processing operations (a–m above) work out in practice can be illustrated by the following example.

Say you were to start up in business on your own as a mechanic repairing cars. On an approach by a prospective customer you would prepare an estimate for the job and then, on its acceptance, would carry out the work, presenting your customer with an invoice for payment on its completion.

Before starting work you will obviously have to buy in a few supplies—say motor oil, a few commonly used spare parts, some cleaning materials, etc. Records you will receive as a result of these purchases are delivery notes and purchase invoices (1). At this point you may decide to keep a record of the supplies you have received—for example, the number of litres of oil delivered, the cost per litre, and the name and address of the supplier (3). You will probably use a separate piece of paper for each product, keeping the papers together in a folder as a file (n). In fact, you may decide to open files for the delivery notes and the invoices as well (b). Within these files you will keep the records in alphabetical order to facilitate easy reference (c, i).

While working on the job, you will keep a record (a) of the time spent on it (hours worked) and a list of the materials used (2), adding the customer's name to each entry to identify the job. On completion of the job you will want to work out how much it has cost you.

To do this you may prepare a cost sheet bringing together all of the items of cost (d), checking as you do so that the same customer name appears against each item (g). You will now evaluate these items of cost, retrieving from your file (j) the prices of the materials and noting these down on the cost sheet and also the hourly rate you are going to charge for your labour. Next some calculations will have to be carried out involving multiplying the quantities by their unit price (e). The sum of the products will then give you the total cost.

Having done all this, in order to be on the safe side, you could well check that every record made during the job's progress has been dealt with, check that you have used the correct prices and also check that the calculations have been carried out correctly (h).

Two other things you may do at this point. You may look up on your file the original estimate and compare this with the total cost you have just arrived at (f). This will give you some idea of the effectiveness both of your estimating procedure and of the job performance. You may also at this point check the balance of, say, the motor oil that remains in stock and review this against the quantity you know you are going to need to see you through to the next delivery (f) and so decide whether you should now place another order for a fresh supply.

With the total cost now known and with reference to your estimate, you will now be able to assemble together (l) the information required to prepare an invoice (4) for presentation to your customer, typing or writing it in a way that can be understood (m).

Inasmuch as your customer will now owe you some money, you will doubtless want to keep an account of what is owed; indeed, you will also want to keep records of money you owe to your suppliers. On sending the invoice to your customer, you will post the amount to his account, adding it to any balance already outstanding and so bringing the account up to date (k).

Periodically, perhaps once a month, you will want to review your business activities. You could do this by arranging and analysing the records you have kept so as to show the total turnover and profitability of the different categories of work you have been engaged in (l), such as repainting, mechanical repairs, servicing, etc. You may use this information to arrive at decisions (5) to discontinue servicing because this is unprofitable and to concentrate in future on repainting jobs because it is in this area that your profit level is highest.

Finally, during the whole of this process of recording facts and figures you will want to monitor that work is keeping up to schedule and that all your records are kept up to date and are accurate—for example, by checking the accuracy of invoices received for supplies and notifying your supplier of any discrepancies (6).

Data processing methods

In the example given above we have assumed that all operations were carried out manually. Of course, in practice, this is seldom the case. As we saw earlier, the volume of records flowing through an organisation is usually so great that mathematical and machine aids of one kind or another have to be relied upon to deal with them. These devices will be reviewed in some detail later on, but the main agencies through which data are processed are summarised below. It would, of course, be wrong to assume that only one of these is used exclusively in any specific data processing situation. In practice elements of them all could well be present.

Manual processing involves the use of mainly handwritten or typewritten records but will usually incorporate the use of ready reckoners, slide rules, calculators, etc., as aids to performing arithmetic.

Mechanical aids. This term generally means the use of mechanical or electromechanical devices such as accounting machines, punched cards, keyboard entry devices, etc.

Electronic aids. This term covers the whole range of electronic computers and calculating devices.

While the data processing operations listed earlier are common to all of these methods, it will be evident that the use of machines, particularly computers, will involve some additional operations, such as:

The *preparation of data* in a form that can be accepted by and worked on by the machine.

The imposition of a comprehensive set of *controls* and *checks* to ensure the accuracy of data items while they are being processed and also that the machines used are functioning properly.

Assembling and communicating to the machine a logical sequence of instructions—a *program*—that will specify the functions it must perform in order to carry out the processing operations required.

Exercises

1.1. Your company manufactures kitchen furniture, purchasing its supplies of raw materials from outside contractors. Suggest: (a) four items of data you would expect to receive from your contractors in respect of purchases made from them; (b) four items of data that would be generated by the internal activity of your company and that would be used to prepare a bill for one of your customers.

1.2. Enumerate the main operations that are likely to be encountered in a system designed for processing data.

1.3. Give an account of any procedure you are familiar with in your everyday life that involves (a) the capture of original data, (b) reference to stored data and (c) arithmetic calculations.

1.4. Each day you make a note of the newspapers delivered to your house and at the end of each week calculate how much you owe your newsagent. Show, in the form of a list of instructions, everything that needs to be done to prepare an accurate statement of what you owe.

1.5. Make a list of the main elements you will find in any data processing situation.

1.6. 'The data arising from activities in your business can in turn be used to control or modify the activities themselves.' Explain this statement, quoting in your answer examples of the type of information you would expect your data processing system to produce in order to accomplish this.

Chapter 2
Data: some characteristics

It could be said that data are the raw material of a data processing system. They consist of the facts and figures that record in detail the many and varied activities with which we are associated. A data item, on its own, however, means very little unless it is related to other items of data and interpreted within the context of the system as a whole. The aim of data processing is to relate and interpret items of data to provide meaningful information in the form of output records.

To enable these processes to take place effectively, certain characteristics possessed by data must be examined in order to determine how the data items are to be handled, how they can be identified and how they should be processed.

With this in mind, this chapter is concerned with:

The structure of data records
Types of data record
The identification of data
The origination of data
The capture of data
The storage of data

To examine these points, we shall start with a fairly simple data record that is likely to be found in any accounting system:

    4972   A.T. Smith, 24 West Street, Newtown   £163.00
(Account (Customer name and address)   (Debtor
number)   balance
                                                                              outstanding)

Structure of data

If we examine this record we find it made up entirely of a series of digits, letters and symbols. Each of these we can call a *character*, which is the smallest indivisible unit in the record. We can further note that these characters are grouped together, each representing a discrete item of data. For example, the account number with four digits, the customer name with ten letters and symbols. Each of these groups of characters we refer to as a *data field*. The whole statement, consisting of a number of data fields, is known as a *data record*. If we had a number of similar records all of which gave customer details and balance outstanding, we would then have a *file*. In this case we would describe it as a sales ledger file (Fig. 2.1).

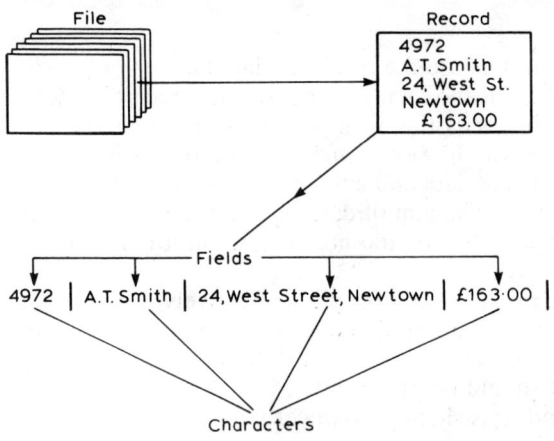

Fig. 2.1. Structure of data

Now, while this structure is patently obvious in a written record which we can see and read, its significance becomes far more important when we are dealing with records that are processed by machine, in which, as we shall see later on, characters are not stored as digits and letters but as magnetic fields or electronic pulses. The problem of grouping characters into fields and records then becomes far more complex.

Types of data

If we look at the record from another angle, we can identify two categories of data.

First, the part which identifies the customer account number, name and address, and is purely *descriptive* by nature. These are data we would not expect to change very frequently; in fact, unless the customer changes his name or address, they will always remain the same. This quality gives rise to data of this type being often referred to as static.

Types of data 17

The second element is the *quantitative* part, the balance outstanding, which we would expect to change quite frequently as a result of trading activities with the customer. This element is often known as dynamic data, since it is constantly being changed to provide a statement of the current situation. For example, assuming the above statement to represent the position at the beginning of the month, if during the month further goods were sold to A.T. Smith:

  4972 A.T. Smith Sales £250.00

then the original record will have to be amended to show a revised balance of £413.00.

This means that in data processing we are concerned with data records of two main kinds. On the one hand, there are the records which contain static descriptive data which remain unchanged for a long period of time and give an up-to-date statement of quantitative values. This type of record is known as a *master record*. On the other hand, there are records relating to the periodic changes in values resulting from current activity such as the sale of goods mentioned above. These are known as *movement records*. We would refer to a collection of similar records as a *master file* and a *movements file* (sometimes known as a *transactions file*), respectively.

Now, there exists an interaction between these two types of record—a data processing procedure—which we call *updating*. This means that the master record and the movement records are brought together by comparing and matching elements of descriptive data and the quantitative element of the movement record is used to amend—or update—the quantitative element contained in the master record. In practice, it is probable not only that this amendment to the balance takes place, but also that the details of the movement records are added to the master record so as to provide a history of transactions over a period of time (Fig. 2.2).

It was mentioned earlier that the descriptive part of the master record was likely to remain unchanged for a long period of time. However, from time to time alterations will be necessary—change of address, for example—and also from time to time it will be necessary to delete some records from the file for customers no longer trading with us and to add new customer details. These are known as *changes* and a collection of such items is known as a *changes file*. These change records are applied to the master records in much the same way as are movement records but in this

18   Data: some characteristics

case to bring the descriptive data up to date rather than the quantitative data.

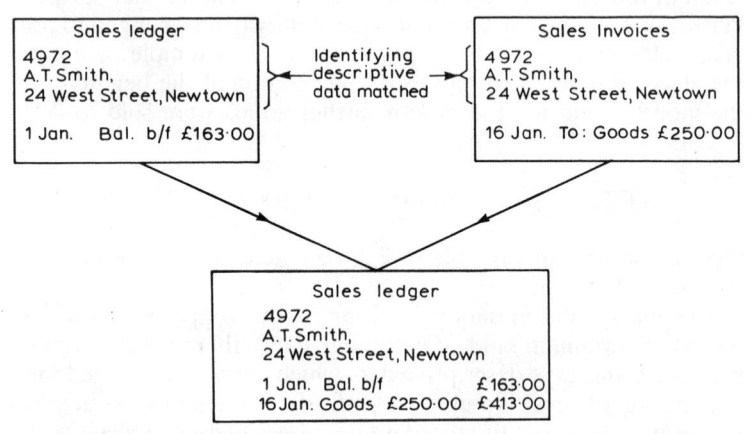

```
┌─────────────────────────┐                          ┌─────────────────────────┐
│     Sales ledger        │                          │     Sales Invoices      │
│  4972                   │    Identifying           │  4972                   │
│  A.T. Smith,            │ ◄─ descriptive ─►        │  A.T. Smith,            │
│  24 West Street, Newtown│    data matched          │  24 West Street, Newtown│
│                         │                          │                         │
│  1 Jan.  Bal. b/f £163·00│                         │  16 Jan. To: Goods £250·00│
└─────────────────────────┘                          └─────────────────────────┘
              │                                                   │
              └──────────────────┐         ┌──────────────────────┘
                                 ▼         ▼
                    ┌─────────────────────────────────┐
                    │        Sales  ledger            │
                    │  4972                           │
                    │  A.T. Smith,                    │
                    │  24 West Street, Newtown        │
                    │                                 │
                    │  1 Jan.  Bal. b/f      £163·00  │
                    │  16 Jan. Goods £250·00 £413·00  │
                    └─────────────────────────────────┘
```

Fig. 2.2. Record updating

Identification of data

Having said that different types of data record are brought together for the purpose of keeping records up to date, there remains the problem of how we can associate related records easily for this purpose. If we are dealing manually with just one transaction, as in the above example, it is easy enough to check that the same name and address appear on both the transaction and master records. However, if we are dealing with a large volume of records, it would be a quite laborious process, and indeed a process very much prone to error, to match up records on a basis of name and address, particularly if we had a number of different customers all with the same name. This problem would be very much accentuated if, rather than doing the matching manually, we required a machine to do it. Not only this, but the full name and address would have to be repeated on every record, which, as we shall see when we are concerned with machine processing, is not really necessary.

It will have been noted that the first data field in the example we have been using is called an account number. This part of the descriptive data is, strictly speaking, not necessary to the identification of the customer. It is really an accountancy convenience to enable us to readily find an account when required and to provide a logical sequence in which the data records can be held on file. For this reason it is often known as *control data*.

If, then, each customer is given a unique number, or reference, which appears on all transactions relating to that customer, we have a ready and effective means of bringing together different records relating to the same account. The name we give to this reference used for identifying a record is a *record key*.

The usual way of providing such a key is to allocate to each record a group of characters known as a *code*. It is a system with which we are all familiar in the form of bank account numbers, social security numbers, etc. In fact, we find that in most aspects of our lives requiring a clear identification a number or code is used. Such a reference system applied to data records in a data processing system can accomplish a number of useful functions.

This is particularly so in the area of computer processing, where records cannot be examined for identification by visual scrutiny. The code will give us the following advantages:

(1) The means of identifying a record without reference to the descriptive data contained in the record.

(2) A medium for sorting records into a predetermined order or into defined groups based on some record characteristic—for example, geographical zones or product groups.

(3) An easy way of matching records that relate to each other such as bringing movement and master records together.

(4) Economies can be effected in capturing data records. The use of a code eliminates the need to repeat descriptive data. For example, no need to record a name and address on a movement record, since the record key it contains will associate it with a master record in which this information is already held.

(5) It makes possible rapid reference to and retrieval of specified records by associating the record key, through an index, with a reference of its physical location.

(6) It can specify a processing routine—that is, how the record should be dealt with. For instance, two digits of the code may specify the trade discount allowed to the customer to which the key relates.

(7) It may specify physical characteristics by relating elements of the code to factors such as size or volume.

(8) It can show relationships with other items by, for example, one element of the code being common to all parts of a subassembly, while the remaining elements identify each individual part of the assembly.

In fact, broadly speaking, a code can be made to do anything. It is simply giving a unique identifying label which may also indicate a quality or series of qualities about a commodity or a record of an activity. Of course, the more we expect from a code the more complex will be its construction and the more unwieldy its size. Also, by definition, the greater the chance of error when quoting it. Since so much reliance is placed on record keys in a data processing system, there is a good argument for keeping the codes on which these keys are based as simple as possible and also for ensuring that adequate checking routines are applied in order to ensure their accuracy.

Types of code

Codes fall into two main categories: (1) non-significant, (2) significant.

NON-SIGNIFICANT CODES

Non-significant codes, as the name suggests, do not attempt to describe the function to which they relate. In themselves they are meaningless and the range of purposes they serve is limited. Such a code may be used to identify a record, to locate a record, to sort records into a sequence and for matching purposes, but for little else. They are simple to construct: for example, all that is needed is a block of numbers, say 0001–9999. They involve the use of a minimum number of digits and, in theory, make use of all the combinations in the series without leaving gaps. These are sometimes referred to as sequential and serial codes.

In a practical data processing situation the use of a continuous series of codes within a single block is inconvenient, since the code needs to be structured to meet the requirements of the multiple number of systems being operated. In this case one or more of the following principles could well be incorporated.

Block codes
Block codes are used to identify groups or blocks of records having a common property. In the simplest form the major groupings are usually indicated by the first digit within the code. The total data processing system of an organization may incorporate a number of sub-systems, records relating to each of which require a positive identification with the relevant sub-system. We could, for example, have the following situation, allocating blocks of codes for each:

Sales ledger records 10000–19999 (the first digit '1' identifying 'sales')
Purchase ledger records 20000–29999
Stores parts identification numbers 30000–39999

Such a coding principle allows for more detailed sub-grouping if required and the second digit may be used for this purpose:

Sales ledger records in S.W. area 11000–11999
Sales ledger records in S.E. area 12000–12999
Sales ledger records in Home Counties 13000–13999

The set of code numbers within each sub-group may be allocated serially irrespective of any other element within the record or will, more probably, be allocated in some logical sequence—say in alphabetical order of customer names.

It will be evident that the greater the degree of analysis required from the coding system the greater number of digits required to form the code. The range of number combinations used serially within a sub-group must be large enough to accommodate the largest group and also must be large enough—for example, in the case of alphabetical arrangement—to accommodate future additions. Since the number of records in each sub-group is likely to vary considerably, a large proportion of the code numbers will remain unused.

This block coding principle is used extensively in data processing systems, having the advantage of simple construction and adaptability. It is comparatively easy to delete and insert groups. The coding system lends itself readily to both visual and machine checks, provides a medium for sorting into any sequence demanded by the data processing system, helps the mechanics of analysing records for management control purposes and also provides a basis for retrieving any record on demand.

SIGNIFICANT DIGIT CODES

Significant digit codes are codes that incorporate a quantitative element in the form of an actual measurement of an attribute of a commodity. For example, the coding of copper piping could be

  264013   13 mm diameter
  264022   22 mm diameter
  264027   27 mm diameter

The significant digits of this code—in this case those defining diameter—are usually part of a longer code which may incorporate a second coding principle—for example, a block code where the first digit, '2', is common to all stores parts.

While this type of code has the advantage that it will, to an extent, specify in detail characteristics of the element to which it refers and is therefore very useful in a visual context, it can become very unwieldy if expected to specify too many such characteristics. Furthermore, it may also become over-complicated if a mixed, alphanumeric, content is called for, as would be the case, for example, with paper sizes A4, A5, etc.

Data origination and capture

We have already seen that any activity, situation or event will give rise to the generation of data. If you are just walking down the road, some of the data items that may be generated are that the pressure on the ground under your feet is x pounds per square inch, the length of your stride is y inches, you take z strides per minute, and so on.

While all of these data may, for certain purposes, be very useful, if we are aiming, as would be the case in a data processing system, to provide specific items of information, then it becomes necessary to *select* those data items generated by the activity that are relevant to the aims we have in mind. If, for instance, we wished to calculate the speed at which you are walking, y and z would be relevant but x would be of no interest for this purpose. The same situation applies to any commercial data processing situation. If one of the objects of a system is to record in our stock inventory the quantity and cost of goods delivered to our factory, while this activity could give rise to an almost endless list of data items (the distance the delivery lorry had travelled, the number of men required to unload it, the weight and type of packing materials, etc.), the essential data that would have to be selected for our purpose might only be the description of the goods, their quantity and their unit price. A data processing system must, therefore, specify those items of data that are necessary to meet the aims of the system.

Next these data items must be *observed* or *measured* in some way. For some items this may just mean looking at and reading, say, the name and address of a supplier on a delivery note. On the other hand, some objective method of assessing quantities, sizes and values may be called for. The time spent working on a specific job must be measured in order to evaluate labour costs; the quantity of materials issued from store must be measured to find material usage. However, these measurements may take a form that is not suitable for further processing. The data may be represented by just counting a number of articles or perhaps by the movement of a needle on a dial to show weight, etc., and so the next stage is that data must be *recorded*.

Recording data

It was suggested earlier that there are basically two types of data record—master records and movement records. In both cases data initially have to be obtained from one source or another.

With the reservation that the quantitative part of a master record will be updated as and when movements relating to it occur (usually a purely automatic process), recording master data is a once-only operation carried out when the activity to which it relates is first started. For example, taking a new item into stock would involve recording its description, size, weight, etc., and this information would remain static all the time the item was held in stock, irrespective of changes in the quantity held.

Recording movement data, however, since these represent a minute-to-minute record of what is happening in an organization, is a continuous process. These movement data records will originate from a number of different sources. We may have records of the movement of stock items from a stores office, records of hours worked from a works office, records of sales from a sales office, and so on. Not only will the data records come from different sources, but also they may originate in a number of different formats.

As we shall see, there are a wide variety of ways in which this data recording can be done and its mode will usually depend upon the techniques we are using to process the data. In a completely manual system the data would probably be recorded in ordinary handwriting or perhaps with a typewriter. In a mechanised system the mode will depend upon the type of machines being used.

It may, for example, be in coded form, such as the bar coding we see on a tin of soup purchased from the local supermarket, or in the form of holes punched into a small card attached to a garment. On the other hand, it may be that the data items are not recorded on any type of document at all but are written direct to some kind of magnetic recording device such as magnetic tape or disc simply by depressing keys on the equivalent to a typewriter keyboard.

Furthermore, for some purposes it may be possible to record the data purely automatically without any human intervention at all by making the activity itself directly generate the data relating to it. Two examples of this are the counting of cars for the purpose of traffic light control, when the car indicates its presence by passing over a pad in the road, and when articles coming off a production line break a light beam focused on to a photoelectric cell to set up impulses to count the number of articles produced.

Whatever technique is used to record these items of data and on whatever medium the recording is made, the one common factor is that data relating to an activity are being captured. The term we use, therefore, to identify this process is *data capture*.

To summarise, then, data may be captured in the following ways:

(1) In ordinary visually readable writing using conventional digits, letters and symbols recorded on a document of some kind.

(2) In coded form on a document but the data are not expressed in conventional readable characters.

(3) Entered through a keyboard and recorded magnetically or electronically on an appropriate medium.

(4) Captured completely automatically and transmitted for recording on an appropriate medium.

While this is not intended to be an exhaustive list of the methods that may be used to capture data (for example, data can be captured acoustically by speaking into a microphone), those quoted represent the methods most likely to be encountered in commercial data processing.

It will be noted that in the first two cases the data are initially captured on a document; in many cases, this also applies to the third method by reading from a document for entry through a keyboard. This medium upon which the recording of data first takes place is known as a *source document*.

Data preparation

In whatever form data items are captured, in the final analysis they must be prepared in a form that is compatible with the requirements of the equipment being used to process the data. If we are using purely manual methods (say writing up a stores ledger from written stock requisitions and supplier invoices), no problem arises, since we can use the source documents in their original form. If, however, we expect a machine to carry out the work for us, it may well be that neither the mode in which the items are recorded nor the medium on which they are captured would be acceptable to the machine. If, for example, we wished to record a passage of music from an original script, it would be pointless to show the script to a microphone and hope that the passage would then be transferred to a magnetic tape. The data on the script representing the music must first be converted into audio signals, perhaps by playing the passage on a piano, before the microphone will accept them.

This principle, as we shall see in detail later on, applies particularly to the use of computers in data processing, when all data must be expressed in a form the computer or its associated equipment will be able to understand. This will often mean that the mode in which the data were originally recorded must be converted to a mode which is machine acceptable, a process known as *data preparation*.

Data storage

An essential feature of any system designed to process data is that the data records must be available as and when demanded by the requirements of the system. In practice, this means that records must be stored in such a way as to be capable of conveniently being retrieved as and when required so that reference can be made to stored information and also so that the information can be amended and brought up to date when necessary. We were thinking of an example of this earlier, when reference had to be made to a stored price list for information to evaluate materials on a stores requisition.

The implication of this is that data records must be assembled into files and that the location, the contents and the order in which records are arranged in the file must be known. Also, as we saw when discussing record keys, a unique identifying factor must be incorporated into each record. In taking these two factors into account, the retrieval of any specific record can be accomplished by associating the record key, through an index, with the location in which the record is stored.

In a manual system this is a fairly straightforward process. If we have a series of files labelled 'Sales Accounts', 'Purchase Accounts', 'Stores Ledger', etc., in which all records are held in record key number sequence, then to find, say, a specific sales ledger account we would have to:

(1) Find the record key of the sales ledger account we wish to refer to (this may be done by looking up an index associating the

customer's name with the record key—in this case the account number).

(2) Go to the file labelled 'Sales Accounts'.

(3) Extract from the file the record with the key corresponding to the one we are looking for. This is easy enough when all the records are on file in numerical key number sequence.

In a manual system this all means visually scrutinising the data to find what we are after. If we are using machine forms of storage, then, of course, this visual scrutiny is not possible and, as we shall see when discussing computer storage later, the process of retrieval becomes more complex, even though the basic principles outlined above may be retained.

Exercises

2.1. What do you understand by a record key? Suggest four purposes for which the record keys in your stock inventory file could be used.

2.2. Devise a code that will provide a unique key for each of your 4000 customers distributed equally over four areas, North, South, East and West. The code should identify the area in which your customer is situated and also show within which of three discount categories the customer falls. Using a maximum of seven characters, suggest coded record keys for: (a) ABC Engineering Co. in South area, with 40% discount; (b) Mann Bros. in West area, with 10% discount; (c) York and Sons in East area, with 25% discount.

2.3. Distinguish between a master record and a movement record. Explain the interaction that takes place between these two records in a data processing situation.

2.4. Some data items can be said to be 'static' and others to be 'dynamic'. Explain what is meant by these two terms, illustrating your answer with examples of each.

2.5. Give an account of four ways in which data items can be captured at source.

2.6. Give an explanation of (a) a data record and (b) a data field.

2.7. Explain what is meant by record updating. Using a procedure with which you are familiar, describe how this process takes place.

2.8. What is a significant digit code? Suggest advantages that accrue through the use of such a code.

Chapter 3
Data processing systems

The purpose of this chapter is to look at some general features relating to data processing activities irrespective of the methods—manual, mechanical or electronic—used to perform them. Details of how procedures are carried out will be considered later.

What is a system?

This is a question not easily answered in a few words. Within the context of data processing systems, possibly the nearest definition we can get is: 'An ordered set of procedures designed to organise, motivate, monitor and control an activity or series of activities to accomplish a predetermined purpose'. There are, nevertheless, different schools of thought in interpreting the extent of the activity understood by the word 'system'. One would have it that there is only one total universal system embracing all physical and human activity and that the various types of activity are sub-systems within this. Another will look at it from an organizational point of view and suggest that the activities of an organization as a whole constitute the system and that manufacturing activities, sales activities, data processing activities, etc., are sub-sets within this overall system.

As a basis for discussion in this section on systems considerations, we shall take a 'system' as referring to a discrete area of activity one would generally expect to find within the spectrum of normal commercial usage, such as a stock control system, a wages system, a market research system, a production planning system, a sales system, and so on. However, there is the reservation that such systems do not work in isolation.

Relationship between systems within the organization as a whole

A system is not an end in itself. It exists within the environment of an organization and should have as its aims the provision of an efficient service—whether this be buying, selling, manufacturing, controlling traffic lights, monitoring a patient, or any other—and the successful conduct of the organisation itself. A system is a service that seeks to provide information at the right time, in the right form and in the right place, and in doing so to promote and guide the controlling mechanism of the organization. This it does by monitoring, recording and processing data relating to the activities with which the organization is involved. It will provide information for the day-to-day running of a business—invoices, accounts, stock levels, wage statements, etc.—and also provide information to guide management policy decisions, control production activities and optimize the use of available resources.

Traditionally, clerical procedures and systems within an organization tended to be departmentalized. An organization would have its wages office, invoicing office, personnel department, cost office, accounts office, etc., with each unit being responsible for its own files, maintaining its own records, processing its own data, producing its own reports. From this way of organizing processing activities some important considerations emerge.

(1) No one section can exist in isolation; there is an interdependency between one and the other (Fig. 3.1). The output of one section may well be the input of another. For example, an invoicing department may be engaged in preparing customer invoices from advice notes it has received from the showroom store. A copy of the invoice is then sent to the accounts office and becomes the input for a sales ledger system.

(2) Such an approach will lead to a duplication of records. The

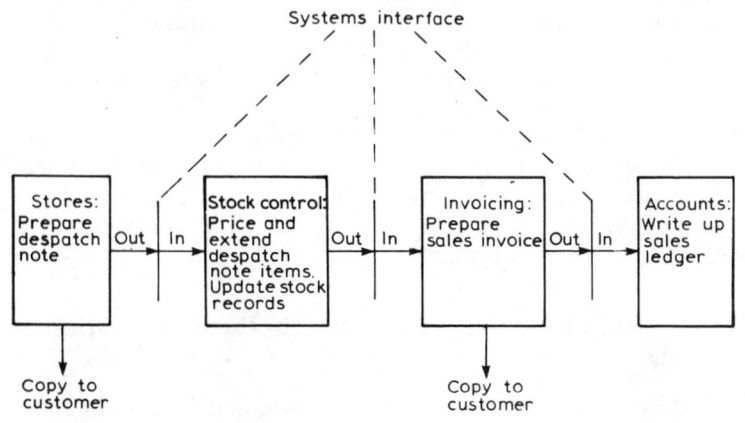

Fig. 3.1. Interdependence of procedures

wages office may keep records of hours worked by operatives for wage calculation purposes, while a cost office may well keep the same records for labour costing purposes.

(3) A time lag arises when the output of one department is to become the input of another.

(4) A variety of data processing methods may be used in the various departments.

(5) There may well be an under-utilization of data processing equipment, as each department needs its own machines to support its own system.

(6) There will be a delay in the provision of management control information when the output of two or more departments has to be brought together to provide the information.

These circumstances may well lead to sound arguments being presented for the centralization of all processing in which records can be held for use in a number of different processing routines. Furthermore, with such an arrangement the number of previously existing offices or sections could well be dramatically reduced. Procedures which were previously an end in themselves could well now become the by-product of a larger system. For example, labour costing could become a by-product of a wages system.

It is in this area of centralized data processing that the computer comes into its own, although with the range of computers available today it is by no means axiomatic that such a system of centralized processing is necessarily the most economic or efficient way of going about it.

Systems structure

In a data processing system it is usually the case that the end-product of the system is arrived at through a number of stages, the output of one stage becoming the input of the next (see Fig. 3.2). This hierarchy of operations is particularly evident in a manually operated system.

The levels into which a system can be broken down can be labelled as follows:

System
Sub-systems
Procedures
Operations
Tasks

Of these, a task is the smallest unit of work we can identify within the system. If we take as an example a wages system in which the primary input is clock cards stating the times of starting and finishing work, then the progressive stages within the system could follow this pattern:

Tasks:	Receive clock cards
	Check cards received for all employees
	Add up the total standard hours worked
	Add up the total overtime hours worked
	Enter standard wage rate
	Enter overtime wage rate
Operation:	Extend standard hours by rate
	Extend overtime hours by rate
	Add to find gross pay
Procedure:	Calculate PAYE deductions
	Calculate insurance, superannuation deductions
	Arrive at net pay
Sub-system:	Prepare wages payment slips

WAGES SYSTEM

Sub-systems

Prepare labour analysis	Prepare wage payment slips	Prepare P.A.Y.E returns

Procedures

Calculate P.A.Y.E. deductions	Calculate pension deductions	Calculate net pay

Operations

Extend standard hours by rate	Extend overtime hours by rate	Calculate gross pay

Tasks

Receive and check clock cards	Add total standard hours worked	Add total overtime hours worked

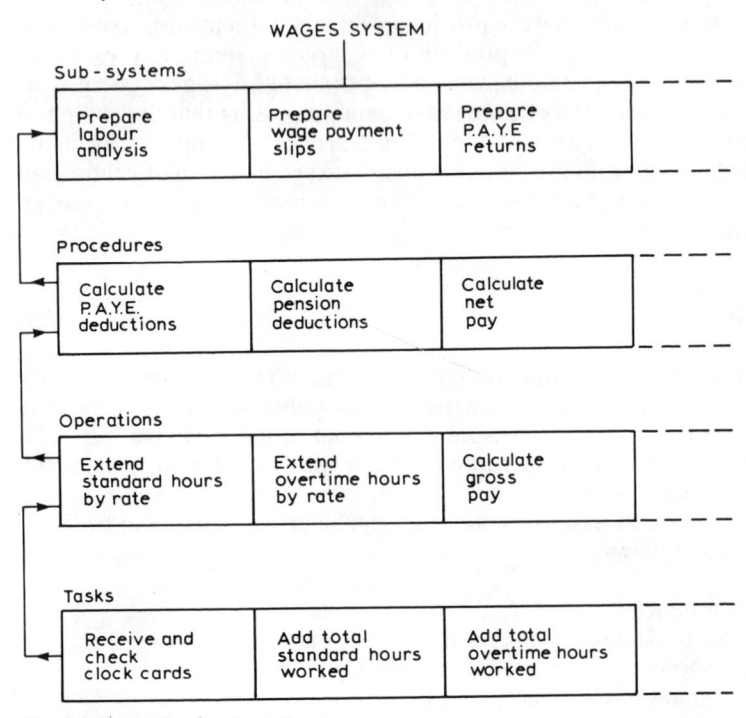

Fig. 3.2. Example of systems structure

Elements of a system

In Chapter 1 we saw that a data processing system accepts data arising from an activity or situation, processes it and provides as a result useful and meaningful information:

Input (data items) → Processing → Output (useful and meaningful reports)

If we now take a simple example of a manual processing routine, we can identify from this some basic factors, or elements, that will be present in any system whether manual, mechanical or electronic methods are used or, indeed, a combination of these three.

A clerk working in a stock control section receives requisitions recording items issued from a materials store. These have to be priced, the quantity issued has to be entered on the relevant stock control card and the balance on the card has to be amended accordingly. The requisitions contain the following information:

Description and part number of the articles issued from store
Quantity issued
Number of the job on which the materials are to be used
Date, requisition number and signature

This information would probably be written by hand on the requisition by the storekeeper and it records, or captures, an account of the activity taking place. Therefore, the name, we give to this process is *data capture*.

On receipt of the requisition, the clerk is required to enter in the relevant column the unit price of the article—this is obtained by reference to the stock control card. He then multiplies the unit price by the quantity, enters the product in the '£.p.' column and makes the necessary entries on the stock control card. Should there be more than one line entry on the requisition, he will later have to add the column and enter the total at the bottom.

If we imagine the clerk (Fig. 3.3) to be sitting at a desk with two trays, one on his left hand and the other on his right, we can then visualize the flow of the requisitions—the source documents—through the procedure. Requisitions to be processed are placed in the left-hand tray—the 'In' tray. This we can call the *input*. By the same token, on completion of work on a requisition, the clerk would place it in the right-hand, or 'Out', tray, and this we can call the *output* of the system.

In between this input and output is a processing area in which the clerk will carry out the procedures called for. This will first entail taking a requisition from the 'In' tray, identifying the material issued and then extracting the relevant card from the stock control file. This brings us to the concept of *stored* information—that is, information held on a file—and the *retrieval* of this information as and when it is required for use. Having looked up the unit price of the material from the card, the clerk will probably note it down on a piece of paper and then refer back to the requisition to find the quantity that has been issued. He will then multiply these two factors to obtain the cost—this brings us to the *arithmetic* of the situation—and copy the answer down in the correct column of the requisition. This illustrates the concept of *file updating*—that is, amending the file records in order to bring them up to date. He will repeat the above process for every item listed, finally adding all the products of his arithmetic to find the total value represented by the requisition. Having noted this down, he will pass the requisition to the 'Out' tray, which now becomes the output of the system.

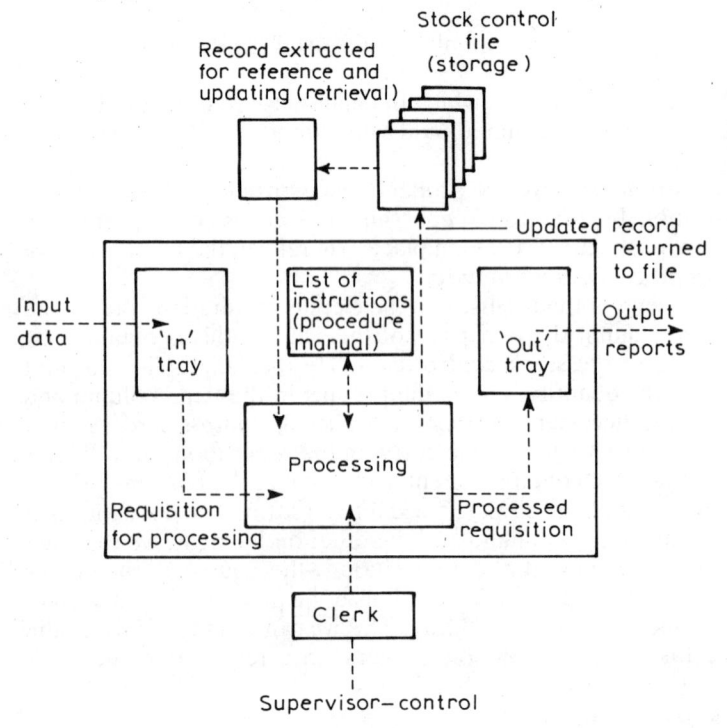

Fig. 3.3. Elements of a data processing system

There are, however, two other basic factors in this situation that are necessary to its successful and accurate completion.

In order to get the correct answer, the operations mentioned above must be carried out in a correct predetermined sequence. We could make a detailed list of instructions in sequence for the clerk to follow something like this:

(1) Take requisition from 'In' tray.
(2) Read part number from requisition.
(3) Extract stock card containing this number from stock control file.
(4) Read unit price and enter on requisition.
(5) Copy unit price to scrap pad.
(6) Read quantity from requisition.
(7) Enter quantity on scrap pad.
(8) Multiply unit price by quantity.
. . . and so on.

This list of instructions represents the logic of the situation, and we can call a list of the instructions assembled logically to accomplish a predetermined aim a *program*. In a manual system this list of instructions would probably be contained in a procedure manual.

The second additional factor which must be present has as its purpose to make sure that the job is being carried out correctly. Indeed, it would be most unusual to have a clerk working away on these requisitions without being supervised in some way. Someone has to make sure that the instructions are being carried out correctly, that the requisitions are available when required, that the correct file is being used, that the arithmetic is being performed accurately, and so on. In other words, there must be an element of *control* over the whole proceedings.

To summarize, then. We have these elements in any data processing operation whether performed completely manually, wholly automated or using a mixture of processing methods:

The initial recording in one way or another of
    facts and figures relating to an activity: *data capture*
The entry of these data into a system designed
    to deal with them: *input*
The application to the data of a logically
    assembled series of operations: *processing*
in which reference may be made to information
    held on a file: *storage*
and from which relevant items of data will be extracted
    for use in the processing cycle: *information retrieval*

and in which calculations are carried out to
provide a required answer: *arithmetic*
The amendment of the file record to
bring it up to date: *updating*
and finally the completed record is passed on
for further use: *output*
The whole of these procedures are carried out
according to a predetermined set of instructions: *program*
and the performance throughout monitored and
supervised to ensure accuracy and completeness: *control*

Systems resources

Having reviewed the processing elements that are present in a data processing system, we can now turn our attention to a broad survey of the resources required to execute these processes. Of course, the weight given to the use of any of these will vary from situation to situation, depending to a great extent upon the degree of mechanization and automation being employed. Manual systems tend to be labour intensive; automated systems, machine intensive. By and large, however, the following basic resources will be present in most systems:
Equipment resources
Human resources
Information resources
Control resources

Equipment resources

The category 'equipment resources' embraces the whole range of devices and supplies used in the data processing function. In a simple manual system requirements will be modest—perhaps just simple calculating devices, a filing system and the stationery upon which data at the various stages of processing can be recorded. In more sophisticated systems a wide range of computers and their associated equipment is available. It would be impracticable to give a complete survey of all the machines available. The more generally used are discussed in some detail in Part 2.

From our earlier discussion on the elements of a system it will be seen that one way of looking at it is as three sub-systems: an input sub-system, a processing sub-system and an output (or reporting) sub-system. In the same way, equipment resources can be categorized into these three sub-sections.

Input: The requirements for capturing data at source and preparing them for the processing stage. Devices in this section range from a simple pad of sales dockets with carbon copies used as data input, tills in which sales may be entered through a keyboard with a tally-roll produced for further processing, to punched card devices, devices for recording on magnetic media—tape or disc, terminals that will capture data automatically and transmit them to a computer for processing.

Processing: Devices used in the process of converting source data into the output reports demanded of the system. The essential requirements are recording media on which data can be held while processing takes place, a filing system to hold data records to which reference must be made and equipment to carry out the required calculations. Again such equipment will range from filing systems holding sheets of paper or cards on which data items are recorded to tapes and discs on which data are held magnetically; from simple calculating devices to fully automated computer systems.

Output: Essentially devices employed to communicate the results of the processing function to those who need to use them. In small-scale manual processing a handwritten or typewritten document may suffice. In large-scale systems high-speed printing devices, photographic techniques for recording on film and cathode ray tube devices for displaying information may be employed.

Human resources

The staff employed in data processing activities fall into four main categories:

(1) Those whose responsibility it is to prepare source data. This task could well be a by-product of an operative's main job—for example, a storekeeper who prepares sales dockets when goods are sold.

(2) Data processing specialists who are employed full-time in processing activities—for example, operating machines used in the processing functions, checking and preparing data as they flow in to the system, checking and distributing the output reports.

(3) Staff who are involved in planning, designing and controlling data processing systems and operations.

(4) Users who receive, interpret and act upon the reports produced by the processing activity.

Information resources

Information resources represent the whole range of data and data records upon which the processing system operates:

(1) Source data arising directly from the activity the system is designed to record and control.
(2) Where appropriate, machine input records prepared from these data.
(3) Systems files holding master data records.
(4) Output reports.

Control resources

Controls are implemented through three main agencies:

(1) The specification of the system itself, defining the procedures and processes that will be applied to the data and the order in which they should be performed.
(2) The list of instructions specifying in detail how each procedure and operation will be executed—the program.
(3) Checking techniques to ensure the accuracy, completeness and timeliness of the processing operations.

Data processing objectives

As mentioned earlier, data processing is not an end in itself. It should be designed to meet objectives that promote the efficient and effective running of the organization within which the processing operates. These objectives can be summarized as follows:

> To promote efficient administration
> To promote operating efficiency
> In a business to maximize profitability
> To promote good relationships

Administration

The product of a data processing system is useful information. Information flow is an essential ingredient in business administration and control. Such information can be said to fall into two broad categories:

(a) The information essential to the day-by-day running of the business, such as despatch notes and invoices to be sent to customers, pay slips for employees, re-order lists to replenish stock, and sales and purchase ledger accounts giving a statement of debtors and creditors. This type of information is often known as *operating information*.

(b) Information that is necessary to the management decision-making process in order to control its activities and formulate its policy. This information, which in many cases may be just a summary of operating information, will include such things as cash flow statements, sales analysis, budget/performance comparisons, profit breakdown, etc. This is known as *management control information*.

The effectiveness of the administration will largely depend upon the qualities of the information it has at its disposal. Any data processing activity should seek to provide information that is:

(1) Accurate to a degree that is sufficient to serve the purpose for which it is designed. An invoice to a customer must be accurate to the nearest 1p. A statement of total sales for the year may, for the sake of clarity, be rounded off to the nearest £1000.

(2) Timely. Out-of-date information will often be useless, as it will be too late to take effective action the information calls for.

(3) Complete. Information must contain all of the factors that are necessary to the decision-making process.

(4) Relevant. Supplying irrelevant information is not only a waste of data processing resources, but also a waste of the time and effort of the person receiving it and, indeed, can mislead by obscuring information that is relevant to the situation.

(5) Up to date. Information should reflect the situation that exists at the time of the production of the report. To be given today information on the levels stocks were at two weeks ago may lead to serious stock shortages.

(6) Concise. Where possible the exception principle should be adopted in the preparation of reports, attention only being drawn to situations departing from a previously determined norm.

(7) Well presented. Information may be presented in a variety of ways: as narrative, as tables, as charts, as diagrams, as graphs, etc. Care should be taken to present any particular information in the manner that is going to prove easy to interpret and act upon.

(8) Cost effective. There is no point in going to a lot of expense to produce information when its cost is going to be greater than any benefits or savings derived from it.

Management information systems

Management at any level implies the supervision, planning and control of an area of activity and the consequent need to reach decisions relating to it. It is unreasonable to expect management to reach the correct decisions without having recourse to information relating to the area of activity controlled. To a great extent a data processing system will be the medium through which this information is obtained, bearing in mind that such information should conform to the criteria mentioned above.

We can look at the decision-making process at three levels:

(1) Routine decisions based on fixed rules.

(2) Planning, problem solving and control decisions at departmental or functional level—these are tactical decisions, usually the province of lower or middle management.

(3) Determination of overall policy—strategic planning—usually the role of senior management.

At the first of these levels, routine decisions can be purely an automatic function of a data processing system, provided that the system incorporates the criteria upon which the decision must be reached. One example is the re-ordering of stock by comparing a fixed stated minimum stock level with the actual stock level and, when necessary, automatically preparing a replacement order. Another example is a credit control system which will automatically compare a balance outstanding with the fixed credit level, drawing a debtor's attention to the situation should the credit limit be exceeded.

At the second of these levels a data processing system may be designed to output summaries and reports of the activity and to highlight any exceptional circumstances arising within the activity. This means that management is aware of what is going on and, being so informed, is able to direct attention to any problem areas and to plan for the optimum use of the resources at command. For example, a materials variance report showing the excessive use of materials on a job could well lead to decisions to use a better quality of material or to introduce measures to cut down wastage. Schedules of machine utilisation, waiting time, stock shortages, etc., could well lead to decisions that will improve work flow and productivity.

At the third level—formulating overall policy—while information relating to the organisation's activities produced through an internal data processing system will be necessary, other external information sources will also play a major role.

Internally generated reports such as turnover analysis, analysis of gross and net profit over product range, production cost trends, etc., will give a picture of current activity but external conditions must also be taken into account. For example, public demand, technological developments, competition, interest rates etc.

Using a computer, all of this information, whether internally or externally generated, can be brought together in the form of a 'model' that will simulate various combinations and levels of activity and will forecast likely results.

Operating efficiency

As we saw earlier, data processing does not just record an activity, but also provides reports to enable decisions to be reached to modify the activity when necessary. These reports can be the basis for increasing the operating efficiency of an organization in a number of ways:

Effective scheduling of work flow.
Increasing machine utilization.
Controlling stock levels.
Making more efficient use of labour by reducing idle time.
Improving communications.
Reducing waste arising from production errors.

Profitability

All of the factors mentioned in the preceding two sub-sections will have the result of providing economies in both administrative and operational activities and so have the direct effect of reducing costs. However, data processing should result in a number of indirect savings working towards maximizing profitability. For example: (a) The efficient control of stores will keep to a minimum the amount of capital tied up in stocks and also provide savings in storage costs. (b) The timely production of customer accounts could well result in earlier settlement of debts, which would reduce the total of sundry debtors at any one time and lead to an improvement in cash flow.

Relationships

An effective processing system could well be an aid to maintaining cordial relationships with customers and other ouside agencies—by, for example:

Reducing delivery time of an order.
Improving the accuracy of quoted delivery dates.
Dealing with enquiries and complaints quickly.

Ensuring that special orders are scheduled for completion with a minimum of delay.
Holding prices to a minimum by providing realistic information for price fixing.
Ensuring the quick acknowledgement of orders.

Other considerations

Processing frequency

A question that needs to be asked in this connection is: 'How soon after the origination of data are they to be processed?' Two answers suggest themselves but in some situations a combination of both may be called for.

(1) If the system is one that lends itself to historical processing (that is, processing the records that relate to the activity after the event takes place), the source records will be collected and assembled over a period of time—a day, a week, a month—and then dealt with in quantity. This is known as *batch processing*. An example of this is a sales ledger system where it could well be the case that statements of accounts are required only at the end of a month. In this case a file of movement (transaction) records may be built up progressively during the month in batches, one processing run taking place at the end of the month to update the sales ledger and prepare statements for distribution to customers.

(2) In some cases it may be desirable to process a record immediately the activity that gives rise to it takes place—indeed, to process it so quickly that the performance of the event itself may be influenced. An example of this is the presentation of a cheque at a branch bank. The data on the cheque must be immediately compared with the up-to-date balance on the account, to enable the branch staff to decide whether or not the cheque should be honoured.

These two ways of processing data are not necessarily mutually exclusive. The bank provides us with an example where in some cases, as outlined above, immediate processing is called for, while the general routine processing is accomplished by collecting together all of the branch transactions for the day—after they have occurred—and processing these in a batch mode to produce revised account balances for the commencement of trading the following morning.

Retrieval of records

Following from the previous discussion it will be evident that when records have to be referred to immediately an event takes place, a system of filing records must be devised to facilitate the rapid retrieval of any one required record. In a manual system this is usually accomplished by filing records in a predetermined order—alphabetical or numerical—so that a file can be quickly visually scrutinized and the correct record selected. In a machine system, when records are held on media in code and so cannot be read by sight, the selection of a storage system that will meet the demands of the system becomes of vital importance.

Feasibility

In considering the methods used to process data, the following three considerations will arise:

(1) *Technical feasibility*. It would be unusual for this to present any major problem. A sufficiently wide range of machines exists today to cope with virtually any data processing problem—computers, with their associated support peripherals; data preparation hardware; and non-computer machines.

(2) *Systems feasibility*. Again it is difficult to envisage any data processing problem for which a system cannot be devised to provide a solution. However, it is important to bear in mind that far-reaching changes may have to be made in administrative organization and an assessment made as to whether or not this is justified.

(3) *Economic feasibility*. Probably the most important factor. How cost effective will be a system devised for data processing? This is a factor needing assessment, not only in terms of direct costs, but also in terms of indirect savings such as improved cash flow, effective control of minimum stock levels, etc.

The question of feasibility and cost effectiveness will be discussed more fully in a later chapter.

Exercises

3.1. What is a data processing system? Suggest how a data processing system can have an effect on the activities to which it relates.

3.2. Using any business application of your choice to illustrate your answer, show how the flow of information though the procedures is essential to their effective performance.

3.3. What do you consider to be the basic elements of a data processing system?

3.4. Describe a procedure for working out your newspaper bill at the end of the week, showing how the basic elements of a data processing system all play their part.

3.5. Suggest the main types of resource that are necessary for the successful operation of a data processing system.

3.6. Give an account of six ways by which you feel the administration of an organization may be improved through an efficient data processing system.

3.7. Data processing is not an end in itself: one of its objectives should be to promote the operating efficiency of an organization. Discuss how, through the medium of its output reports, a data processing system can help achieve this aim.

3.8. Describe how you would set about estimating the cost of redecorating your dining-room, showing how all the elements found in a data processing system play their part.

3.9. A questionnaire completed by 1000 people showing the mode and distance they have travelled over the past month has as its object the calculation of average travel costs per person. Show how the main resources required in a data processing system play their part in this procedure.

Chapter 4
Data processing methods

We have earlier considered the basic factors that must be present in a data processing situation:

Input—Storage—Processing—Output—Program—Control

The purpose of this chapter is to show how these factors are present irrespective of the methods used to process data.

There is no direct relationship between the size of an organization and the volume of data it has to deal with. For example, a car distributor with a turnover of £1m may be involved in the movement of only 2000 units of sale—cars; on the other hand, £1m turnover in a supermarket may well represent the sale of two or three million items. Generally speaking, the greater the volume of data the greater the economic advantages arising from automation and the greater the benefits arising from improved accuracy, timeliness and control that automatic methods offer. The levels of data volumes will, therefore, play an important part in deciding the methods used to process data. In the case of the car distributor, manual processing with, perhaps, the aid of simple calculators may be perfectly adequate, while the supermarket may need a quite sophisticated computer system.

Manual processing

Manual processing is mainly in the form of handwritten or typewritten records, with the processing techniques performed manually by clerks. The input is the source documents, used in the form in which they originate, so that no data preparation procedures are necessary. Processing is carried out by hand-sorting, matching, updating master records, etc., while any calculations may be carried out mentally, although it would be usual to use some form of aid, even if only a ready reckoner. However, electronic calculating devices are almost universally used nowadays. Storage takes the form of sheets of paper bound into books or cards held in filing cabinets, and output is often on the original source document, represented by writing, in the relevant spaces provided, the results of processing. Clerks operating the system will usually work from a memorized list of instructions—the program—which follows a routine designed at some time in the past when the system was first introduced. Control is exercised partly through self-checking by the clerk himself and partly by the manual reconciliation of control totals—for example, through a cash control account or ledger control accounts. Overall control and supervision is usually exercised through a supervisory clerk.

Systems are available which are designed to minimize the number of handwritten entries to the system and to help eliminate the transcription errors which are very prone to occur in manual systems. They involve taking a number of copies, each copy being used for a different purpose. The principle is to use documents perforated down one side and assembled with interleaved carbon paper on a 'peg-board' to give positive registration. As an example, the top copy may be a cash receipt for sending to a customer, the second copy the entry into the customer's personal account and the third copy an entry to the cash book.

Accounting machines

Accounting machines are mechancial or electromechanical machines which can perform some of the functions of a data processing system, but they do not have the speed, the storage capacity or the range of operations offered by electronic devices. Basically, they are rather like a typewriter with a keyboard for the manual input of data read from the original source documents. Storage of data is usually in the form of cards or sheets held on a file which can be individually extracted and inserted into the machine through a platen so that printed entries can be made on the cards or sheets as keys are depressed. In addition to the normal typewriter mechanism, limited arithmetic processing is accomplished through mechanical add/subtract registers incorporated into the machine, the contents of which can be printed out on program or keyboard command. The number of registers tends to vary from machine to machine. Output is through printed record on the cards themselves and also through carbon copy listings giving control totals. Control is exercised through these totals, although more sophisticated machines may provide for an automatic check on the correct entry of quantitative data and on whether the posting is made to the correct account. A limited number of program instructions can also be stored in the machine in the form of 'keys' fixed to a control bar. These keys trip the appropriate mechanism designed to perform the function they represent—add, subtract, print, etc.—as the control bar, attached to the carriage, proceeds through the machine. Program bars may be interchangeable—that is, a separate bar for each system processed by the machine.

Punched card systems

In a sense, these systems were the forerunners of computer systems, and punched card processing installations were extensively used for processing data before the advent of the computer. Their great advantage is that they provide a great deal of automation in data processing. Input is in the form of punched cards prepared by the manual entry of data from source documents through a card punch keyboard, while the cards themselves are the medium for the storage of data in coded form, represented by the holes they contain. There is a range of machines available for processing the data held in the cards, among the more important of which are:

Sorter: For arranging the punched cards into a predetermined sequence, a 'key' field punched into the card being used for this purpose.

Collator: Used for merging two sets of cards in key number sequence. This is a prerequisite for an updating run when movement record cards must be associated with their corresponding master record card.

Tabulator: The machine that carries out the logical, arithmetic and printing functions of the system. It contains arithmetic registers in which add/subtract functions can be carried out on quantitative data. Output is in printed form, through a printing head or the automatic punching of processing results into the existing cards or into a new set of cards. The sequence of operations performed by the tabulator is determined through a stored program in the form of an electrically wired plug-board—that is, a board into which plugs may be inserted to determine the operations the machine will carry out and their sequence.

Control is exercised through verifying procedures at the punched card preparation stage and also through the reconciliation of control totals built up in the arithmetic registers of the tabulator.

Electronic calculators

Bearing in mind that data processing systems will usually incorporate some arithmetic processes, one very widely used device today in processing is the electronic calculator. First generally introduced in the 1960s, electronic calculators have now virtually supplanted all other forms of calculating device. The three main types of electronic calculator are:

(1) *Non-programmable calculators.* Early types of calculator were designed to perform only the basic arithmetic functions—addition, subtraction, multiplication and division, usually up to around six decimal places. Non-programmable calculators are now available to perform a very wide range of arithmetic functions automatically simply by entering the variable data through the keyboard and then depressing the relevant function key. Examples of such automatic operations are calculating square roots, percentages, metric/Imperial conversions. This type of calculator has a visual display readout and also incorporates a limited memory facility in which constants or the intermediate results of processing can be held and recalled as and when required.

(2) *Programmable electronic calculators.* The main disadvantage of the basic electronic calculator is that if a series of similar calculations is to be carried out, not only the variable data, but also the series of operations required to perform the calculations must be keyboard entered each time. To overcome this need to keep repeating the entry of operations, calculators are available that will store, once they are entered, a series of instructions in their memory—a program—and automatically repeat these on the variables as they are entered. With some machines the program can be written to and stored permanently on a magnetic card for future automatic entry to the calculator when required.

(3) *Printing electronic calculators.* While most electronic calculators output results through a visual display, a permanent record is sometimes required. Machines are available incorporating a printing head, using a tally-roll, on which the results of processing are recorded as a hard copy. However, in principle, these machines operate in the same way as those described above.

Computers

Computers are discussed in some detail in Part 2.

Exercises

4.1. Give an account of the machines that would normally be found in a punched card installation, describing the purposes of each.

4.2. What controls do you suggest should be applied in a manual data processing system in order to ensure accuracy of postings?

4.3. What advantages do you think accrue by using an accounting machine to process your sales ledger as opposed to manual processing?

4.4. What are the six essential features that will be present in any data processing situation irrespective of the methods used to process the data?

4.5. Give a description of the three main types of electronic calculator, emphasizing the ways in which they differ from one another.

PART 2
Data processing practice

Chapter 5

Introducing computers

Some of the characteristics of data and the principles underlying data processing having been reviewed, it would be difficult to see how these principles are applied in practice without reference to the equipment commonly used for handling and processing data records.

It was suggested earlier that data processing activities can be performed manually, that they may involve the use of mechanical aids or that electronic devices may be used. In practice, more often than not, all three systems will be present in any data processing situation. It could well be that data items are recorded manually at source by the completion of a form in ordinary handwriting, which is then entered through some kind of mechanical keyboard machine and written to a machine acceptable medium such as punched cards, magnetic tape or magnetic disc. In turn, the processing may be carried out by an electronic computer and the results output to another mechanical device, a printer.

It is electronic equipment that is by far the most important and widely used element in data processing today. It embraces a very wide range of devices, from simple electronic adding and calculating machines to fully automatic computers of varying sizes and power. Bearing in mind that, irrespective of the type of equipment being used, the basic principles of data processing remain the same, the main task of this chapter is to review how, in practice, computers and their associated equipment carry out these processes.

Perhaps it would be best to start off by identifying the type of computer we shall be considering. There are two main types, known as *analogue* computers and *digital* computers.

Analogue computers

Analogue computers are concerned with the continuous measurement of physical properties and with performing computations on these measurements, using the physical properties of the computer itself to provide an analogy with the problem to be solved.

Digital computers

As the name implies, a digital computer is a machine that works in discrete digits, or numbers. All processing is carried out in terms of a numerical representation of the information being processed. This means that, since data items when they originate are usually expressed in digits, alphabetic characters and symbols, a converting process is usually necessary in order to present them to the computer in the numerical form it is designed to deal with. In the event, a computer uses a very simple number system known as *binary*, a system with a base (radix) of 2, which means that it has to deal with two characters only—0 (zero) and 1 (one)—and can be represented by any two-state device that can be set at will to either of its two states. This binary system is explained more fully later.

The basic difference between the two types of computer—analogue and digital—can be explained by the following simple example. If you wanted to measure the speed at which your car is travelling, you could do so by measuring out on the road the distance of a mile, placing someone at each end with a stop-watch and then driving over the measured mile while the time taken was recorded on the watches. You would finish up with some numerical data—distance and time—from which you could compute your average speed over the distance. This is a digital approach to the problem. On the other hand, you could rely on your speedometer, which is an analogue device continuously measuring the speed of shaft revolutions on your car and converting this through its own mechanism to a miles/hour reading on a dial.

It is, then, the digital computer with which we are concerned in data processing, although in some situations an analogue device may be used to capture data. If, for example, we wanted to measure and record light intensity in an industrial process, an analogue device would be employed, probably using photoelectric cells through which an electric current would be induced proportional to the light intensity. However, to record and process these measurements their values would have to be expressed digitally, and this would be done through an analogue/digital conversion process.

While there are a number of different types of digital computer (microcomputers, minicomputers and the larger 'mainframe' computer), and while these may be operated in a number of different modes to process data (for example, batch processing, time-sharing, real time, etc.), there are a number of factors common to the use of all these models and modes, and it is these factors we shall consider first, with the specialized aspects being developed later.

Basic elements of a computer

Earlier we listed the basic factors that are present in a data processing situation irrespective of the agency used to perform the processing. It follows, therefore, that these basic functions must be capable of performance by a computer used for this purpose. We suggested that a clerk working on a requisition pricing routine would be concerned with an input to the procedure on which he is working, with an output of the completed results and with retrieving information that was held on files in storage. He would have a working area on his desk where he would process the data by applying to them a logically arranged series of instructions—a program. This would involve some arithmetic and some kind of control would have to be exercised to monitor the accuracy of his work (Fig. 5.1).

A digital computer works in much the same way. Its main device is known as a *central processor*, in which—something like the clerk's desk—the instructions are carried out. This processor has the capacity to store, and to refer to, a program of instructions and to

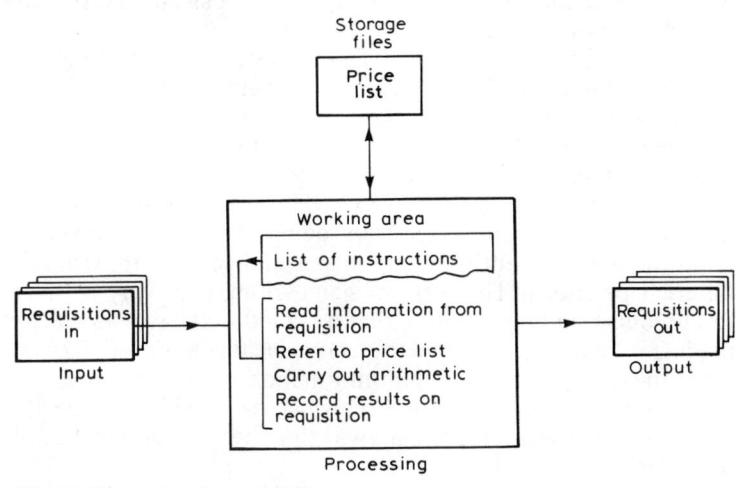

Fig. 5.1. Processing data manually

store data temporarily while the instructions demanded by the program are executed on it, and the ability to communicate the results of its processing to another device—for example, a printer. It must also be able to perform arithmetical and logical operations as part of its processing routine and also have an inbuilt control mechanism to ensure that everything is being carried out as demanded by the system. (See Fig. 5.2.)

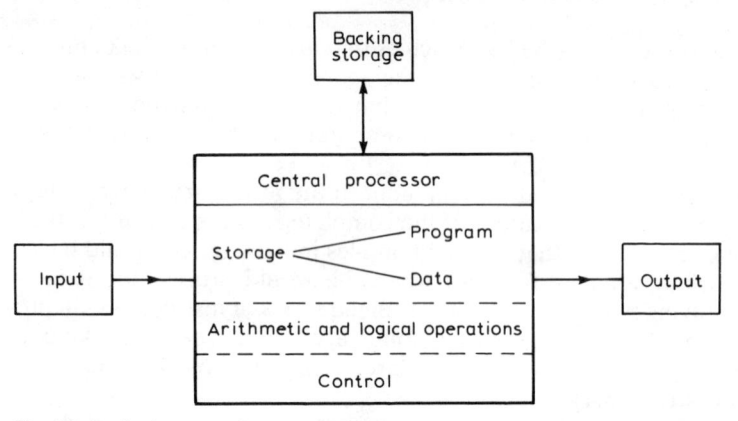

Fig. 5.2. Basic elements of a computer

Carrying the analogy of the clerk a little further, it will be remembered that he had an 'In' tray on one side of his desk, into which requisitions needing attention were placed. This represented the input to the system.

With a computer, it is usually not possible, unfortunately, to feed data to it in the form in which they originate. If we could feed the actual requisition into the machine, get the machine to do the required 'working out', write the answer in the correct place, and then eject the completed requisition from the other end, things would be a lot more straightforward. However, there are difficulties that prevent a computer from doing this. For example, the requisitions may be of different shapes and sizes, with writing in different positions. The form of handwriting may vary so much from requisition to requisition that we could well have difficulty in reading it ourselves, let alone expect a machine to do so. To overcome these problems the input information must be (a) prepared on a standard size and type of form which the machine will be able to accept, and/or (b) entered in a way that the machine will be able to recognize and read.

There are a number of specialized machines capable of handling information so prepared—we call these *input devices*. They are not part of the central processor, but are connected to it and are capable of transferring the information they accept to the processor.

It will be noted also that the clerk took only one requisition at a time from his 'In' tray, transferring it to his desk, where he worked on it. In other words, he was extracting it from a file of requisitions that were stored awaiting attention. This brings us to the concept of computer storage which is external to the central processor and from which data can be transferred to the processor as and when required. There are a number of types of storage device that are used for this purpose—we shall be reviewing these in detail later. The machines that handle these files are known as *backing storage devices*.

Finally, the clerk had to communicate the results of his work by placing the completed requisition in his 'Out' tray. In the same way a computer will have to communicate the final results of its processing. This is done through the medium of *output devices*. A number of different types of output device may be used for differing purposes and these will be looked at later in detail.

We can, therefore, regard a computer as being, not just one machine, but a collection of devices, the main one of which is the central processor, supported by input, output and storage devices connected to it. The name we give to these supporting devices is *peripherals*, and the whole collection, including the processor, we refer to as a *computer configuration* (Fig. 5.3).

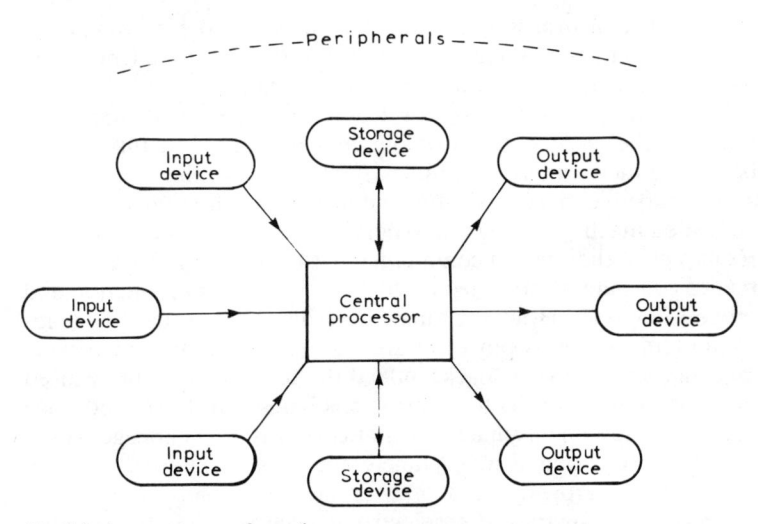

Fig. 5.3. A computer configuration

At this point, perhaps it would be as well to introduce two terms that will be frequently used throughout the rest of this book.

Hardware refers to the machines that make up a computer—the central processor and the input, output and storage peripherals.

Software is the term given to the programs that tell the computer what to do. There are a number of different types of program, and these will be considered in detail later.

Types of digital computer

Three terms encountered in computer descriptions and specifications are 'microcomputers', 'minicomputers' and 'mainframe computers'. In principle they have much in common:

(1) A central processor containing circuitry to deal with the processing function—arithmetic and logic unit, timing unit, instruction decoding circuits, control registers, etc.

(2) A resident immediate access memory containing read and write random access elements and also read only memory elements.

(3) An interface consisting of input and output ports to link on with external peripheral devices.

(4) A range of input, output and storage peripherals.

From a data processing point of view, while the mechanics of input, output and storage may vary from machine to machine, the basic principles discussed in Part 1 are common.

It was once possible to draw fairly clear lines of demarcation between these three types of digital computer, but this is now becoming increasingly difficult, particularly so in the case of mini and mainframe machines. Minicomputers were first introduced as dedicated machines designed to perform a specific processing task. Examples of their use in commercial data processing was as visible record computers and in technical applications for production and process control. However, machines described today as minicomputers can be as powerful and as versatile as the mainframe machine of a few years back; indeed the term 'super-mini' is used by some manufacturers to describe machines that in size and price are much the same as machines that two or three years ago would have been regarded as mainframe computers.

The fastest-growing area of computer technology is the field of microelectronics. Microelectronics circuits, only recently developed and known as integrated circuits (ICs), are constructed from wafer-thin slices of a semiconductor material, usually silicon. A small chip can contain a large number of electronic components with their associated circuitry. Large-scale integrated circuits (LSIs) can now be produced containing tens of thousands of components on a chip no larger than 5 millimetres square by 0.1 millimetre thick. The availability of these chips holding the circuitry for processing and storage functions allowed of the construction of very small computers to which has been attached the name 'microcomputer'. The original concept of a micro was of a machine built around silicon chip technology contained in a small box with integrated input and output devices having fairly slow operational speeds with a small—8 bit—word length. However, microelectronics have now found their way into all sizes of computer, and, on the other hand, microcomputers have developed to a point where machines at the top end of the range are claimed to be as powerful and as fast as machines falling nominally into the minicomputer range.

From the point of view of a user concerned with the performance and suitability of a machine to perform his data processing requirements, we are, perhaps, reaching a point where the terms 'mainframe', 'mini' and 'micro' are almost becoming redundant as attempts to categorize digital computers. After all, the user's interest is centred around a cost/efficiency basis rather than labels attempting to place machines into discrete categories, the demarcation lines between which appear to be becoming more hazy. Recognizing, however, the general usage of these three terms, the following comments seek to put these machines into some kind of framework, although it is appreciated that any attempt to categorize them can probably be refuted by quoting specific examples.

Mainframe computers

The term 'mainframe computers' generally refers to medium- or large-size machines designed for large-scale data processing, handling very large volumes of source documentation and coping with a wide spectrum of systems. The main features of this type of machine include the following:

(1) It supports a wide range of fast input and output peripherals and has backing storage of high volume capacity.
(2) It has a large, fast central processor.
(3) It provides support services for data preparation, data con-

trol, programming systems design, etc.

(4) It is usually a centralized service department in its own right.

(5) It is subject to environmental control—for example, air-conditioning, and dust and temperature control.

(6) It often is a centralized machine supporting remote satellite computers and terminals.

Mainframe machines are very expensive to install and are justified only where large volumes of data are processed.

Minicomputers

As the name suggests, minicomputers are generally regarded as being a smaller version of the digital computer, with the central processor and the range and capacity of peripherals on a smaller scale. Features of this type of machine may well include:

(1) Physically smaller hardware units.

(2) In early machines the central processor store tended to be small, although, with the introduction of semiconductor memories, more recent models have tended to substantially increase memory capacity.

(3) Backing storage peripherals, if used, tend to be smaller—for example, small flexible disc units rather than the standard rigid disc pack used with mainframe machines and smaller magnetic tapes of perhaps 600 feet rather than the standard mainframe tape of 2400 feet.

(4) The range of input/output peripherals tends to be limited.

(5) A minicomputer will probably operate on a shorter word length than mainframe machines—say 16 bits—and the range of machine functions—the machine code—tends to be smaller. These two factors may result in lower operation speeds.

(6) The controlled environment necessary with mainframe machines is not necessary with minicomputers.

In general, minicomputers are less expensive than mainframe machines but are capable of coping with most of the routine processing jobs done on the larger computers, although, in many cases, lacking the speed and the range of operating modes and storage facilities offered by them. Software for minicomputers has reached an advanced state of development, with a wide range of standard programs available from manufacturers. Some machines offer multiprogramming facilities, and a range of utility programs and compilers is available.

Microcomputers

The past few years have seen a dramatic decrease in the cost and size of computers. The equivalent of a machine requiring a whole room to house it ten years ago will now sit comfortably on a small desk, while microcomputers can be purchased today for as little as £200 that would have cost, ten years ago, £100000 or more for a machine of equivalent power. All this means that microcomputers are now within the price range of quite small organizations, with the result that their use in data processing is becoming increasingly widespread. The employment of these machines in no sense means that the basic principles of processing data have changed but rather that another tool is available, inexpensive and very reliable, for carrying out these operations.

As we saw earlier, the basic building block of a microcomputer is the silicon chip, containing in a very small space a very large number of electronic components. While it is possible to build a complete microcomputer on a single chip, it is usually the case that the microprocessor is held on one chip, another chip contains ROM (read only memory) elements for the storage of permanent information and RAM (random access memory) for holding current data and programs is contained on a further chip, or chips. This means that memory capacities can be readily updated by the addition of further chips. In addition, the processor will have input and output ports to interface with peripheral units. (See Fig. 5.4.)

There is on the market today a very wide spectrum of machines described as microcomputers, ranging from the small processor with a keyboard input which can be plugged in to an ordinary television set and costs just a few pounds, to far more sophisticated systems that will support a range of peripherals and have quite extensive resident memories, costing up to around £5000.

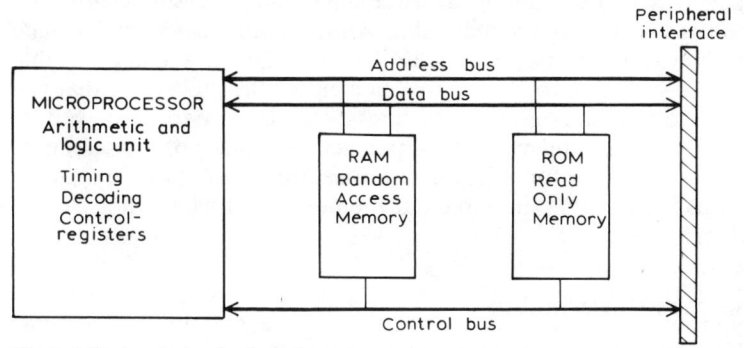

Fig. 5.4. Basic microcomputer elements

Memory capacity varies very much from model to model. Memory capacity is measured by the number of words the memory can hold. The unit 1 K = 1024 words is often used in the computer world, to express memory sizes. Microcomputers at the lower end of the range offer a basic 8 K of RAM, which in many cases is upgradable by additional elements to about 48 K. At the top end of the range, 64 K appears to be the basic capacity with again an upgrading capacity to, in many cases, 526 K or more. Smaller machines tend to use an 8-bit word, or byte, and larger machines 16 bits, although in a few cases the word length is as much as 32 bits. This means that the operation speeds in the smaller machines tend to be fairly slow. Machines at the lower end of the scale tend to be restricted to the use of one computer language, usually BASIC, and the interpreter is 'hard wired' into ROM elements so that as language statements are entered through the keyboard they are automatically translated into machine code. Larger machines will cope with a range of languages (for example, BASIC, FORTRAN, COBOL, RPG, etc.) with compilers supplied by manufacturers. Most microcomputers incorporate an interface for linking up with external peripherals.

MICROCOMPUTER INPUT

The most generally used input medium is a manually operated keyboard. While this means a slow rate of data entry, it is no slower than other devices using keyboards, for example key-to-disc entry or entry through a Teletype. In many machines the keyboard is an integral part of the computer, while in others it is a separate 'plug-in' unit. Keyboards tend to follow the standard layout of typewriter keyboards, although in some cases numerical characters are concentrated into a separate section of the keyboard. This leads to a faster input rate in cases where data records have a high numerical content. Another device that can be used with some machines is a light pen. This is a small portable device, wired in to the control element of the processor, that can be used to modify graphs and charts, etc., as they are displayed on a VDU screen, by moving the pen across the face of the screen. It can also be used for indicating options from a list of displayed data items by touching the screen at the position at which the selected item appears.

MICROCOMPUTER OUTPUT

Virtually all microcomputers incorporate a visual display unit

(VDU) on which output data may be displayed. A very wide range of these is available—black on white, white on black, colour—of varying sizes, of varying character densities, etc. Of course, the major disadvantage of a VDU is that it does not give a hard copy. To meet this requirement small printers have been developed mainly of the Teletype, Daisy Wheel and matrix types. Of these, the matrix printer seems to be the most popular, being relatively cheap and fast. Most matrix printers use a 9×9 dot matrix and the resultant type print is somewhat lower in quality than that of machines using solid type faces. A Daisy Wheel printer will give a higher-quality print and so is often used to prepare documents for external distribution.

MICROCOMPUTER BACKING STORAGE

As with larger computers, backing storage devices are required to hold data and programs for transference to and from the central processor as required. In principle, microcomputers use the same type of device—magnetic tape and magnetic disc—but they are constructed on a smaller scale. Magnetic tape cassettes are commonly used (that is, a tape sealed and stored in a container) and are virtually identical with the cassettes used in audio systems. They tend to be rather slow, with transfer rates of about 1500 characters per second, and, in many cases, are not particularly reliable.

A more popular medium for holding large volumes of data is the magnetic disc, which brings with it the facility for directly accessing records. The two types of disc commonly used with microcomputers are floppy discs and the Winchester disc. These are described in some detail in the chapter on computer storage.

Exercises

5.1. What are the basic elements of a computer? Using any illustration of your choice, explain how these play their part in processing data.

5.2. A computer consists of a central processor supported by a number of peripheral devices. Give examples of the different types of peripheral device, explaining their purposes in relation to the central processor.

5.3. Differentiate between an analogue computer and a digital computer. What is the essential difference between an analogue watch and a digital watch.

5.4. Give an account of the development of the main aids to

calculating up to the introduction of the modern computer.

5.5. What do you consider to be the main functions of a computer's central processing unit.

5.6. Explain the main differences in principle between a mechanical accounting machine and an electronic computer.

5.7. Explain what is meant by the terms 'hardware' and 'software'.

Chapter 6

Representing data in a computer

Before we go on to examine in detail how the components of a computer configuration set about processing data, it would be as well to consider how these data can be expressed and communicated in a form the computer can deal with (Fig. 6.1).

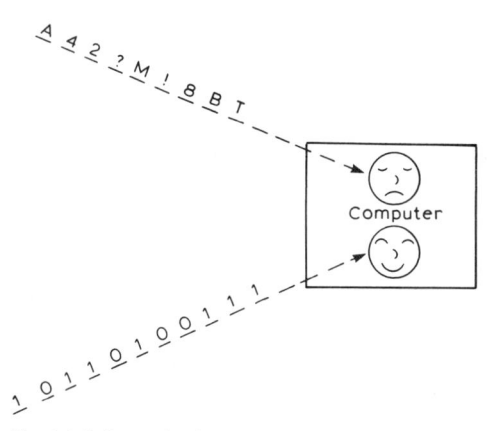

Fig. 6.1. Information into a computer

Three points we should bear in mind are:

(1) Data items generally originate and are captured in terms of the digits (0–9), letters (A–Z) and symbols (?, £, &, etc.) that we normally use in written communications.
(2) A digital computer will, by definition, work only in discrete numbers (or digits).
(3) While we have not as yet discussed the mechanics of how it is done, we are dealing with devices that store and manipulate data magnetically or electronically. Put simply, this means that their capacity to handle data is limited to the absence or presence of an electric potential, the direction—clockwise or anti-clockwise—of a magnetic field. This means that all data items are represented in and

manipulated through two-state devices that can be used only to indicate one of two available conditions: on or off, yes or no, or, expressed digitally, zero or one. All information dealt with in a computer must, in the final analysis, be expressed in one of these two terms. A number system based on two variables only is called a *binary system*.

Binary arithmetic

There are, in common use, a variety of numbering systems with which we are familiar. For example, when measuring time, we know that 60 seconds equal 1 minute, 60 minutes equal 1 hour and 24 hours equal 1 day. In linear measurements 12 inches equal 1 foot, 3 feet equal 1 yard, and so on. In money we know that 2 halfpence equal 1 penny and that 100 pence equal £1.

In all of these systems a 'carry-over' occurs when a given number is reached:

50 seconds + 40 seconds = 30 carry 1 = 1 minute 30 seconds
6 inches + 9 inches = 3 carry 1 = 1 foot 3 inches
£0.57 + £0.66 = 23 carry 1 = £1.23

The most common number system that we use is that having a carry-over of 10. This is known as the decimal or denary system. The value of each digit in a decimal expression is determined by its position in relation to the others. We sometimes call this its place value. For example, in the number 2345 we know that the digit on the extreme right is equal to 5 units; the next to its left equals 4 tens; the next, 3 hundreds; and the next, 2 thousands. Each digit, then, reading from right to left, represents the multiple of a successively higher power of 10, where $10^0 = 1$, $10^1 = 10$, $10^2 = 100$, and so on.

$$2345 = (2 \times 10^3) + (3 \times 10^2) + (4 \times 10^1) + (5 \times 10^0)$$
$$= 2000 + 300 + 40 + 5 = 2345$$

A number system based on 10 (the base in any number system is known as the radix) involves the use of ten variables—0, 1, 2, 3, 4, 5, 6, 7, 8 and 9. As we saw earlier, a computer is unable to cope with such a wide range of digits, being limited in fact to two—0 and 1. It uses a number system with a radix of 2—the binary system.

In a decimal system, carry-over occurs each time 10 is reached and is indicated by moving a 1 to the left followed by a zero. In a binary system a carry-over occurs every time 2 is reached and is indicated in the same way by moving a 1 to the left followed by a zero.

In decimal 5 + 5 = 10 (decimal 10)
In binary   1 + 1 = 10 (decimal equivalent 2)
and
            1 + 1 + 1 = 1 carry 1 = 11 (decimal equivalent 3)

In a decimal system place values increase by an additional power of 10, moving from right to left of an expression, while in a binary system these place values increase by additional powers of 2. Place values in a decimal system = $10^4, 10^3, 10^2, 10^1, 10^0$ and in a binary system = $2^4, 2^3, 2^2, 2^1, 2^0$ (remember $2^0 = 1, 2^1 = 2, 2^2 = 4, 2^3 = 8$, and so on). This means that in the binary expression 11011 we have, reading from left to right:

$$(1 \times 2^4) + (1 \times 2^3) + (0 \times 2^2) + (1 \times 2^1) + (1 \times 2^0)$$
= 16 + 8 + 0 + 2 + 1 = decimal 27

Conversion from decimal to binary notation

The principle used here is to divide the decimal number successively by 2 until it is reduced to zero. When, on division by 2, a remainder of 1 occurs, this becomes a binary digit 1; when there is no remainder, this becomes a binary digit 0. The binary expression is built up from right to left.

Example: To convert the decimal number 349 to binary.

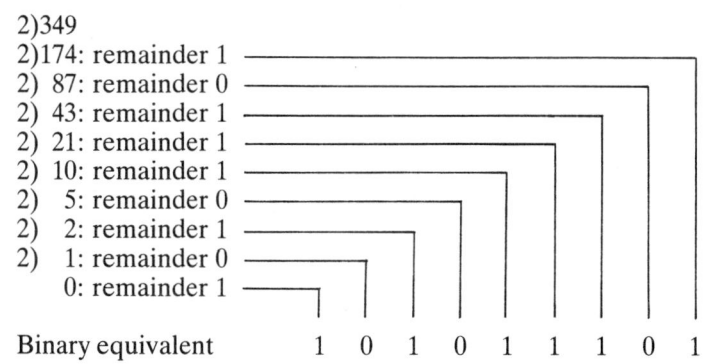

```
2)349
2)174: remainder 1
2) 87: remainder 0
2) 43: remainder 1
2) 21: remainder 1
2) 10: remainder 1
2)  5: remainder 0
2)  2: remainder 1
2)  1: remainder 0
    0: remainder 1

Binary equivalent      1  0  1  0  1  1  1  0  1
```

Conversion from binary to decimal notation

The decimal value of a binary expression is equal to the sum of the decimal values of the binary digits.

Example: To convert binary number 101011.

$$\begin{aligned}&1\quad 0\quad 1\quad 0\quad 1\quad 1\\ &= 2^5 + 0 + 2^3 + 0 + 2^1 + 2^0\\ &= 32 + 0 + 8 + 0 + 2 + 1 = \text{decimal } 43\end{aligned}$$

Binary fractions

In a binary integer (whole number) successive places to the left increase in value by an additional positive power of 2. In a fraction successive places to the right decrease their value by an additional negative power of 2.

Binary fraction					Decimal fraction	
.1	=	2^{-1}		=	½	= 0.5
.01	=	2^{-2}	= $\dfrac{1}{2 \times 2}$	=	¼	= 0.25
.001	=	2^{-3}	= $\dfrac{1}{2 \times 2 \times 2}$	=	⅛	= 0.125
.0001	=	2^{-4}	= $\dfrac{1}{2 \times 2 \times 2 \times 2}$	=	¹⁄₁₆	= 0.0625

CONVERSION OF DECIMAL FRACTION TO BINARY FRACTION

Multiply the decimal fraction successively by 2, counting each 1 carry-over as a binary 1, and if there is no carry-over, as a binary 0. Discard the carry-over for the purpose of the next multiplication. The binary expression is built up from left to right.

Example: To convert decimal 0.375 to a binary fraction.

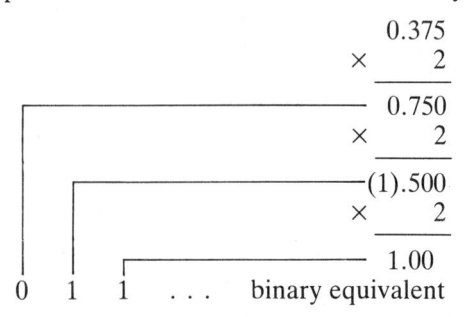

$$\begin{array}{r}0.375\\ \times \quad 2\\ \hline 0.750\\ \times \quad 2\\ \hline (1).500\\ \times \quad 2\\ \hline 1.00\end{array}$$

0   1   1   ...   binary equivalent

CONVERSION OF BINARY FRACTION TO DECIMAL FRACTION

The decimal value in the binary expression is equal to the sum of the decimal values of the binary places.

Example: To convert binary fraction .1101 to a decimal fraction.

$$\begin{aligned}
&\ \ 1 1 0 1 \\
&= 2^{-1} + 2^{-2} + 0 + 2^{-4} \\
&= \tfrac{1}{2} + \tfrac{1}{4} + 0 + \tfrac{1}{16} \\
&= 0.5 + 0.25 + 0 + 0.0625 \\
&\ \ = 0.8125 \text{ decimal fraction}
\end{aligned}$$

It will be evident from this that any decimal number, integer, fraction or mixed number can be converted into a binary expression, and, indeed, the converse is true: binary may be converted to decimal.

Principles of binary arithmetic

Without for the moment concerning ourselves with the mechanics of how binary is stored in a computer and how it is manipulated through arithmetic processes (this will be looked at later), let us give some thought to the principles the machine makes use of in working out its sums.

It is true to say that however complex a mathematical problem, if it is capable of solution, it can be solved by the application of the four basic arithmetic rules—addition, multiplication, subtraction and division. In manual calculating reducing a problem to these simple terms could well be too lengthy a process, and so more advanced principles are used to speed things up. However, one great advantage a computer has is that it is easily capable of coping with a mass of simple arithmetic in a very short space of time. In saying that, we are thinking in terms of perhaps millions of calculations a second. The computer can make use of the great speed at which it works to simplify its internal arithmetic processes.

Of our four basic rules, multiplication can be eliminated by repetitive addition. The answer to 63 × 34 can be found by adding 63 to itself 34 times. This is the basic principle the computer uses in its binary multiplication, although short-cuts can be taken by using a 'shift' technique. This, in principle, means moving the whole binary statement one digit to the left and adding a zero, which has the effect of multiplying the statement by the radix—that is, 2.

Subtraction can also be eliminated by a process known as complementary addition. In decimal calculations the complement of a number is that number which must be added to it to give a zero total. For example, the complement of decimal 473 is 527. On addition the sum of these is 1000—in other words, zeros in the three significant digits. To subtract 473 from another number, say 982, we add the complement of 473—that is, 527. 527 plus 982 =

1509. Ignore the first digit and the correct answer results: 509. The usefulness of this method when calculating in binary lies in the fact that a binary complement can easily be found. This is done by reversing the value of all the digits (1 becomes 0 and 0 becomes 1) and adding 1 to the result.

Here is an example of complementary subtraction using numbers expressed in binary form:

```
111010 − 100111
Find the true complement of    100111
reverse digits                 011000
add                                 1
                               _____

true complement                011001
then add                       111010
                               _____
                             (1)010011
111010 − 100111 =               10011
```

Now, using complementary addition to subtract, we can perform division by repetitive subtraction. The answer to 1467 − 49 can be found by counting the number of times 49 can be subtracted from 1467. Again, as was the case in multiplication, shift techniques can be used by moving the whole statement one digit to the right and so dividing by the radix—that is, 2.

Using these techniques in computer arithmetic means that all four basic arithmetic rules can be carried out in terms of simple binary addition.

So far, all of the binary expressions we have used have been in what is known as pure, or serial, binary—that is, one complete series of binary digits the value of which is numerically equivalent to the original decimal expression. The binary numbers dealt with in a computer are not necessarily stored in this form. While computers almost universally use binary as their base number system, variations in the construction of binary expressions are often used for reasons of convenience and economy. Perhaps it would be as well to note here that different techniques may be used in different makes of machine. The following is an account of some of the ways in which binary is used other than in its serial form.

Binary coded decimal

One alternative way of recording numbers using the basic binary principle is to convert each individual decimal digit into its binary equivalent rather than convert the whole number into a continuous binary expression. For example, the decimal number 569 in pure binary is 1000111001.

Converting each individual digit to binary gives:

5   6   9
0101 0110 1001

It is usual when storing numbers in this form in a computer to allocate a standard number of digits for each of the ten numbers 0–9, giving the following pattern:

0 = 0000
1 = 0001
2 = 0010
3 = 0011
4 = 0100
5 = 0101
6 = 0110
7 = 0111
8 = 1000
9 = 1001

Referring back to the example above, 569 in binary coded decimal (BCD), it is important to remember that the place value of each binary digit within each group is measured in terms of the power of 2, but the groups themselves in terms of the power of 10:

$$(2^2 + 0 + 2^0)^{10^2} + (2^2 + 2^1 + 0)^{10^1} + (2^3 + 0 + 0 + 2^0)^{10^0}$$

Octal number system

An octal number system has a radix of 8. This means that the range of different characters required to express a number in octal is only eight—equivalent to the decimal numbers 0–7. It will be noted above that the number of binary digits needed to express any decimal digit between 0 and 7 is only three and furthermore that all of the binary patterns containing three binary digits are used—that is, 000 to 111. This is not the case when using BCD, since four binary digits will give a total of sixteen patterns, 0000–1111, and only ten of these are used.

A decimal number can be converted to octal in much the same way as to binary except that a division by 8 is used.

Example: To convert 6189 to octal.

```
8)6189
8)  773: remainder ─────────────────────┐
8)   96: remainder ──────────────────┐  │
8)   12: remainder ───────────────┐  │  │
8)    1: remainder ────────────┐  │  │  │
8)    0: remainder ─────────┐  │  │  │  │
      Octal expression      1  4  0  5  5
```

This, of course, may be expressed as

$(1 \times 8^4) + (4 \times 8^3) + 0 + (5 \times 8^1) + (5 \times 8^0) = 6189$

Individual digits within this octal expression—14055—can now be expressed in binary groupings. This is known as *binary coded octal*.

001   100   000   101   101

Remember that the same principle applies as in BCD—binary digits within each group are expressed in powers of 2 but in this case the values of groups are expressed in powers of 8.

Hexadecimal number system

It was mentioned earlier that the use of binary coded decimal utilizes only ten of the sixteen patterns available in a group of four binary digits. The use of a hexadecimal system, since this has a radix of 16, gets around this problem, although, in turn, it raises a further one, as sixteen different characters are needed to express it. Thus, in addition to the ten digits we normally use we require another six; the letters A–F are usually used for the purpose. This means that when hexadecimal is expressed in ordinary open language, A becomes the symbol for 10, B for 11, and so on, to F for 15.

In converting decimal to hexadecimal the same principle is used as in the case of binary or octal, except that successive divisions by 16 are made.

Example: To convert 15352 to hexadecimal.

```
16)15352
16)  959:   remainder 8 ─────────────────────────────┐
16)   59:   remainder 15 represented by ──────────┐  │
16)    3:   remainder 11 represented           ┐  │  │
       0:   remainder 3              │   by    │  │  │
    Hexadecimal equivalent 3         B         F     8
```

that is: $(3 \times 16^3) + (B \times 16^2) + (F \times 16^1) + (8 \times 16^0) = 15352$
  12288   +   2816   +   240   +   8   = 15352

Individual characters within the hexadecimal expression may be expressed in binary groupings known as *hexadecimal coded binary* as follows:

0011   1011   1111   1000

Here the value of successive groups from right to left increases by additional powers of 16.

Alphabetic characters in binary

Up to now we have been concerned only with seeing how numbers can be expressed in terms of binary. However, a computer, of course, also has to cope with alphabetic characters and with symbols, each of these being represented by a unique binary expression. There is no standard way of doing this, in the sense that there is a code pattern common to all makes and types of computer, but the following illustrates one approach to the problem.

As we have seen, the ten digits 0–9 can be expressed in binary coded decimal expressions, 0000–0001. We can then adapt this principle by dividing the alphabet into three groups of 9, 9 and 8 characters consisting of A to I, J to R and S to Z, respectively. The numbered position of the letter within the group can be indicated by using the range of binary patterns as for numbers—for instance, A = 0001, I = 1001. The group can then be prefixed by two additional digits to indicate the group within which the letter falls. For example, we might use 01 for the group A to I, 10 for the group J to R and 11 for S to Z, leaving the prefix 00 to represent a digit—0 to 9. In this case the letter A would be represented by 010001, K by 100010 and U by 110011 and the digit 7 would then become 000111.

Exercises

6.1. Give an account of how alphabetic characters can be expressed in binary for storage in a computer.

6.2. Explain how a number may be held in storage in these three ways: (1) serial binary, (2) binary coded decimal, (3) binary coded octal. Express the number 156 in each of these three modes.

6.3. What do you understand by the binary number system? Explain two ways by which a number and one way by which a letter can be expressed in binary. Illustrate your answer by expressing the decimal number 125 in the two ways you suggest and show a binary equivalent for the letter N.

6.4. Describe what is meant by binary coded decimal. Express the following decimal numbers in BCD form: (a) 478; (b) 810; (c) 4078; (d) 1000.

6.5. Express the following decimal expressions in serial binary: (a) 387; (b) 512; (c) 17.25; (d) 64.375.

6.6. Differentiate between binary coded octal and binary coded decimal. Illustrate your answer by expressing in these two binary modes the decimal number 1365.

Chapter 7
Data input

The point was made earlier that data items, when they originate, must be captured in some way. In commercial data processing this is usually done by recording the data on a document of one kind or another—known as a Source Document. Basically, the data may be recorded in one of two ways:

(1) By using the ordinary characters—digits, letters, etc.—that we normally use in our day-by-day written communications, handwritten, typewritten or printed. However, data recorded in this way present a very wide variance not only in character shapes and sizes, but also in the documents on which the characters are recorded. This means they are not capable of acceptance or reading by a machine.

(2) By using standard stylized character shapes and sizes or by recording the data in coded form, both of which are machine readable, and also recording the data on a standard-sized document that a machine is able to accept.

In the final analysis, a computer is only able to accept data that are expressed in a representation of binary coding. It follows, therefore, that we must interpose between the data items in their original written or coded form a machine that will read them and convert them into the required binary representation. Such a machine is usually known as a *document reader*.

This process presents little difficulty in the case of data captured in the modes suggested in (2) above, since the original source document can be fed directly into the reader. However, data captured in the mode suggested in (1) do present a problem, in that they must first be converted into a form that is machine acceptable before they can be presented to a reader for entry to the computer. This conversion—known as data preparation—is usually accomplished by sight reading the original items from the source document and entering them to a machine through an alphanumeric keyboard giving one of the following two results:

(1) The machine will prepare a second document containing the

74 Data input

data in code or printed in stylized characters that can, in turn, be accepted by a document reader. For example, punched cards, punched paper tape, MICR documents.

(2) The machine will directly convert the keyboard-entered data into their appropriate binary coding, storing this in turn on a magnetic storage medium and thus by-passing the need to prepare a second machine acceptable document. The data stored on the magnetic medium are subsequently read into the computer. For example, key-to-disc or key-to-tape encoding.

Fig. 7.11 gives a summary of the more commonly used computer input methods, relating each to the comments given above. The following is a more detailed description of each.

Punched cards

This, in common with punched paper tape, is a very costly and time-consuming process, as it involves the preparation of a second document that is machine acceptable to replace the original non-acceptable source document. It has been supplanted in newer computer installations by data preparation systems that by-pass this need to prepare a second document. However, until recent years, punched cards were used extensively in computer operations and, indeed, they are still to be found in many established computer installations. For this reason a description of their use is included.

A punched card is a piece of high-quality cardboard made to exact size and standard thickness. The accuracy of its dimensions is critical for machine processing. The principle underlying the use of punched cards is to record data in the form of holes which a machine can readily sense. Each position on the card where a hole may be punched is given a predetermined value or meaning. Thus, when sensing the presence of a hole, the machine will interpret it in terms of the value it is intended to represent. The most widely used type of punched card, known as an 80-col card, is divided into 80 vertical columns (Fig. 7.1), each column having twelve positions into which holes may be punched. Each column will record one character—a digit, a letter or a symbol—by means of a pattern of one, two or three holes unique to each character. These patterns of holes representing characters are known as a punching code. The code varies slightly from system to system. An example of how data can be recorded in punched cards is shown in Fig. 7.1. The digits 0–9 are punched into columns 1–10, the alphabet into columns 18–43 and a number of symbols into columns 11–17 and 44–64.

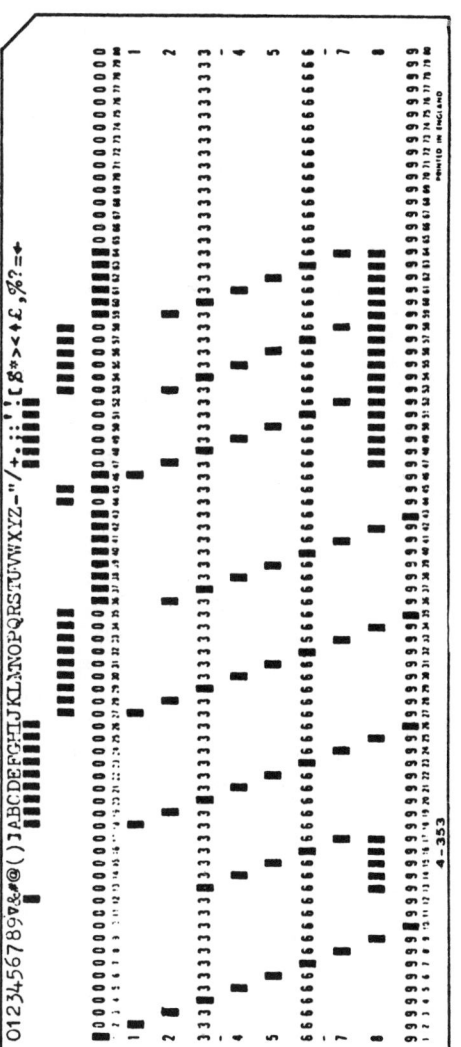

Fig. 7.1. 80-column punched card, with ICL 64-character card code

While each position in a vertical column has a predetermined value, if we are to make sense of all the holes punched, we must also know what each column or group of columns represents. For instance, suppose that we wish to represent the following information on the card:

Reference number   Description   Quantity   Value

We must allocate a fixed number of columns to contain each of these data fields. These fields are usually distinguished from each other by printing vertical lines on the card to mark the extent of each field, with a field heading (for example, Description) printed at the top of each group of columns. The whole of the information printed on the card, in this case consisting of four data fields, is a *data record*.

From a machine point of view, entering source data into the computer via punched cards is a three-stage affair (Fig. 7.2):

(1) Cards are prepared on a *card punch* by an operator reading data from an original source document and entering it through a keyboard. At this stage the card is perforated with the holes representing the data.

(2) The same information is punched a second time into the same card by a different operator using a *verifying punch*. In this case the machine will not actually perforate the card but will, on depression of a key, sense whether the relevant holes are already present and whether the pattern of holes is correct for the particular character entered. Should there be any difference in the two punchings, then an error state is signalled, and the card removed, checked back to the original source document and, if incorrect,

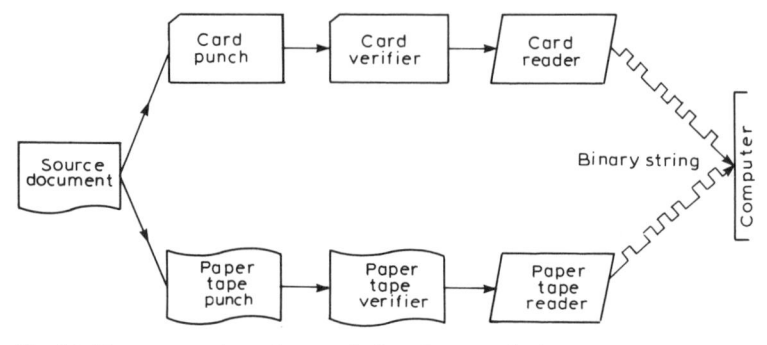

Fig. 7.2. Data preparation using punched cards or punched paper tape

punched again. It is important that cards repunched to correct errors should in turn be verified to ensure the accuracy of the correction. This second punching process is known as *verification*.

(3) The verified cards are then fed into a *punched card reader* which will sense the position of the holes and convert the information they represent into its binary equivalent and transmit this as a series of electric pulses to the computer central processor.

Card reading speeds vary from machine to machine—from about 300 cards per minute in the older, slower types of reader to more than 1500 per minute in newer, faster machines. An average reading rate would probably be in the neighbourhood of 900–1000 cards per minute, giving a maximum reading rate of around 1300 characters per second, although, of course, the effective reading rate will depend on the number of characters on the cards.

Punched paper tape

In principle the method of recording data on paper tape is much the same as that using punched cards but a continuous strip of paper is used rather than a number of separate cards. Each character is represented by a unique pattern of holes punched across the width of the tape—known as a *frame*. The number of tracks (that is, positions for holes) across the tape varies from system to system but the most commonly used is an eight-track tape, of which seven tracks are used for recording data. This allows for 128 different patterns of holes representing digits, letters, symbols and control instructions (Fig. 7.3).

The eighth track is used for checking purposes and is known as a *parity track*. Its purpose is to provide a safeguard against errors caused by faulty transcription of the data. A hole is automatically punched in the parity track when necessary, to ensure either that every complete pattern consists of an odd number of holes (known

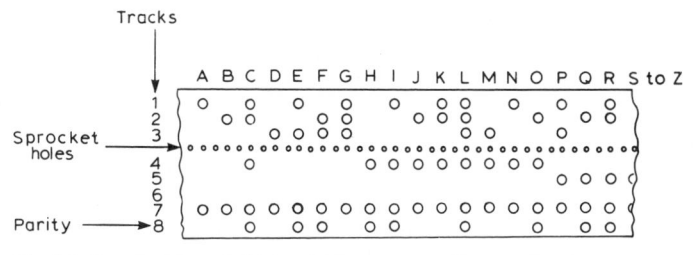

Fig. 7.3. Punched 8-track (7-data-bit) paper tape (International Computers Ltd)

as an 'odd' parity check) or that every pattern consists of an even number of holes (an 'even' parity check). When the tape is read, a check is made on each pattern by counting the number of holes to ensure that it conforms with the correct principle. If this is not so (if, for instance, a pattern with an even number of holes is found on a tape using the 'odd' parity check system), the presence of an error is signalled and an investigation must be made.

Entering data into a computer via punched paper tape is, again, a three-stage affair following the same pattern as with punched cards. A keyboard punching operation is followed by a keyboard verifying operation and the data are then read into the computer through a punched paper tape reader. Reading speeds for paper tape vary between 1000 and 2000 characters per second.

Magnetic ink character recognition (MICR)

The MICR system is a system designed to eliminate to a great extent expensive data conversion procedures, such as are necessary with punched cards and punched paper tape. However, while there is no need for a second document, it does entail a limited degree of source data conversion.

The MICR system is based on the use of a stylized set of characters printed in an ink containing a ferromagnetic substance. This ink can be magnetized, and the shape of the characters can subsequently be detected through their magnetic fields by a reader designed for this purpose.

The two most important magnetic character founts at present in use are the E13B and the CMC7; the former originates in the USA and the latter is of French origin. The E13B fount is most generally used in the UK, and the CMC7 fount is more widely used in European countries. Examples of these founts are shown in Fig. 7.4.

The main development of MICR using the E13B fount has been in banking, and specialized machines have been developed to meet the needs of banking systems. Its use in these systems is restricted to a range of 14 characters—ten numeric digits and four symbols.

Essential considerations in the preparation of MICR documents are:

(1) Since the source document is also the machine input form, its size must fall within the tolerances imposed by the machine used for processing, although in practice these machines will accept a fairly wide range of shapes and sizes of document.

(2) The successful reading of the characters depends upon the accurate reproduction of the character shape and constant ink

a 1 2 3 4 5 6 7 8 9 0 ⋯ ⫶ ⸗ ⫼

b 1 2 3 4 5 6 7 8 9 0 ⋯ ⫶ ⸗ ⫼

The E 13 B fount

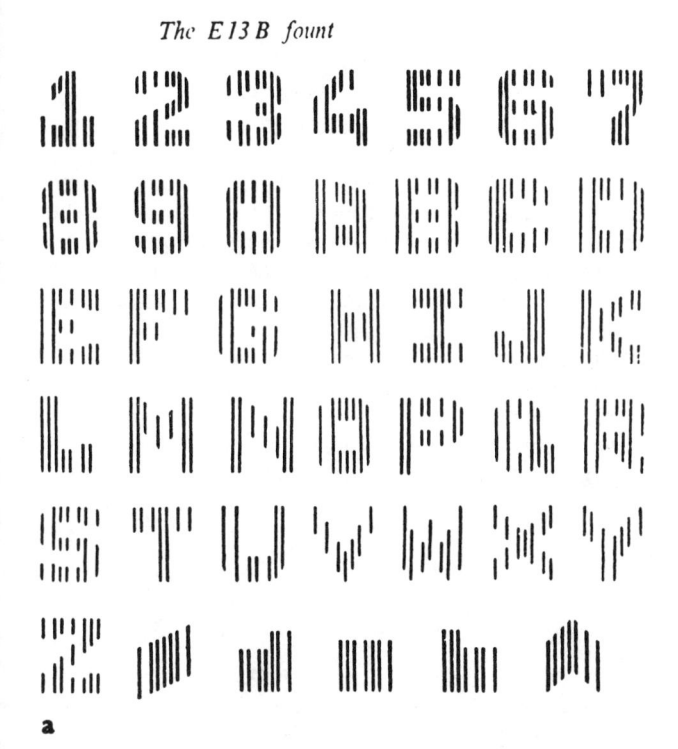

a 1 2 3 4 5 6 7 8 9 0 A B C D E F G H I J K L M N O P Q R S T U V W X Y Z

b ⌇⌇⌇⌇ 1 2 3 4 5 6 7 8 9 0 A B C D E F G H I J K L M N O P Q R S T U V W X Y Z

The C.M.C. 7 fount

Fig. 7.4. Examples of magnetic ink characters

80 Data input

density. This necessitates printing of very high quality.

(3) The characters must appear in predetermined positions on the document to ensure their correct positioning at the reading head during processing.

Magnetic ink characters may be encoded on the document at two stages.

The first of these is when the document is initially printed. This encoding is limited to non-variable data such as, in the case of cheques, the cheque number, the branch reference number and the customer account number. This is known as pre-encoding.

The second stage occurs after the variable data have been entered, which, in the case of a cheque, would be after the insertion of the amount by the drawer. This is known as post-encoding (see Fig. 7.5). The method used is to pass the cheques one by one through a keyboard machine, where the cheque remains visible while the operator reads the amount and keys it in. The cheque then passes through the machine, where the characters are printed in magnetic ink. As a precaution against error, the machine adds the amounts on the cheques and gives a total for a batch at the end of the run. This can then be checked against a total prepared by pre-listing before the documents are processed. MICR documents can be read at about 1200 a minute, which, on a basis of, say, 75 characters on each, gives a reading rate of 1500 characters per second.

MICR sorting machines are also extensively used in this system to sort, by use of the MICR encoded branch code, into branch batches.

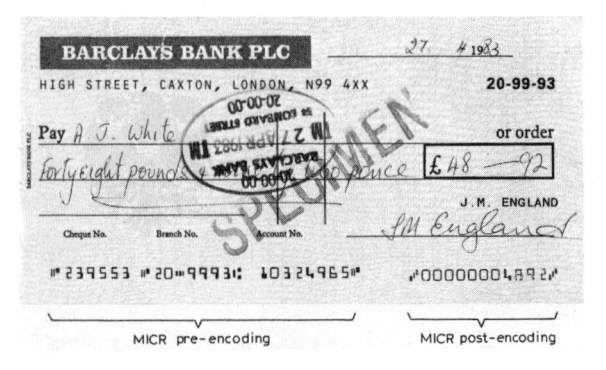

Fig. 7.5. MICR encoding on a cheque

Data input 81

Optical character recognition (OCR)

OCR is another way of encoding data direct on to a machine acceptable document but one that relies solely on the shape of the character rather than the properties possessed by the ink. It is far more adaptable than MICR in that it can be prepared on almost any printing device fitted with a special OCR typeface. The characters are not as stylized as are those in MICR and so are more easily read by human sight. An illustration of an optical character fount is given in Fig. 7.6.

1234567890-*.
a
1234567890-*.
b

Fig. 7.6. An OCR fount

The data contained on OCR documents are transferred to the computer through an optical character reader in which characters are scanned by an artificial light source and on recognition converted into the relevant binary code for entry to the computer. With the most up-to-date machines reading speed for these documents can be around 3000 characters per second.

As is the case with MICR documents, data can be pre-encoded or post-encoded, although with OCR documents the post-encoding stage usually takes the form of a technique known as *optical mark reading*. A series of columns of digits, 0–9, is printed on the document and numeric data are recorded by making marks through the relevant digits. On passing through a reader the positions of the marks are sensed and their values attributed by virtue of their position.

One important application that combines the principles of optical characters and optical mark reading is in gas and electricity billing. A document printed in optical characters is prepared on a computer printer quoting the customer name and address, reference number and last meter reading. Also printed on the form is a series of columns of digits, as described above. The meter reader can then record the current reading by striking through the relevant digits. The completed form is then fed into an optical mark reader, which means that the computer will now have available all the information required to compare previous and current

82   Data input

meter readings, compute consumption, prepare a bill for submission to the customer and also print another form for use at the next meter reading (Fig. 7.7).

By virtue of the fact that the document is initially prepared by the computer, circulated for additional information to be entered and then fed back into the computer, it is known as a *turn-around* document.

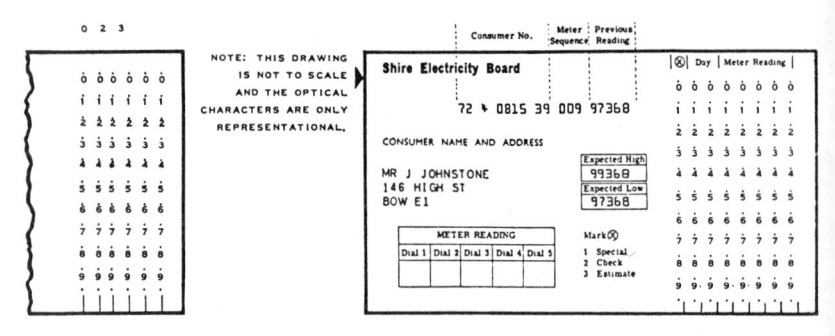

Fig. 7.7. OCR mark reading document

Punched tags

Punched tags are small punched cards on which source data can be pre-recorded. A widely used tag of this type is known as a Kimball tag, and one of its most popular applications is to record the sale of garments. Data relating to the garment—for example, production reference number, size, colour, price, style, etc.—are punched into a tag which is attached to the garment at the manufacturing stage. The information is also printed on the tag in ordinary readable characters.

Tags normally consist of three or four sections with the information repeated on each so that one section can be detached at each stage of marketing—that is, wholesaler stage, retailer stage, etc. The tags can then be entered directly to the computer through a tag reader, which obviates the need for data conversion procedures. Major advantages in the use of tags include:

(1) In a mass production situation the tags themselves can be mass produced when relating to identical units of production.
(2) This mass production of tags minimizes errors and reduces costs.

(3) There is no delay in processing the information they contain, as data conversion procedures are not needed.

Bar coding

Bar coding is a point-of-sale data capturing technique. Methods vary but basically it consists of a printed code in the form of lines, or bars, of varying thickness and spacing to represent a binary coding (Fig. 7.8). The bars are printed on the product container or

Fig. 7.8. Example of bar code

label and can be scrutinized optically with a portable device—a light pen—which generates a pattern of pulses conforming with the bar coding for automatic transmission to computer storage. Validation procedures programmed within the reading device will signal any misreading, so that a second attempt can be made. This has become a very popular method of recording the movement of goods from retail outlets, and examples of this bar coding can now be seen on many products. It has the advantage that the coded data can be printed at source when the containers or labels are prepared and so, again, no data conversion procedures are required.

Badges

Badges represent a further method of entering data direct to a computer without the need for data conversion. A badge consists of a small plastics card on which identifying data are embossed and contains a magnetic stripe, usually on the reverse side of the card, into which control data are encoded. An example of this is a bank card (Fig. 7.9), which can be inserted into a cash dispensing machine. In this case it is used in conjunction with a touch-pad keyboard through which variable data may be entered while the control data items are read automatically from the magnetic stripe when the card is inserted. Data items are immediately transferred to the computer, validated and processed, and the results, in the form of dispensing the cash required, transmitted back to the machine.

It will be appreciated that all of the input methods discussed so far involve the need for machines that will read documents. This is not the case in the following methods.

Fig. 7.9. Bank credit card

Key-to-tape

In principle, the key-to-tape system consists of a keyboard very similar to an ordinary typewriter keyboard, a magnetic tape unit and a small store (known as a buffer store) in which the data entered can be held temporarily before they are written to the magnetic tape. An operator, reading from the source document, will key in the data, which will then be held in the buffer store until a block of data has been completed, and the whole block will then be written to the magnetic tape. Magnetic tapes used in this system are usually small cassette tapes rather than the larger open-reel type. Errors can be corrected by back spacing and retyping, and most systems incorporate a visual display on which data can be visually checked for errors.

A positive verification system is incorporated by rewinding the tape to transfer the data, a block at a time, back to the buffer store. The same data, from the same source documents, are then keyed in a second time but by a different operator. The original entry and the second entry are then compared, and in the event of any difference between the two, an error state is signalled. The use of tape cassettes rather than the conventional open-reel type used in the main computer system makes loading and handling the tape much more convenient. The data on these cassette tapes can then be transferred to the tape system employed by the computer.

Advantages claimed in the use of the key-to-tape system are:

(1) It is faster than punched card or punched paper tape, because it is less mechanical.
(2) A magnetic tape can be used over and over again, whereas a card or paper tape can be used only once.
(3) Error correction and verification procedures are easy.
(4) It is a much quieter process than card or paper tape punching.
(5) Less storage space is required for magnetic tape than for cards and paper tape.

Key-to-disc

Key-to-disc is another, and far more popular, method of entering data from a source document direct to a magnetic medium but this time a magnetic disc. While, from an operator's point of view, a key-to-disc system is similar in many respects to key-to-tape, it is a rather more sophisticated system in two major respects:

(1) A number of operators at keyboard stations (32 would not be unusual) can simultaneously key in data items, which are passed through a minicomputer to one magnetic disc unit (see Fig. 7.10).
(2) A validation program can be held in the minicomputer to check the validity of field and records formats—that is, to check that each data item contains the correct number and type of characters. It will also check that quantitative data fall within preset limits, perform check digit verification checks and generate batch totals. These validation procedures ensure that fully validated data items are eventually entered into the computer and so save time by making it no longer necessary to perform these procedures on main computer runs.

A key-to-disc system consists of:

(a) A number of keyboard devices for entering data from source documents.
(b) A minicomputer in which there are control and validation programs.
(c) A magnetic disc drive.
(d) A magnetic tape deck used for transferring the data from the disc to the main computer backing storage.

86   Data input

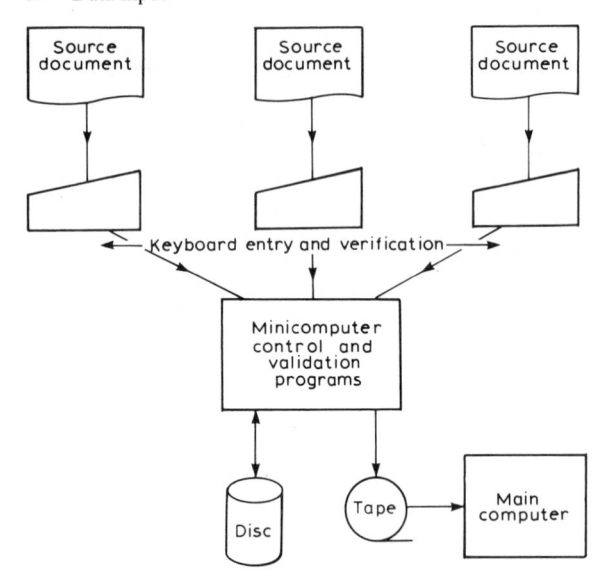

Fig. 7.10. Key-to-disc data preparation

A typical key-to-disc preparation routine is as follows:

(1) The first operator reads from source documents, keying in information through keyboard.
(2) Information is shown on a visual display unit for visual checking so that any obvious errors can be corrected.
(3) Validation checks are carried out by minicomputer.
(4) A block of data is written to disc.
(5) The second operator performs the verification procedure by retrieving data from disc and keying in for a second time the original source data. Comparison of the two versions will reveal errors for correction.
(6) Verified data items are written back to disc.
(7) At the end of the run data on disc are transferred to tape for entry to the computer's main backing storage.

Teletype terminals

Teletype terminals provide a means for direct entry to a computer through the medium of a keyboard similar in many ways to an ordinary typewriter keyboard. It contains a full range of alpha-numeric keys and also incorporates a number of 'command' keys for conveying instructions to the computer. These devices are extensively used for communicating with a computer from remote points. In addition to a keyboard, the device has a printing mechanism that will prepare a printed record—a 'hard copy'—of all the information passing through the terminal. Having entered the data, the operator depresses a 'send' key and the data items are conveyed to the computer over transmission lines. A description of data transmission to and from terminals is given in Chapter 11. Strictly speaking, a Teletype terminal is usually both an input and output device, being able to both transmit and receive data, the data emanating from the computer being automatically reproduced on the machine's printing head. Data entry through a manual keyboard is necessarily slow, being limited to the rate of key depressions, and therefore unsuitable for large-scale data entry.

This type of machine is also often used as a computer operator console providing a means for the operator to communicate with the computer and, in turn, for messages generated by the computer itself to be conveyed to the operator. The printed record provides a permanent record of computer operations. In many cases messages originating from the operator are printed in black and computer-originating messages in red.

Visual display units

The visual display unit (VDU) is another combined input/output device with a keyboard for data entry and a cathode ray tube on which data are displayed on entry and on which data output from the computer are shown. Like the Teletype described above, it is extensively used as a remote computer terminal. Most microcomputers incorporate a VDU as an integrated component, although many such machines are also able to drive additional VDUs as terminals.

Compared with a Teletype terminal, the cost of VDU hardware is lower, but this is partly offset by the fact that more complex and therefore more expensive programming is required. A VDU will, in itself, only give a 'soft copy', in contrast to the printed hard copy of the Teletype.

Major advantages of VDUs are that output of data is very much faster than can be obtained through the mechanical printing mechanism of a Teletype and that a VDU is not restricted in its display to conventional alphanumeric characters but can also display charts, graphs, diagrams, etc.

As with Teletype devices, input rate through the keyboard is very slow, being limited by the rate at which the keys can be depressed, and therefore VDUs are not suitable for large-scale data entry.

Teletype and VDU terminals are extensively used in an 'interrogating' capacity—that is, requesting information held on computer files and updating individual selected records. For example, on presentation of a cheque at the bank, such a terminal could be used to communicate with the computer on which the account is held in order to ascertain whether the balance on the account is sufficient to meet payment on the cheque.

Microcomputer input

Keyboard entry is the standard method used for microcomputer input. In some cases the keyboard is an integral part of the microcomputer and in other cases it is a separate component connected to the computer through an input port. As data items are entered, they are displayed on a screen—a visual display unit—so that checking can take place before data entry to the computer memory.

Acoustic (voice) input

While still very much an area of development, it is possible to communicate, in a very limited way, with a computer by voice. This is done by converting the analogue sound signal, resulting from speaking, into a numeric binary expression, holding this in store and associating it with the meaning the sound is intended to convey. For example, a number ('one', 'five', 'nine' etc.) or a command (say 'add', 'read', 'stop').

However, it is only able to recognize sounds for which it has a stored binary counterpart, which means that this form of communication is usually limited to those people who can pronounce the sound in precisely the same way as the original recording.

One application of the use of voice input is in stocktaking. A person wishing to record stock levels, having initially 'taught' the computer to recognize the sound made when voicing the digits 0 to 9, can then dictate into a microphone the digits necessary to identify the stock and the stock level. This analogue voice signal is then passed through an analogue/digital converter and the resultant digital pattern compared with those already held in the computer.

Data capture	Input method	Data preparation	Machine input document	Computer input device
Source document	Key-to-disc	Keyboard entry Key-to-disc encoding and verifying		Magnetic tape or magnetic disc
Source document	Key-to-tape	Keyboard entry Key-to-tape encoding and verifying		Magnetic tape
Source document	Punched cards	Keyboard entry Card punching and card verifying	Punched card	Punched card reader
Source document	Punched paper tape	Keyboard entry Paper tape punching and paper tape verifying	Punched paper tape	Punched paper tape reader
Source/input document	Terminals – Teletype VDU	Keyboard entry		Direct through transmission lines
Direct	Acoustic (voice)			Analogue/digital converter
Source/input document	Badges	Keyboard entry for supplementary data	Badge	Badge reader
Source/input document	MICR Pre-encoding		MICR encoded	MICR reader
Source/input document	MICR Post-encoding	Keyboard entry	MICR encoded	MICR reader
Source/input document	OCR		OCR encoded	OCR reader
Source/input document	OMR		OM encoded	OM reader
Source/input document	Punched tags		Punched tag	Punched tag reader
Source/input document	Bar code		Bar code document	Optical reader

Data origination

Data arising from an activity, event or situation

→ Computer

Fig. 7.11. Summary of input methods

Exercises

7.1. Briefly describe three ways of recording data at source on documents that can be read directly into a computer without the need for data preparation procedures.

7.2. Two ways in which data may be prepared for entry to a computer are: (1) punched cards and (2) key-to-disc encoding. Briefly compare these two methods and show what advantages you feel accrue by the use of the latter.

7.3. What do you understand by a turn-around document? Describe an application with which you are familiar in which this technique is used.

7.4. What is a visual display unit? Explain how data may be input and output through this device.

7.5. Explain the meaning of 'verification' in relation to the preparation of data. How is verification applied in the case of (a) punched cards and (b) key-to-disc systems?

7.6. Describe an application in which you feel bar coding to capture data could be used with advantage.

7.7. What are the main differences between the preparation of data in MICR and OCR? Mention any advantage you feel one system has compared with the other.

7.8. Explain what is meant by optical mark reading. Give examples of the type of data that can be conveniently captured in this way.

7.9. Identify and explain three ways by which data can be captured at source in a machine acceptable form.

Chapter 8
Output

We can look at output from a computer from two different points of view:

(1) The final output, which must be communicated to people in a humanly comprehensible form—that is, in ordinary printed writing, or as diagrams, charts, graphs, etc., of one kind or another. For example, the former case would include a sales invoice to be sent to a customer or a wages slip for an employee, and the latter a graph to show fluctuations in some area of activity.

(2) Intermediate output arising from data processing routines, held in coded form in the computer's storage. For example, the output of a run to update purchase ledger balances made during the second week of the month. These balances would probably not be required unless specifically requested, and it would therefore be pointless to print out a list of them. They are best retained in store until all of the processing for the month has been completed and then printed out as an end-of-the-month list of creditors.

In this chapter we are going to concentrate on devices falling within the first category. Storage devices that cope with the intermediate outputs of processing are dealt with in a later chapter on 'Storage'.

Printers

By far the most widely used output device is a printer, the basic purpose of which is to convert the binary coded output of the computer into the printed digits and letters used in everyday writing. There are two main categories of printer: (1) impact printers and (2) non-impact printers.

Impact printers

For computer output purposes, impact printers can be of two

types: (1) those that print a line of characters virtually simultaneously, known as 'line printers'; (2) those that print one character at a time in succession, known as serial printers or character printers.

LINE PRINTERS

The most important feature of the line printer is, as its name suggests, that it prints a whole line of characters (known as a print line) simultaneously. The types of printer most generally in use for computer work are known as chain, band, barrel and matrix printers. In the first three of these, the type faces are moving continuously even while the printing operation is being performed.

The printing mechanism of a chain printer consists of a closed metal loop, or chain, carrying the typefaces and revolving continuously, parallel to the print line, while a band printer uses a rotating steel band with sets of characters embossed around its circumference. Behind the paper is a row of hammers, released individually as the required character on the chain or band reaches its printing position. The speed of the hammer strike is such that a clear impression is made on the paper, even though the typeface is moving at high speed.

In a barrel printer the characters are embossed on the surface of a metal cylinder, or barrel, each character being repeated along the length of the barrel, one for every printing position (Fig. 8.1). The barrel revolves at high speed, so that each character is presented to the print line in turn. When, for instance, the row of As is lined up in the printing position, hammers are fired simultaneously at all positions in the line where the letter A is required, impressing the paper against the typeface. Next the whole row of Bs moves into position and is printed, and so on through the whole range of characters. This means that a line of type is built up progressively, character by character, during one revolution of the barrel.

Printing speeds of chain, band and barrel printers, while dependent to an extent on the number of characters in a print line and the number in a character set, vary between 300 and 2000 lines a minute, although the most widely used models operate at around 1200 lines of 132 characters a minute. The character set usually has 64 different characters, 26 alphabetic, 10 numeric and the remainder symbols.

The matrix line printer is another type of impact printer, but instead of the impression on the paper being produced by a solid block of metal in the shape of the required character, it is made by

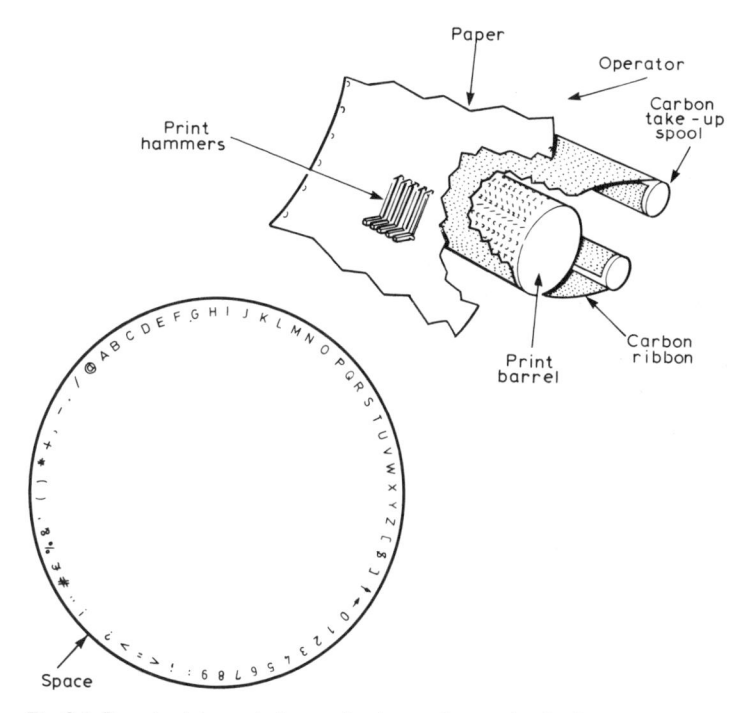

Fig. 8.1. Barrel printer; printing mechanism and example of print barrel character layout

the projecting end of a number of wires carried in an open-ended box the size of one character. The shape of the character is formed as a number of small dots by selecting the pattern of wires necessary to form it and impressing these on the paper. With a number of these boxes arranged side by side along the length of the print line, a complete row of characters can be printed simultaneously. Again, printing speed varies from model to model, falling within the range 125–500 lines a minute.

Continuous stationery is necessary for high-speed line printing, sheets being separated from one another by a line of perforations across the paper. Down each side of the paper is a series of holes (sprocket holes) which engage in sprocket wheels to drive the paper through the printer. These also give a positive registration of the position of the paper. For many output reports preprinted stationery is used. It is important that weight, length of sheets and sprocket hole spacing should conform with the computer manufacturer's specification. Multiple copies may be obtained by the use of

Output device	Extent of use	Hard copy	External distribution	Interrogation	Permanent file	Intermediate output	Turn around for re-input	Information retrieval
Line printer	Extensive	✓	✓		✓		✓ using OCR	✓
Terminal (typewriter)	Extensive	✓		✓	✓			✓
Visual display unit	Extensive			✓			✓ Using light pen	✓
Microfilm and microfiche	Widespread and developing	✓ Two-stage	✓ with viewing device		✓			✓
Graph plotter	Limited	✓	Limited		✓			✓
Punched media	Very limited				✓	✓	✓	
Magnetic media	Extensive					✓		
Audio-response	Developing (limited)			✓				✓

Fig. 8.2. Summary of output devices

interleaved carbon paper, or NCR (no carbon required) paper—say up to six copies for the former and eight for the latter.

The arrangement and layout of output data in printed form is subject to a number of considerations:

(1) Printing time does not depend on the number of characters in a line but on the number of lines printed. It takes as long to print a line of two characters as it does a line of 120. It is an advantage, therefore, to get a maximum number of characters in a line by using stationery as wide as possible. If, however, the stationery must be narrow, consideration should be given to printing two forms simultaneously, side by side.

(2) Spacing a line (that is, leaving a line blank) takes less time than printing a line, but the first in a succession of space lines takes longer than the others. It is, therefore, uneconomic to use too many single space lines.

(3) Wherever possible, in order to save printing time, all predetermined data, such as the title of the form and headings of columns, can be preprinted.

(4) The assembling, layout and presentation of data for printing is subject to program control. This process is known as *editing*. It involves the insertion of symbols such as £ signs in the correct places, and correct spacing of data items and arranging them appropriately to conform with the layout of the form being used.

Ancillary machines for line printer output
It is too laborious and time-consuming a task to deal manually with the very high volume of printed matter coming off a high-speed line printer, and therefore equipment has been developed to deal with it automatically. The more important of these devices are mentioned below.

Bursters   Bursters are designed to pull apart the sheets making up continuous stationery at the lines of perforations. They operate by passing the paper over rollers running at different speeds, so submitting the paper to sufficient tension to burst the line of perforations. They can usually be adjusted to take paper of various sizes and of varying strengths. An additional facility in many of these machines is the incorporation of cutting wheels to trim off the sprocket holes on the sides of the paper.

Guillotines   Guillotines are used for cutting or trimming continuous stationery. They may be used in place of bursters by cutting either side of the row of perforations and trimming the edges.

They are sometimes used in conjunction with bursters, when, for instance, two reports are printed side by side and need separating by a cut down the centre of the paper.

The purpose for which output reports are to be used (that is, for external or internal distribution) will usually determine the method used for handling the printed output.

Decollators Decollators separate multiple copies of continuous stationery, and, if necessary, extract their interleaved carbon paper before the bursting process. The machine removes the carbon paper from the copies by winding them on separate rollers. Depending on the type of machine used and, of course, the number of copies, this may be done in one pass or the operation may take a multiple number of passes.

Folding and mail handling equipment Many of the output reports prepared on a line printer are in finished form ready for external distribution. After decollating and trimming, the forms need to be folded and inserted into envelopes. Machines are available which will only fold the forms, which are subsequently put manually into envelopes, but a more complex machine, known as a mail handling machine, will cope with both the folding and envelope insertion operations.

SERIAL PRINTERS

Serial printers print one character at a time along a print line in much the same way as a typewriter. Compared with line printers, they are fairly slow printing devices. They fall into three main types:

(1) Machines using the conventional typewriter print bar with a separate character embossed on each. The maximum input rate of this type of machine is around 5 characters per second; and when used as an output device, about 10 characters per second. Their main area of use is as terminals linked to a central computer—the Teletype or VDU terminal mentioned in the previous chapter—or as a console for operator/computer communications.

(2) Machines using a wheel with a number of spokes radiating from the centre on the ends of which characters are embossed. This is known as a Daisy Wheel. The wheel revolves until the relevant character is in the printing position, when it is impressed upon the paper. This type of printing device is often used for the printed output of microcomputers. Printing speed is far faster than

that of the conventional Teletype, being in the region of 35–55 characters per second. The faster machines use a bidirectional printing mode—that is, printing one line from left to right, the next from right to left, and so on.

(3) The matrix character printer operates on the same principle as the matrix line printer mentioned earlier, except that one matrix only is used. There is a very wide range of these printing devices on the market. Generally speaking, they are somewhat faster than daisy wheel printers, with average speeds around 110–120 characters per second, with bidirectional printing offered by the faster models.

Non-impact printers

The printing devices so far considered all rely on the impression of typefaces upon the paper through carbon ribbons, to reproduce an image. This can also be done by (a) electrolytic, electrographic and electrostatic techniques; (b) xerographic printers; (c) photographic means.

The main difference between these categories is that (a) and (b) produce a final printed copy on paper, while (c) reproduces the data on film which, in turn, needs to be projected on to a screen, although techniques exist to take a permanent paper copy when necessary.

ELECTROLYTIC, ELECTROGRAPHIC AND ELECTROSTATIC PRINTING

The main disadvantage is that it is necessary to use special chemically treated paper, which is fairly expensive. Maximum printing speed is around 3000 lines per minute, although many slower machines operate at only about 500 lines per minute.

XEROGRAPHIC PRINTERS

Xerographic printers have the advantage of using ordinary paper to record the image. The image is projected on to a revolving drum having a photoconductive surface. As the drum turns, paper that is continuously in contact with part of the drum surface moves in pace with it. Toner powder dusted on to the drum adheres to the areas covered by the projected image and is, in turn, transferred to the paper. It is then fixed by a heat process, which gives a permanent image. Printing output speeds for this type of printer can be as high as 20 000 lines per minute. Their use can only be justified in situations of very high data volume output.

MICROFILM

As a method of capturing computer output data, the use of microfilm is growing in popularity as an alternative to the printer. A number of systems are on the market, but the basic principle is to photograph data displayed on a cathode ray tube, capturing the image on film. It is known as COM—Computer Originated Microfilm, or Computer Output to Microfilm. In some cases the microfilming is done off-line by the data first being written to magnetic tape, the tape then being fed into a microfilmer, where it is displayed on a cathode ray tube and photographed. On the other hand, an on-line method may be used by the computer displaying the data direct on a cathode ray tube for photographing, its recording on magnetic tape being by-passed. Some systems use rolls of 16 millimetre film photographing 'pages' of data serially throughout the length of the film, while others use a microfiche principle. This is a sheet of film, say 4 inches × 3 inches, on which up to 80 pages of data can be recorded.

Output on microfilm or microfiche can only be read by the use of a special viewing device. Each frame is indexed to facilitate retrieval, and some systems are fully automatic, enabling a frame to be retrieved by keying in its reference. Electrostatic or xerographic document copiers can be attached to the viewing device to enable hard copies to be prepared if required.

Advantages in the use of these photographic techniques are:

(1) Speeds are well in excess of those of line printers and can be up to 100 000 characters per second.
(2) They will reproduce diagrams and charts as well as the usual range of alphanumeric characters.
(3) They are relatively cheap.
(4) It is easy to produce a printed copy if required.
(5) They are very compact, and demands on storage space and cost are therefore reduced.

Disadvantages are:

(1) Viewing equipment is needed to project and enlarge the image.
(2) They are not suitable when a printed document is required for circulation and use—for example, an electricity bill or a wage statement.

Generally speaking, microfilm comes into its own from the bulk storage of inactive files to which reference is not frequently required. Microfiche provides a very convenient means of circulating information from a central computer to remote points. It is easily mailed and will contain a vast quantity of information. Two examples in common use are the recording of car parts lists, which can be circulated to local depots, and lists of clients' account balances, circulated to branch banks from a central computer.

Visual display units

As explained in the previous chapter, the visual display unit displays data on a cathode ray tube, but it does not produce a permanent output record unless the data are fixed by microfilm or photographing.

Digital increment plotter (graph plotter)

The digital increment plotter is a specialized device used for communicating the output of a computer in printed graphic form, as, for example, a diagram. The machine consists basically of a drum which moves a sheet of paper mounted in it backwards and forwards. To provide accurate positioning the paper is sprocket controlled. Suspended from a slide above the drum is a drawing-pen, able to move left or right across the width of the paper. This will give movement in four directions, the paper backwards and forwards and the pen left and right. By altering the relative speeds of the paper and pen, a line of any direction and curvature can be drawn on the paper. The dimension and shape of the line are determined by the output data. However, it should be mentioned that a far quicker and cheaper method of reproducing charts and diagrams could well be provided by the other methods outlined above.

Acoustic output

Mention should be made of one of the more recent developments in output—that involving the use of voice systems, known as acoustic output or voice output. Although there is no wide use of this in commercial data processing, the system is increasingly being used in microchip-based teaching machines. Voice synthesizers in the form of sophisticated tape or disc recorders have been in use for some time, and it is a comparatively straightforward process to play back selected sounds under computer control. More recent developments involve the storage of sounds, words, etc., in digital form. These digital signals are read out of store when required, and fed through a digital-to-analogue converter, thus producing an analogue audio signal for playing through an amplifier or loudspeaker.

Exercises

8.1. List the main types of output devices used in commercial data processing and in each case give one example of an application in which you feel the device could be used to advantage.

8.2. What is the difference between a serial printer and a line printer? Give examples of each of these types of printer.

8.3. What is a visual display unit? Describe how permanent records may be obtained from this device.

8.4. Give an account of the ancillary machines commonly used to deal with printed output from a line printer.

8.5. Explain the differences between microfilm and microfiche. Suggest three commercial situations in which you would advise the use of one or other of these techniques.

8.6. Suggest the type of computer output you would use in the following cases, giving reasons for your choice: (a) preparation of wage pay slips; (b) recording stock balances at the end of a daily stock inventory updating run; (c) request for information on a customer's credit status; (d) distribution to a number of scattered depots of lists of stock held in a central store.

Chapter 9
Computer storage

Our main concern, from a data processing viewpoint, lies in the way data can be organized on files; how data records can be retrieved from these files as and when required; how the records can be used in the processing function and then the results of processing filed for future use or for output as information. It is within this context that the devices used in these processes will be reviewed and it is not the intention to become over-involved in their mechanics.

One of the most significant characteristics of a computer, and one that distinguishes it from mechanical and electromechanical machines, is its capacity to store large volumes of data. We have seen that it is not necessary to store all of these data in the central processor itself, since external backing storage devices are available for bulk storage and only those data required for immediate processing need be held in the central processor. We have also seen that in the final analysis all data are expressed in terms of binary digits (referred to as BITs—an abbreviation of Binary digITs). The purpose of this chapter is to discuss (a) the devices that are commonly used to hold all these bits representing data, (b) how these bits can be marshalled together into the characters, data fields and data records they represent, and (c) how they can be located and retrieved for use in the processing cycle.

Central processor store

The term 'memory' is often used to distinguish the store of the central processor from bulk backing storage. Furthermore, since the data held in the central processor are immediately available for processing through the processor's arithmetic and logic circuitry (in contrast to data held on backing storage, which must first be transferred to the central processor), the processor store is known as an immediate access store.

Having established that all of these data items held in store are represented in terms of bits, it follows that the store must basically consist of a number of two-state devices, each capable of representing one bit—0 or 1.

Until a few years ago, magnetic devices were almost universally used for this purpose, the central processor memory consisting of a large number of ferrite rings, each capable of being magnetized in either of two directions in order to represent a binary 0 or 1. Although ferrite core storage has now been superseded by semiconductor storage elements, there are still a number of operational computers incorporating this type of storage and so a brief description is given.

Ferrite core storage

Use is made of the elementary electrical principle that when an electric current is passed through a wire, a magnetic field is created around it in a clockwise direction in relation to the current flow. Reverse the direction of the current and the direction of the magnetic field will be reversed. If a wire is threaded through the centre of a small ferrite ring capable of being magnetized, then, on a current being passed through the wire, the north-seeking ends of the particles of ferrite will point in a clockwise direction following the lines of force of the magnetic field and will remain in this state even when the current is switched off. If a sufficient current is then passed in the opposite direction, the polarity of the magnetism in the ring will be reversed. This gives a convenient and relatively easily operated two-state device which, by virtue of the direction of its magnetism, can represent a 0 or a 1 bit.

It must, of course, be possible to change the magnetic condition of each individual core so as to accommodate different items as they are read in. This is done by arranging the cores in a matrix (Fig. 9.1) so that each is threaded by two wires at right angles to each other. The critical level of current required to change the state of any individual core can then be achieved by passing half-pulses through the two wires intersecting at the selected core. If a number of these matrices are mounted vertically, each vertical column of cores will represent a computer word in which all the cores can be accessed simultaneously for reading and writing purposes.

Semiconductor storage

There are a number of different types of semiconductor and the following is a very much simplified illustration of the use of one of these in a computer memory.

Central processor store 103

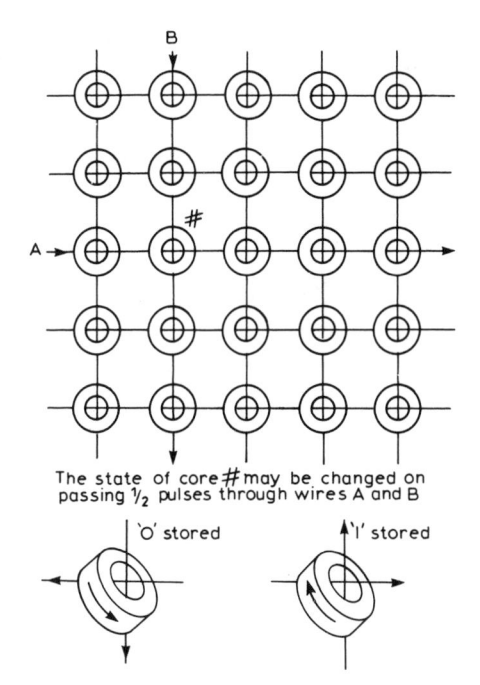

Fig. 9.1. Section of a magnetic core store matrix

Pure silicon is a poor electrical conductor, but the addition of impurities—for example, boron—to a silicon crystal will render it conductive. If wires are attached at each end of a piece of this doped silicon—a source (S) and a drain (D) wire, respectively (Fig. 9.2)—and a voltage is applied across them, a current will flow from S to D. It is possible to inhibit this current flow by applying a voltage to a gate (G) between the source and the drain wires. This results in a two-state device that can be controlled by the application of a voltage to the gate. In other words, a binary 1

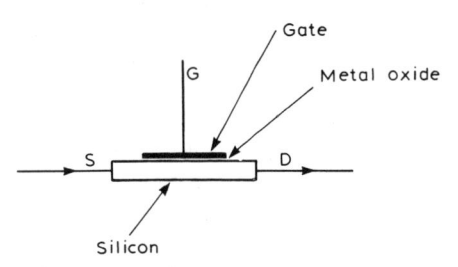

Fig. 9.2. Metal oxide semiconductor field effect transistor (MOSFET)

can be represented by the current flow arising from the absence of a voltage at G and a binary 0 by the absence of current flow arising from a voltage applied to G.

To test or 'read' the state of the device, the drain wire is tested for current flow. The device is known as a field effect transistor (FET). In practice, the gate is usually insulated from the semiconductor by a layer of metal oxide which has the effect of increasing the resistance to current flow between S and D. It is then known as a MOSFET (metal oxide semiconductor field effect transistor).

These devices are assembled into a matrix (Fig. 9.3) and wired so that each semiconductor can be accessed individually to enable reading and writing operations to take place.

Organization of central processor store

Before we go on to discuss how the central processor immediate access store is organized, it must be said that it is impossible to talk about a 'typical' central processor, because of the very wide range of types and sizes available and the different methods of organizing the processing function. The following descriptions are, therefore, of a general nature.

We know that every numeric or alphabetic character stored must be represented by a group of bits, which, in practice, means its representation by the physical state of a group of the storage devices mentioned above. We have also seen that, in turn, a data field is made up of a group of characters and that each data record is made up of a number of data fields, all of which is represented in store in terms of bits.

Now, a store holding tens of thousands of these bits will be completely meaningless in terms of information unless we can define the beginning and the end of each character, field and record. It would be rather like having a page of a book completely covered with characters. This would be meaningless unless the characters were marshalled into words, the words in turn arranged into sentences and the start and finish of each word and sentence defined.

For example, unless we know the particular convention being employed and where each group of bits begins and ends, the string of bits 100101000011 could equally well represent 3371, 943, 2371 or N3. Another problem is that it must be possible to locate each separately stored item of data so that it can be referred to and used whenever required.

We start off, then, with two main problems: (1) to define the extent of each character, data field and data record, and (2) to be able to locate any data item in store. The solution to the first of

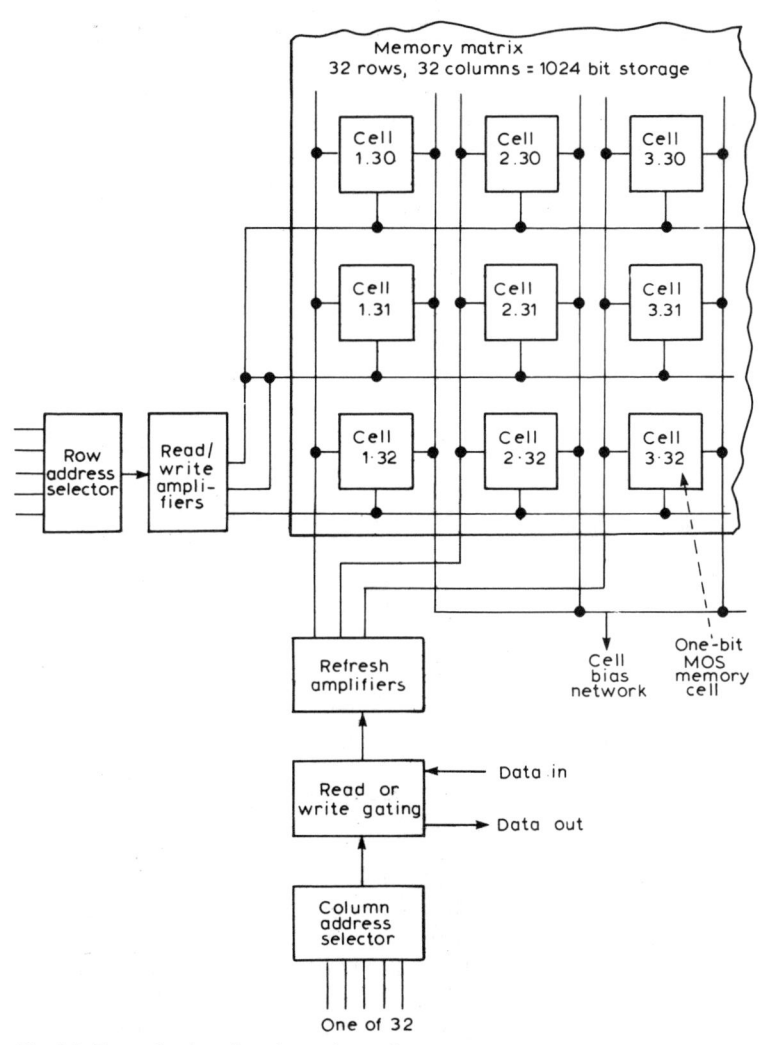

Fig. 9.3. Example of semiconductor immediate access memory

these problems lies in dividing all the devices holding bits into groups of a standard size, each group containing sufficient bits to represent one or more characters. This means that the limits to each group are fixed. The second problem is resolved by giving each group a unique reference and then associating an identification of the contents of the group, through an index, with the group's reference. In practice, the index is created by the computer

106　Computer storage

itself and there is no need for us to keep a record of what each group contains.

It is rather like having a lot of small boxes, each having a reference number, as shown in Fig. 9.4. In this case each box contains sufficient bits to hold one character and the character is located by the box number. The name given to this number is an *address*.

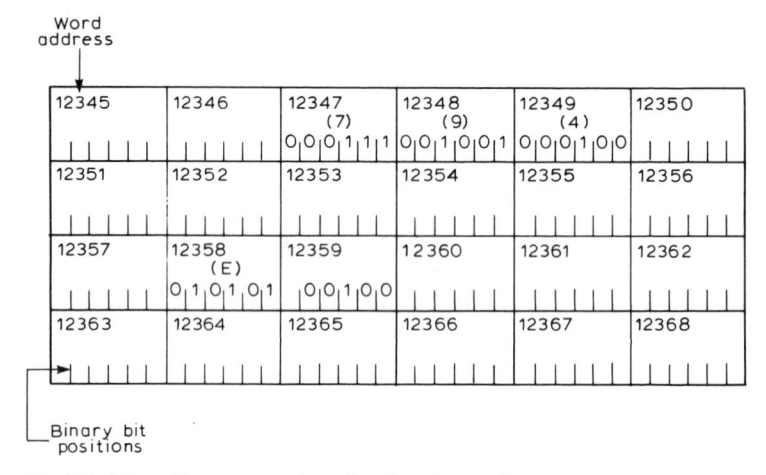

Word address					
12345	12346	12347 (7) 0,0,0,1,1,1	12348 (9) 0,0,1,0,0,1	12349 (4) 0,0,0,1,0,0	12350
12351	12352	12353	12354	12355	12356
12357	12358 (E) 0,1,0,1,0,1	12359 ,0,0,1,0,0	12360	12361	12362
12363	12364	12365	12366	12367	12368

Binary bit positions

Fig. 9.4. Schematic representation of section of central processor store. The number '7' is stored at address 12347; the letter 'E' at address 12358

It having been decided to divide the store up into groups of bits, the next problem is to decide the size of the groups. We saw earlier that the number of bits required to store a decimal digit is 4 and the number to store an alphabetic character is 6. Thus, a 6-bit grouping would appear to be sufficient to hold any number, and since with 6 bits we can get 64 unique patterns (from 0000 to 1111), we could throw in a number of symbols as well, to give a range of 64 different characters.

This principle of arranging bits into groups of 6 is used in some computers. Each group is capable of holding one character and each group has its own address. These machines are often referred to as character addressable or character machines.

But what now happens if we want to use a binary expression containing more than 6 bits? The biggest number we can represent with 6 bits in binary is 63; 7 bits are required up to 127; 8 up to 225; and so on. One answer, of course, is to overflow from one location to the next, and, indeed, this can be done, provided that in our programming we let the computer know we are going to use a number of locations to contain a single expression. Because of this facility for increasing the size of a location to accommodate one large binary expression, this type of store organization is known as variable word-length storage.

Of course, another way of getting around the problem is to increase the size of the bit groups, but on first thought, to do this, we would have to sacrifice the convenience of a 6-bit grouping. Why not, then, have a group containing a multiple of 6 bits—say 18, 24 or 30—so that it can contain either a number of 6-bit characters or one longer pure binary expression? Many machines organize their storage in this way. For example, if we decided to have groups of 24 bits one group could contain either four 6-bit characters or one pure binary expression (see Fig. 9.5).

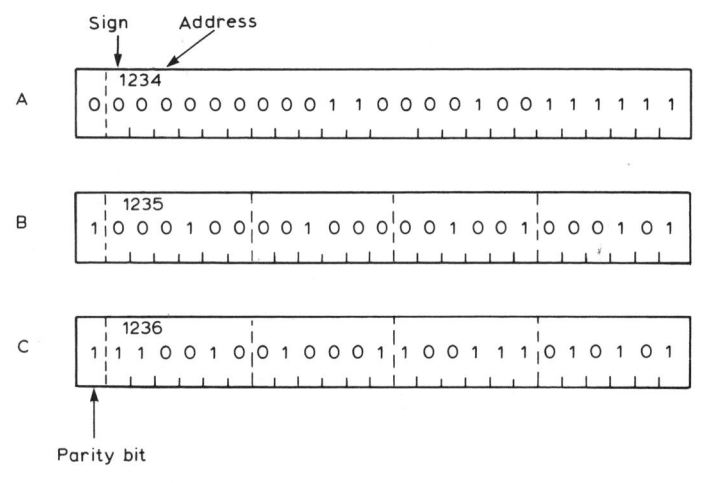

```
           Sign     Address
                ↓    ↓
           | 1234
A          |0|0 0 0 0 0 0 0 0 0 1 1 0 0 0 0 1 0 0 1 1 1 1 1 1

           | 1235
B          |1|0 0 0 1 0 0|0 0 1 0 0 0|0 0 1 0 0 1|0 0 0 1 0 1

           | 1236
C          |1|1 1 0 0 1 0|0 1 0 0 0 1|1 0 0 1 1 1|0 1 0 1 0 1
            ↑
         Parity bit
```

Fig. 9.5. Examples of a 25-bit word. (a) contains the pure binary equivalent of 24895. In the sign bit position 0 positive, 1 negative. (b) contains the binary coded decimal equivalent of 4895. (c) contains the alphabetic characters TAPE

As we saw earlier, numeric data can be either descriptive or quantitative, only the latter type being the subject of any calculations in the processor. The construction of a 24-bit word in this manner will give the facility for storing descriptive data in BCD (binary coded decimal) and the quantitative data in pure binary expressions.

This arrangement, however, brings with it a further problem in that we can no longer give an individual address to each character. But does this really matter? If the first character to be read always appears in the first position in the group and succeeding characters are arranged in sequence, the machine need only refer to the address in which the first character is contained and keep reading until instructed to stop. This can be done with a program instruction to read a defined number of characters, or by using a special group of 6 bits to hold a stop marker.

Perhaps it would be as well, at this point, to attempt to organize our terminology. We have been using the term 'group' to indicate a sub-division of the central processor's store and have seen that a store organized into 6-bit addressable locations is known as a character machine and can be said to have a variable word length. We have also suggested that a group may contain a multiple number of 6 bits. The name given to a group of this nature is *word,* and a machine with a central processor divided up in this way is known as a *fixed word-length* machine. The sub-divisions of the word into character locations are often known as *bytes.* Each word is addressable but individual bytes are not.

Another way of organizing storage is based on a group of 8 bits. The recording mode used divides the set of characters into ten zones, each containing ten characters. The first 4 bits indicate the zone number and the second 4 indicate the position of the character within the zone group. An arrangement of this nature is known as a zone/numeric code. For instance, zone 0001 may contain the letters A–J, and so the binary coding for the letter H would be 00011000.

At first sight this may seem an uneconomic way of utilizing store space, since, as we have already seen, BCD representation needs only 6 bits per character. However, recognizing that a large proportion of data is in numeric form, this allows two digits to be packed into one 8-bit group by discarding the zone element of the code and so using 4 bits only for each. (See Fig. 9.6.)

Zone 4-bits	Numeric 4-bits
0 , 0 , 0 , 1	1 , 0 , 0 , 0

The letter H recorded

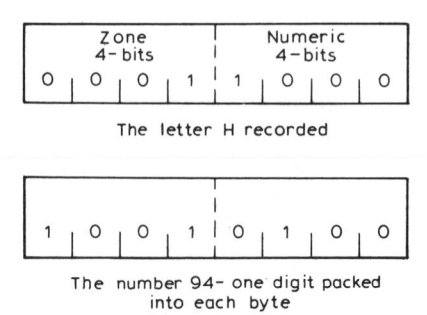

1 , 0 , 0 , 1	0 , 1 , 0 , 0

The number 94 – one digit packed into each byte

Fig. 9.6. Use of 8-bit word

Eight-bit locations in this type of machine are known as bytes, and a machine using this type of storage organization is usually referred to as a byte addressable machine or a byte machine.

Fig. 9.5 gives an example of a 24-bit word that can be subdivided into four 6-bit bytes. Stored numbers will be positive or negative, and a method must exist for distinguishing between these two alternatives. This is usually done by reserving one bit in the word to indicate the sign: 0 equals plus and 1 equals minus. For example, in the 24-bit word illustrated the left-most bit is used for this purpose, which leaves 23 bits to record the value of the expression. With numbers recorded in BCD, the use of a 6-bit byte leaves two spare bits, one of which can be used to indicate the sign.

Calculations in the central processor are carried out in terms of pure binary expressions rather than BCD. It is common practice to simplify input and output procedure by reading and storing data in BCD form, and when calculations are required to convert these BCD expressions into pure binary statements and then convert the answers back again for output purposes.

One further consideration arises in the storage of data in the processor. In order to provide a check on the accuracy of data as they are transferred from one location to another, or to and from the processor itself, additional space is provided in each word to hold a *parity bit*. A test is made on the transfer of each word for an odd or an even number of bits, depending on the system used (see Fig. 9.5).

It was mentioned earlier that the central processor must contain a large number of devices, each capable of representing one bit, and that these devices are assembled into groups known as 'words'. The storage capacity of the processor store is defined by the number of words it contains. This is expressed in terms of K, 1K representing 1024 words. Stores are usually constructed in multiples of 4K; thus, we would have a 4K, 8K, 32K store, etc. This means, assuming a word size of, say, 24 bits, that a 4K store would be made up of, any other factors being ignored, over 24 such devices.

What is stored in the central processor?

So far we have limited our discussion to the storage of data items only in the processor. However, a number of other factors will also be present. These are summarized below and will be expanded upon later in the description of how the central processor works and in Part 3.

(1) The *control function* is permanently stored in a number of locations reserved exclusively for this purpose whose addresses remain fixed. It includes the machine's operation (or function) code—a series of binary statements that individually determine the operations the machine will carry out within the finite range of operations it is designed to perform.

(2) *Arithmetic and logic unit.* These locations are reserved for holding data on which arithmetic and logic operations are to be performed.

(3) *Data.* By and large, data may be stored anywhere in the processor's store. Usually, however, one part of the store is reserved for receiving and holding input data awaiting processing, while another part is reserved for marshalling together and holding output data for transfer to an output peripheral.

(4) *Program.* Again the list of instructions comprising the program can be stored in any part of the processor's store not being used for any other purpose, provided that these instructions are stored in the sequence in which they will be worked through.

(5) *Operating system.* This is a program designed to generally supervise and monitor the whole of the computer's operations. It is stored in the same way as the program mentioned above.

One factor that emerges is that there must be the facility for transferring data from one location to another within the processor. For example, data items having first been read into the reserved input area, they may then have to be transferred to the arithmetic unit for processing and the results transferred back to the output area. In some machines the bits making up a word are transferred one at a time until the whole word has been moved, while in others all of the bits are transferred simultaneously. On the other hand, transfer of an expression in BCD could well be done one complete character at a time. The first method is known as serial transfer, the second as parallel transfer and the third as serial/parallel.

Another point arising from the above list is that some of the information held in the central processor is unchanging and, once stored, must remain there permanently. An example of this is control information such as the machine operation code.

The state of the semiconductor memory device described earlier is capable of being changed on demand, and therefore the binary coding represented of being altered. It will accept (write) data submitted to it, transfer (read) these data to another medium or location and then, in turn, accept a completely new and different item of data. For this reason it is referred to as read/write memory. It is also known as a random access memory (abbreviated as RAM).

It will be evident, then, that this type of memory is unsuitable for holding permanent and unchanging information. To do this, devices are required that will hold a binary representation which is incapable of being changed once the information has been entered. These are known as read only memories (ROM). The state of these memories in binary terms is constant and their output will always be the same whenever input pulses are presented to them.

The essential features of a central processor store are:

(1) Each device representing a bit must be capable of individual access in order to change its state, when necessary, to represent an 0 or a 1.

(2) These devices must be arranged into standard-sized groups, each group capable of holding one or more data fields.

(3) Each group must have a unique address so that the data held in it can be located.

(4) Each group must be capable of direct and immediate access without reference to the contents of the groups coming before or after it. This capacity on the part of the processor to gain immediate access to any item of information gives rise to the store being described as an *immediate access store,* in contrast to backing storage, where each data item, after it has been located, must be transferred to the central processor store.

External storage

In carrying out a manual procedure—say to keep stock records cards up to date—the records we would need are:

(1) A file containing a record card for each item of stock on which would be recorded issues, receipts and the balance in stock.

(2) A file of issue notes identifying the item of stock issued and quoting the quantity.

(3) A file of advice notes for receipts of stock items, identifying also the item and quantity.

We earlier gave names to these different types of file: (1) a master file, and (2), (3) movement files.

In the process of updating we would be working at any one time on only one record card in conjunction with either one issue note or one advice note. The rest of the record cards, etc., will remain on file until we need them.

Computer processing works in much the same way. Only those items currently being worked on are held in the central processor; the files containing the bulk of the records are held on storage devices external to the processor. These are known as *backing storage devices*. Records can be extracted from them and returned to them as and when demanded by the central processor.

Current computer technology has produced a mass of different types of backing store, but it is beyond the province of this book to give a comprehensive review of all of them. We are more concerned with the principles that underlie the part they play in processing data. Basically, there are two types of backing store, one known as serial access and the other as direct or random access. The difference between these hinges on the way in which data can be stored and, in turn, located on them. Perhaps this difference can be appreciated by comparing the recording of music on a tape and on a disc. In the first case, if we wanted to play back a specific passage, we would have to run through the tape until we reached the passage looked for. In the latter case, all we need do is place the stylus of the record player at the beginning of the track on which the passage is recorded. In other words, with the tape we can only access the recording serially, but with the disc we can access it direct.

Serial access storage

MAGNETIC TAPE

Magnetic tape is a very convenient way, and an extensively used way, of storing large volumes of data in a comparatively small space. Magnetic tape decks can be linked permanently to the computer, but the reels of tape containing different files are interchangeable. This means that a library of tapes can be built up containing data files and programs relating to the systems being operated.

Characteristics of magnetic tape
There are two types of magnetic tape commonly in use on computers today: the 'open reel' type is used extensively on the larger mainframe computers, and cassette tapes—almost identical with the commonly used audio cassette—are used on microcomputers. The following description relates to the 'open reel' tape but the principles underlying its use apply much the same to cassette tapes.

Most open reel magnetic tape used for computer backing storage is ½ inch wide and made of a tough plastics which can be coated with a material capable of being magnetized. It is held on spools of varying lengths up to 2400 feet. The information recorded on the tape is transferred to and from the computer through a device known as a tape deck, which is 'on-line'—that is, connected directly to the central processor. Several tape decks can be linked to the processor at the same time. The tape deck has three main elements:

(1) A recording, reading and erasing head.
(2) A driving mechanism to move the tape past the read/write head.
(3) Two reels, one to hold the unprocessed tape and the other to take up the tape after processing.

On either side of the read/write head are loops, or reservoirs, of tape, which help to ensure that the tape passes the head at a constant speed when reading and writing.

All information is recorded in the form of binary bits, each bit being represented by the absence or presence of a small area or dot magnetized in the opposite direction to the permanent field of the tape. A row of such dots across the width of the tape represents a character and is known as a *frame*. The positioning of the bits longitudinally on the tape is on what are known as *tracks*. Each character is represented by a unique pattern of bits, often using the same binary code as that used for storage in the central processor. One track is used for parity checking purposes.

The number of characters recorded on a given length of tape is known as the *packing density* and varies from system to system. It is expressed in terms of characters per inch (cpi), common packing densities being 200, 550, 800 and 1600. Information is written to and read from the tape on program command through the central processor.

Other important characteristics are:

(1) A reel of tape can hold a very large volume of information. This, in the case of a 2400 foot tape, could be in the region of 20 million characters.
(2) Reels of tape can be used repeatedly by erasing data no longer required and recording new data.
(3) While the transfer speed of data to and from the tape will vary to an extent with the way in which the recording is organized, it could well be in the region of 300 000 characters per second.
(4) Data can be preserved for an indefinite length of time until deliberately erased.

(5) The information held on magnetic tape can only be accessed in a serial mode—that is, by running through the tape until the record sought is found.

Organization of data on tape

It will be evident that data must be recorded in a way that conforms with the basic construction of a data file—that is, a number of characters making a field, a number of fields making a record and a number of records making a file. One other factor that needs to be considered when data are being organized on tape hinges around the fact that it is impractical to read a continuous flow of data into the central processor, because, on the one hand, only those records required for immediate processing need be held in the processor, and on the other hand, the processor's store will not be large enough to accept an unrestricted flow of data. It is, therefore, necessary to define the volume of data that can be transferred at any one time. This may be just one record or a predetermined number of records. The name we give to this unit of transfer is *data block*.

On completion of the transfer of a data block, the tape will come to rest and then, when the next block is called for, speed up to reach the critical speed necessary for read/write operations. This means that a gap must be left between blocks to allow for the period during which the tape is coming to rest and then accelerating to reach this speed. This is known as an *inter-block gap* (see Fig. 9.7).

We were concerned earlier with the problems associated with defining the limits of characters, fields and records held in the central processor. The same problems are evident with data recorded on magnetic tape, except that the extent of a character is automatically defined in the form of a frame across the width of the tape. However, some method must be devised of defining the limits of each field, each record and each data block. Two ways of doing this suggest themselves.

One way is to use fixed length fields and records, which means that the number of characters allocated to each field and the number of fields allocated to each record are always constant. If we then write into the program a definition of these field and record lengths, the processor will be able to tell where each ends by counting the number of characters and fields as they are transferred. This method has one obvious disadvantage. When sizes are being set they must be adequate to accommodate the longest data item that is likely to occur, which means that a lot of space is likely to be unused. One way of getting around this problem is in the use

External storage 115

of variable length records. This means that only the precise number of frames required to record a data item are used, but, of course, this raises the problem of defining where fields and records start and end. This is done by inserting special 'markers'—that is, a special pattern of bits the computer will recognize as such—at the end of each field, record and block: at the end of each field, an End of Field Marker (EFM); at the end of each record, an End of Record Marker (ERM); and at the end of each block, an End of Block Marker (EBM) (Fig. 9.7).

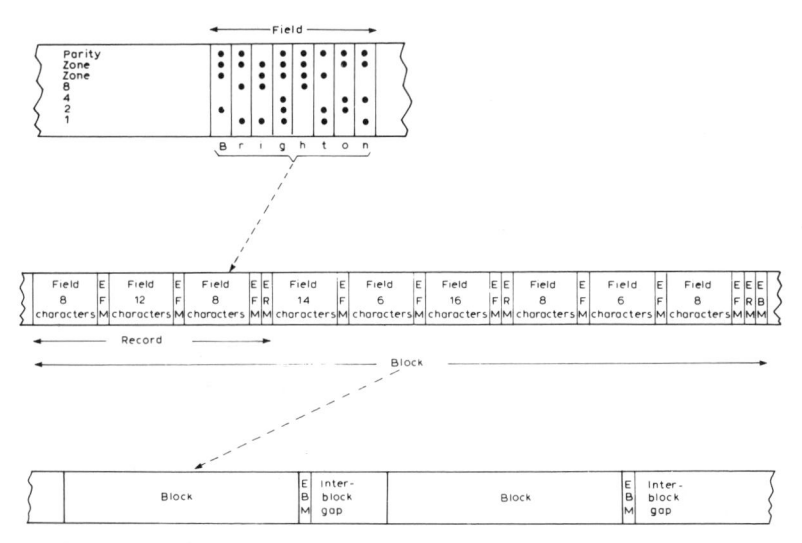

Fig. 9.7. Organization of data on magnetic tape

Within these two basic modes of recording, variations may well exist, as follows:

(1) Fixed-fixed blocks—a fixed number of fixed length records.
(2) Fixed-variable blocks—a fixed number of variable length records.
(3) Variable-fixed blocks—a variable number of fixed length records.
(4) Variable-variable blocks—a variable number of variable length records.

On the magnetic tape provision must be made for indicating the point at which recording may start and, to avoid overrunning at the end of the tape, where it must finish. This is done by siting markers on the tape known as load point marker and end of tape marker, respectively.

Another feature incorporated into the tape is labels occupying the first and last recording blocks. The first of these, at the beginning of the tape following the load point marker, is known as a header label and will contain the following information:

(1) A code identifying the block as a header label.
(2) Tape serial number (identification of the tape itself rather than its contents).
(3) File identification by name and the reel number within the file (should the file consist of two or more reels).
(4) The generation or version reference of the file.
(5) The purge date, which, for security purposes, indicates the earliest date on which the data can be destroyed by overwriting.
(6) Control software.

The other label, occupying the final block on the tape and known as a trailer label, will contain

(1) A code identifying the block as a trailer label.
(2) A repeat of the file name, sequence number within the file and version reference.
(3) File control information specifying whether end of file or referring to file continuation tape.
(4) A data block count (number of blocks of data contained on the tape).

These two labels are of particular importance in data processing, since they provide a medium for security checks when the tape is loaded and run. File identification is communicated to the computer through the program and a check is made against the detail in the header label to ensure that the correct file is being used. To ensure that all records have been dealt with, a count of the blocks is made during processing and this total is checked against the block count in the trailer label. The computer will also check the purge date, and should this be later than the current computer run date, overwriting will not be allowed to take place.

As an additional safeguard, read and write checks are also incorporated into a tape system, although the mechanics of these checks may vary from system to system. It is usual to make parity checks as data are transferred, to guard against the corruption of data as they are being moved. An echo check is also made—that is, each character is read twice and the two results are compared for any discrepancy. This is often described as a read after write check.

Tape operation speeds and capacity
Two main factors will govern the transfer rate of data to and from magnetic tape: (1) the packing density of the data and (2) the speed of tape movement over the read/write heads. This transfer rate is expressed in thousands of characters per second, abbreviated as k ch/s. For example, the theoretical transfer rate of a tape moving at 120 inches per second with a packing density of 800 cpi is 96 k ch/s, but, of course, the average transfer rate for the whole tape will be considerably less because of the time spent in stop/start operations at interblock gaps. Probably a fair average for the bulk of the systems used in commercial data processing is about 150–200 k ch/s.

The criteria which determine the total recording capacity of a reel of tape of given length are the packing density, file design considerations such as the use of fixed or variable length records, the size of data blocks and the frequency of interblock gaps. To quote a standard for, say, 2400 foot tape is impractical, but with a packing density of 800 cpi it could well be in the region of 200 million characters.

Processing using magnetic tape
We saw earlier that when data are organized on magnetic tape, perhaps the most distinctive feature is that data can only be recorded serially along the length of the tape. This means that if, during the course of processing, it becomes necessary to increase the length of a record by adding, say, an additional transaction, this cannot be done without overwriting and destroying the following data record. This means that a completely new tape must be prepared to accommodate the expanded records. If, for example, we have a master file and a movements file representing transactions relating to the master records over a period of time, then these two files will have to be processed together and the results written out to a third blank tape. A necessary precondition to this, since all the records are stored serially, is that the records on both tapes must be stored in the same order—that is, in the sequence of the factor that identifies individual records, which is normally the record key.

Perhaps it would be as well at this point to make clear the difference between these two storage modes—serial and sequential. *Serial* means the storage of records in a continuous series of physical locations, irrespective of any logical order in terms of record keys. *Sequential* means the storage of records in a logical order, usually in record key sequence.

One reservation must be made here. Records that are stored serially may be accessed sequentially, provided that the physical qualities of the storage medium enable this to be done. As we have seen, this is not the case with magnetic tape but is possible, as we shall see later, with other storage devices coming within the direct access category. Thus, with magnetic tape it is usual to store records serially in sequence.

When records are processed by magnetic tape, the following routine will be observed (see Fig. 9.8):

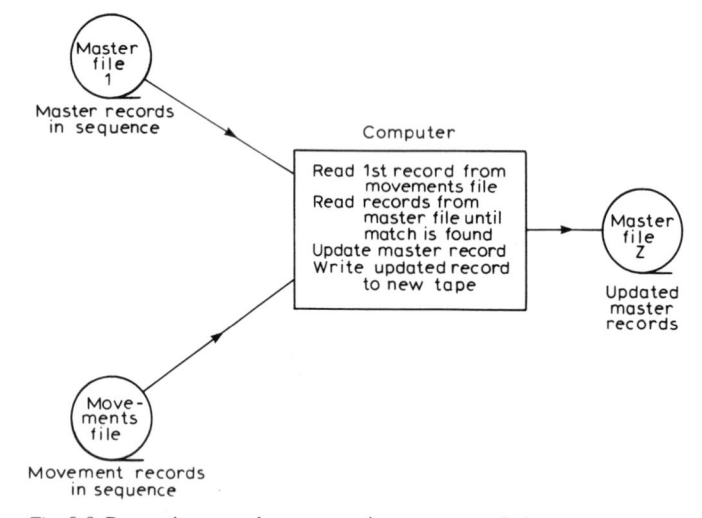

Fig. 9.8. Processing records on magnetic tape—an updating run

(1) The first record will be read from the movement file.

(2) Master records will be read from the master file until a record is found whose record key matches that of the movement record. (Master records whose key does not match will be written out unchanged to a third file.)

(3) Processing will take place by means of applying the movement record to the master record, updating and expanding the latter as necessary.

(4) The updated master record will now be written out to the third file, this file now becoming a new, or updated, master file.

The product of this kind of processing is a series of versions or generations of master tape, each one more up to date than its predecessor. It is customary to keep on file at least three consecutive versions together with the movements tapes used for their updating, so that in the event of destruction or corruption of a file the means exist to reconstitute it. This practice is often referred to as a 'grandfather–father–son technique'.

Magnetic tape cassettes
A cassette tape is one stored in a container—a cassette—in many cases virtually identical with the tape cassette used in audio systems, although the tape tends to be of somewhat better quality. Cassette tapes have the virtue that they are easy to store and can be easily loaded into a cassette handler. They are widely used in small microcomputer systems for the storage of files and programs and also in key-to-tape systems.

Direct access storage

Direct access storage gets around the limitation imposed by magnetic tape of restricting access to records serially. It makes it possible to select any record at will, irrespective of what comes before or after it. This characteristic gives rise to this type of store being described as *random access,* although, in practice, as we shall see, records may be accessed serially, sequentially or at random.

MAGNETIC DISCS

A very wide range of types of disc storage unit is available, from large-capacity fixed disc stores to small minifloppy discs for use mainly with microcomputers, but the basic principles underlying the storage and retrieval of records are, broadly speaking, much the same. The most widely used type of disc storage with the conventional mainframe computer is known as an exchangeable disc store. The following comments relate to this type of store, although a brief summary of other types is given on pages 128–130.

Physical characteristics
In an exchangeable disc system a number of discs are mounted parallel to one another on a central spindle, so providing a multiple number of recording surfaces. A set of discs assembled in this way, known as a disc cartridge or a disc pack, can be mounted or removed at will from a disc transport which is connected on-line to the computer processor. This makes it possible to keep a library of disc packs containing the data files and programs relating to the different systems being operated.

120   Computer storage

The discs themselves are around 14 inches in diameter, and while the number of discs in a pack varies with the manufacturer, the most popular is a pack containing six discs. Of the twelve surfaces available, only ten are used for recording purposes, the exposed top and bottom surfaces not being used. Each surface has on it a number of concentric recording tracks, say 200, and the tracks are, in turn, divided into a number of sectors, usually known as blocks. Therefore, it becomes possible to give each individual block a unique address by reference to the block number within the track, the track number on the surface and the surface number in the pack. (See Fig. 9.9.)

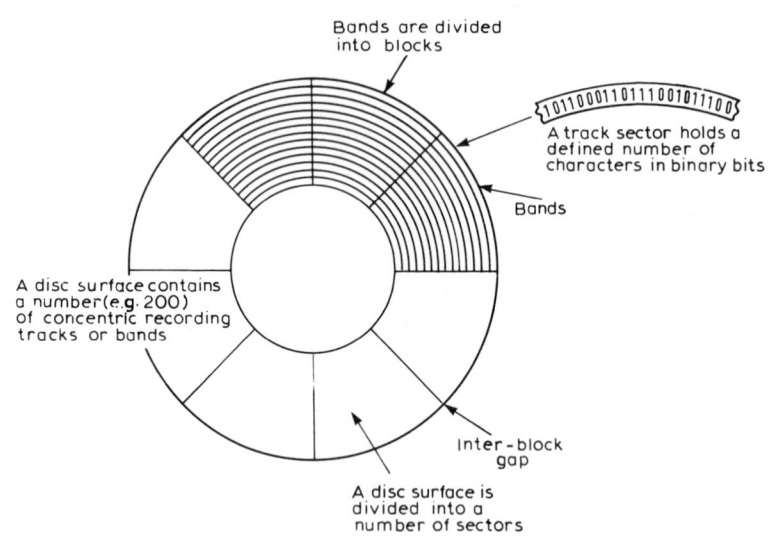

Fig. 9.9. A disc surface

The disc transport contains a number of read/write heads, one for each recording surface. These are fixed on the end of retractable arms so that they can be moved in and out within the spaces between the discs, one head scanning each surface. These arms are, in turn, fixed to a retractable assembly known as a tracking arm. Individual read/write heads are unable to move independently; all move at the same time with the tracking arm. The disc pack rotates at high speed in relation to the read/write heads, conveying every sector of the track to its head in turn (Fig. 9.10).

Mode of recording
All data are recorded in the form of magnetized spots, represent-

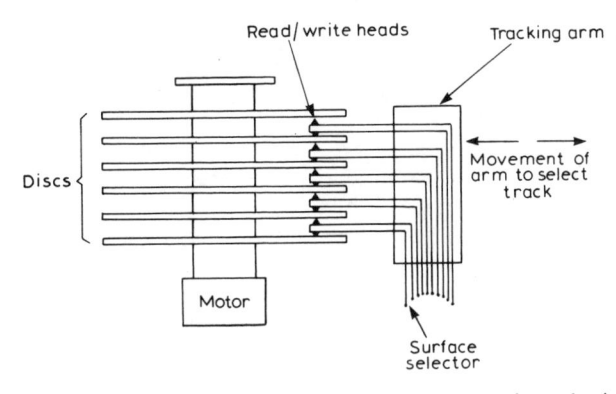

Fig. 9.10. Exchangeable disc unit showing track and surface selection

ing binary bits, longitudinally around the track. Each block in the track has a fixed standard recording capacity—for example, 512 6-bit grouping, each group capable of holding one character. Read/write operations are by program command transferring data between the disc and the processor store. Such commands will specify the address on the disc that has to be accessed. On initiation of a read/write operation the following operations take place:

(1) The tracking arm moves all the read/write heads together until they are positioned over the addressed track. The time taken for this operation is known as seek time, and will, of course, depend upon the distance the heads have to travel. A typical time is about 30 milliseconds.

(2) An electronic surface selector switch (see Fig. 9.10) activates the read/write head that is in conjunction with the surface addressed. The time taken for this is negligible.

(3) The disc, which is continuously revolving, turns until the addressed block is under the read/write head. The time taken for this operation is known as rotational delay, a typical time being around 10 milliseconds.

Data can then be transferred to or from the addressed block.

Organization of data on disc
Bearing in mind that a disc may contain a data file and that the file is made up of a number of data records, then in order to retrieve any specific record it must be (a) identified and (b) located. Identification is by its record key, and its location can be traced by

indexing the record key against the address of the physical location in which it is stored.

Since we are dealing here with a fixed unit of storage (a block), in contrast to a magnetic tape, where a record can extend as far along the tape as may be necessary, it would be unrealistic to expect a situation in which a data record, or a multiple number of data records, fit neatly into a single block. Systems considerations will determine the number of blocks needed to conveniently hold a record; the name given to this unit of systems defined storage is *bucket*. Should a data record in the course of its processing outgrow its bucket, it would obviously be impractical to continue the record into an adjacent bucket, as this will probably contain another data record.

The problem is resolved by reserving on the disc a number of tracks known as overflow tracks. Should a record become too large for its original location, it is moved to one of these overflow tracks and a redirection notice is inserted in its original location. This redirecting reference, known as a *tag* or a *pointer*, quotes the new address of the relocated record. (See Fig. 9.11.)

When a file is first written to disc, it may appear that the best way would be to start recording on the outermost track of a selected disc; when that was full, proceed to the next track inwards; and so on. Further consideration would reveal that, in

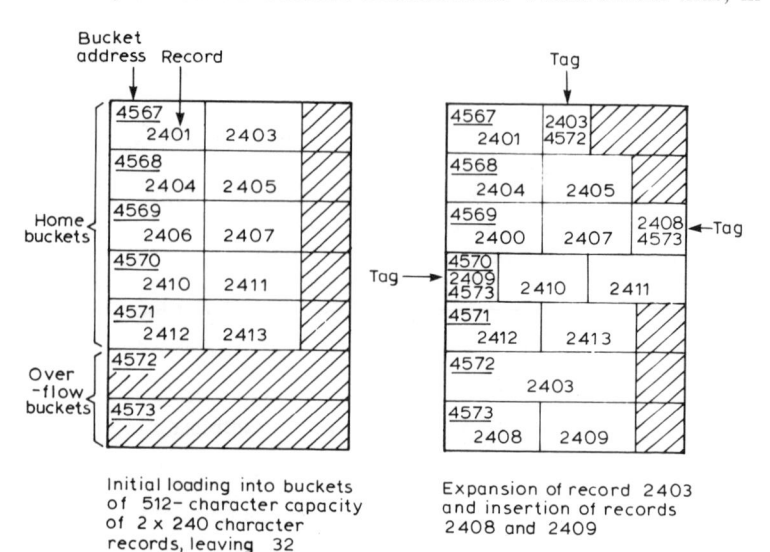

Fig. 9.11. Storage of records on disc

this situation, every time we wished to refer to a record on another track the read/write head would have to be moved, which would take around 30 milliseconds. If, however, we use the same relative track on each of the ten recording surfaces, which gives a vertical rather than a horizontal array of tracks (Fig. 9.12), we have a situation where ten times the number of records are accessible without any movement of the read/write heads. The name given to a set of tracks used in this way is *cylinder*. Of course, a number of adjacent cylinders may be required to accommodate a data file, involving a degree of head movement to access different cylinders. Nevertheless, the frequency of head movement is dramatically reduced, which minimises the total seek time.

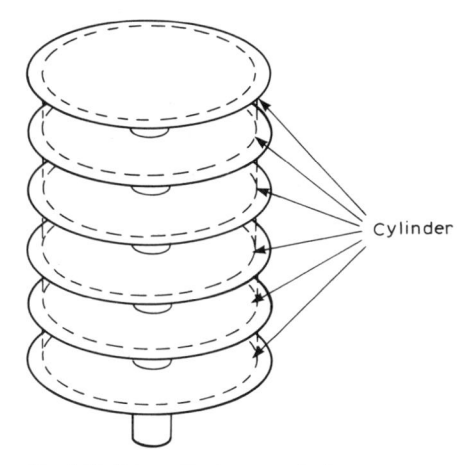

Fig. 9.12. Schematic storage cylinder

File organization
By contrast with a magnetic tape, on which, as we have seen, the only practical way of organizing file records is serially in sequence along the length of the tape, magnetic discs provide a number of alternative ways of organizing files.

Serial file organization The principle in serial file organization is to store records in key sequence order in consecutive storage locations—a principle rather similar to that adopted for magnetic tape. A fixed number of records are allocated to each track, and in a system where tracks are divided into blocks, each block may contain only one record or, to take greater advantage of the available storage space, records may be blocked—that is, a fixed number may be fitted into each block. Since read/write commands will usually only operate down to block level, all the records in an individual block will be transferred to the central processor, where they will be scrutinized to locate the specific required record.

Now, although, in a data processing situation involving updating master records with movement records sorted into the same sequence, this system has the advantage of speed, there are two main disadvantages:

(1) As is the case with magnetic tape, the system does not permit the insertion of new records in their correct place in the sequence.

(2) The system does not permit the expansion of a record beyond the fixed storage space allocated.

In both events a complete rewrite of the file becomes necessary.

Sequential processing In principle, processing in sequential mode follows the sequence of record keys irrespective of where the records may be physically stored on the disc. However, in the interests of economy in storage space and of optimizing processing speeds, it would be usual to initially organize the records serially, as above.

If it becomes necessary to insert a record within the sequence or if a record outgrows its original location, it is stored in the overflow section of the file area. A tag is inserted into the 'home' track (that is, the track in which the record would otherwise have been located) immediately after the record with the preceding key, the address of the overflow track in which it is now situated being quoted. At this point processing is diverted from a serial progression through locations to the overflow track in which the next sequential key appears. Of course, the insertion of tags presupposes that there is room for them in the home location track. If this is not so, the preceding record in key sequence is moved to the overflow area to make room for it and an additional tag is inserted giving this record's new address.

Files organized serially and sequentially are generally used in a search mode of access. This means that, in an updating run, movement records are sorted into the same sequence, and both sets of records read sequentially into the central processor in blocks, where keys are compared for a match. Where matching takes place, the file record is updated and the revised record written back to disc together with those records for which no movement data exist and which have consequently not been updated. In the case of sequential processing, the revised record is written back to the same disc, although this may mean moving it to an overflow area, while in serial processing it is usual to rewrite the whole file on to a new disc area.

Sequential processing is very fast and efficient, provided that a substantial proportion of the records have matching movement records and are to be updated. This factor, known as the *hit rate*, is said to be high when a large proportion of records is updated and low when only a small proportion is involved. It will be appreciated that processing with a low hit rate could be uneconomic, because a large proportion of the records will be transferred to the processor, will go through the matching routine and will then be written back unaltered.

Given, then, a file medium having a direct access facility and a low hit rate situation, it is of advantage just to 'pick out' and transfer to the processor only those records needing processing, even though they may be stored sequentially. This cannot be done unless the physical location of each record is known, which means that some kind of address/record key indexing system is necessary.

Self-indexing Files organized in a serial or sequential processing mode can lend themselves, within the limits of the coding system used to generate record keys, to a fairly simple form of index known as self-indexing. If, for example, we allocated cylinders 56–65 to hold a given file, then, discounting space reserved for control information, the address of the first record could be stated as 5600. That is, cylinder 56, the first surface = 0 and the first block in the track on that surface = 0. All we have to do is to allocate 5600 as the key to the first record and follow this principle throughout the sequence of records and we have what is known as a self-indexing direct addressing system.

Of course, the direct relationship does not apply if more than one record is located in each block, but we can get around this problem by devising a record key coding which, on the application of a simple arithmetic process, will generate the address of the record. Assuming four records to a block, we could have the following situation:

> Block location 5600 holds records with keys 22400, 22401, 22402, 22403
> Block location 5601 holds records with keys 22404, 22405, 22406, 22407
> Block location 5602 holds records with keys 22408, 22409, 22410, 22411

It is then a simple process to divide the keys by the blocking factor, 4, to obtain the address of the record.

The address of record 22406 is $\frac{22406}{4} = 5601$

Any remainder from the division is ignored.

Although this addressing technique appears a simple and logical approach to the problem, there are major difficulties which often make its use in commercial data processing undesirable:

(1) It presupposes an unbroken sequence of record keys. This may not happen in practice. Gaps will occur—for example, when records are deleted, leaving, since locations have to be allocated for every key within the sequence, 'empty' store locations.

(2) It is inflexible. Records must always remain at the same address; otherwise the arithmetic generation principle will be upset.

(3) In practice, record keys do not always lend themselves to self-indexing. For example, they may be mixed alphanumeric and under these circumstances it becomes far more difficult to devise an address generating formula.

However, self-indexing does combine with the advantages of sequential processing a facility for direct access.

Indexed sequential organization Indexed sequential organization is an indexing system that seeks to overcome the shortcomings of self-indexing by providing a method of locating the address of records even though no affinity exists between the location address and the record key. It is therefore suitable for any key coding system. Nevertheless, it still works on the principle, as the name suggests, that the records are stored sequentially.

It is based on a hierarchical structure of search levels, the highest being a search to locate the disc unit, assuming more than one, the next level the cylinder within the unit, and the next the track within the cylinder. It works in principle as follows:

(1) In a reserved part of one of the disc units holding the file an index is held listing the highest key number held on each unit against the unit number:

Unit Level Index

Highest key	Unit number
19672	1
37846	2
56231	3

For instance, if it is required to locate the record with the key 20235, then, by comparison with the listed highest keys, the nearest one above is selected, directing the search to the relevant unit.

(2) Within the unit a section of store will be allocated to hold an index listing the highest key held on each cylinder against the cylinder reference:

Cylinder Reference Level

Highest key	Cylinder number
19965	1
20163	2
20473	3
20714	4
37582	99
37846	100

Again, by comparison with highest keys, the one nearest above 20389 is selected and the next level of search directed to that cylinder—in this example cylinder 3.

(3) A section of the cylinder will be allocated to hold an index listing highest key number on each track against disc surface numbers:

Surface Level Index

Highest key	Surface number
20194	1
20236	2
20261	3
20473	10

A further comparison of key number with highest track key index will direct search to track 2, where a search through the track will locate the record sought.

The description above takes the addressing down to track level. This is not always the case, as some discs use a variable format track and others, as we have seen, are physically divided into sectors. In this case, addressing could well extend down to sector level by incorporating a sector index on the same principle as for cylinders and surfaces.

DIRECT ACCESS PROCESSING

While the above indexing and addressing system works for records stored sequentially, a different method is required for tracing the location of records that are stored on the disc in no particular order at all—that is, stored at random. In this case there are a number of techniques that can be used, usually incorporating an arithmetic formula, which can be applied to the record key in order to generate its address. To review all of the methods in depth would be far too big a task, and so just one of the simpler methods is described, as an illustration.

A file is held on 20 cylinders numbered 20–39, each cylinder containing 8 tracks holding 4 buckets, each containing 4 records. This gives a total record capacity of 2560 held in 640 addressable buckets. We wish to calculate an address for the record with the key 14936.

If we take the prime number nearest below 640 (that is 631) and divide it into the key number, then the remainder must be within the range 000–630. With key reference 14936 the remainder is 423. This number is called the relative bucket address, and it now has to be converted into cylinder, track and bucket addresses.

If we then divide 423 by the number of cylinders, 20, the remainder will fall within the range 00–19; in this case it is 3. On adding 20, the lowest cylinder number, a cylinder address is derived, 23. If we now divide 423 by 32, the number of buckets in a cylinder (8 tracks of 4 buckets), the remainder will be between 0 and 31, giving the address of the bucket within the cylinder; in this case it is 7. The location address would, therefore, be expressed as 2307, the seventh bucket on cylinder 23. This could be taken a stage further by dividing 423 by 8, with the remainder 7 identifying the track within the cylinder, and a further division of 423 by 4, with a remainder of 3 giving the bucket reference in the track. In this case, the location address is 2373, bucket 3 in track 7 of cylinder 23.

One problem is that the same location may be generated for two different records. In the example given above, the record key 15567, on being divided by the prime number 631, would have the same remainder, 423, and so would address the same bucket. Of course, the problem is reduced if records are organized four to each bucket, as this enables four synonyms to be coped with. Should the same address be generated more than four times, overflow techniques would have to be used.

SMALL DISC SYSTEMS

Following the introduction of microcomputers, small disc systems have been developed to provide them with an on-line direct access backing storage facility. The two types of disc commonly used are known as *floppy discs* and *Winchester discs*. In principle, they operate in much the same way as the larger disc systems already described. The floppy disc is a single exchangeable disc system, while Winchester systems may consist of just a single disc or a number assembled on to one spindle. In most cases the Winchester discs are not removable from the disc drive, although recently removable disc cartridges have come on to the market.

Floppy discs The floppy disc is a flexible disc housed in a square sleeve that is not removed when the disc is loaded on to the drive. The sleeve contains a slot through which the recording tracks can be accessed for reading and writing purposes as the disc revolves. Two sizes are commonly used—8 inches and 5¼ inches in diameter, the latter popularly known as a minifloppy disc. Disc drives of less than 4 inches are now becoming available also. In some floppy disc systems recording is limited to one side of the disc, while others will have recording surfaces on both sides. In view of the very wide range of disc units available, with their varying degrees of bit and track packing densities, it is impractical to quote a 'typical' disc storage capacity. This, in fact, may vary from as low as 90 kilobytes (thousands of 8-bit bytes) on a one-sided 5¼-inch disc to in excess of 1 megabyte (1 million bytes) on the larger 8-inch disc. Similarly, there is a wide variance in access times and data transfer rates, although, as a generalization, these may well be slower than with the larger disc systems described earlier.

Winchester discs The Winchester disc is a rigid disc system offering a far higher storage capacity than is the case with floppy discs, consisting of either a single double-sided disc or a number of discs mounted in a cartridge, each recording surface having its own retractable read/write head. In a Winchester system these heads are floated in extremely close proximity to the recording surface, thus decreasing the width of the band scanned by the head and making possible a very high track density. This can be as high as nearly 500 tracks per inch, compared with the maximum of around 80 in the case of floppy discs. The gap between the head and the disc surface is so small that even the smallest particle of dust can upset the read/write operations, which makes it necessary to encase the discs in a sealed container. Three disc sizes are available—5¼ inches, 8 inches and 14 inches in diameter, the 5¼-inch being the most commonly used in small desk-top microcomputers. Again it is very difficult to quote typical capacities. In large systems capacity is quoted in terms of gigabytes (one thousand million bytes)—for example, a 14-inch disc pack with 32 recording surfaces will hold in excess of 2 gigabytes. At the other end of the scale, a 5¼-inch disc surface could be expected to hold 2 megabytes or more.

Storage back-up systems

In any backing storage system it is important to keep duplicate copies of data files as a safeguard against the corruption or loss of data arising from damage to the storage medium or from systems failures. Magnetic tape processing poses no major problem, as a duplicate copy is a product of the system. For example, in an updating run, master and movements tapes are merged and processed, which produces a third, an updated master tape. The records on the original tapes remain the same, and so their retention provides a back-up from which the newest master tape version can be reconstituted should the need arise. It is common practice to keep three generations of magnetic tape files, to provide a foolproof back-up system—a practice popularly known as a grandfather–father–son technique.

On-line direct updating of records on magnetic disc poses a different problem, since the original disc record will be destroyed by overwriting with the new updated record. In this case, it becomes necessary to make a copy of the disc file to fall back on should the new file version become corrupted.

One way of doing this is to copy the whole of the file on to another disc pack, and another is to dump the file contents to magnetic tape. With small microcomputers using floppy discs, disc-to-disc copying is often adopted, although, of course, this involves dual disc drives. Copying can be made to cassette magnetic tape, although this is rather a slow process and there may be difficulties centred around the different capacities of the tape and the disc. Systems using high-speed, high-capacity Winchester discs do not lend themselves to copying to either floppy discs or the conventional cassette tape. These systems make use of another type of cassette tape, known as a *streamer tape*. This is a tape that will accept a continuous stream of data at a very high transfer rate and has a very high storage capacity. These streamer tapes may be provided as an integral part of a Winchester disc drive.

Exercises

9.1. Differentiate between an immediate access store and backing storage. Describe the interrelationship between these two types of store.

9.2. Explain the cylinder concept of storing data records on disc, mentioning any advantages you think accrue from this technique.

9.3. Draw a diagram to show how data are recorded on magnetic tape. What is the difference between fixed and variable length fields? Give examples of the use of each of these.

9.4. Give an account of how the computer's central processor store is organized so that data items can be accessed on demand.

9.5. Distinguish between RAM and ROM memory units.

9.6. Explain how data are recorded on a disc, describing in your answer the meaning of the following terms: (a) track, (b) block, (c) bucket.

9.7. What is the purpose on magnetic tape of (a) a header label and (b) a trailer label? Suggest the information you are likely to find in these two labels.

9.8. What do you understand by the term 'hit rate'? Suggest how this factor might influence the way in which data records are retrieved from store.

9.9. Distinguish between the storage of records serially and at random. Suggest the type of backing storage you would use in each case, giving reasons for your selection.

9.10. What do you understand by the term 'sequential' when applied to the storage of data records? Give an example of an application in which you feel storage in a sequential mode would be of advantage.

9.11. Describe a routine for locating records on disc that are filed on an indexed sequential principle.

9.12. What do you understand by a 'data block'? Give an account of how the recording of a block of records is organized on magnetic tape, assuming that all data items are held in variable length format.

9.13. A computer immediate access store could be said to consist of 32K words of 24 bits, each individually addressable. What do you understand by 32K, the term 'addressable' and the term 'bit'. Suggest two ways in which the number 1432 could be held in one 24-bit word.

Chapter 10

Processing by computer

The purpose of this chapter is to bring together some of the features of data processing we have already discussed in previous chapters and to see how they all fit into a processing situation.

We have seen that data have to be initially captured, that they must then be stored in some way (this may involve their conversion to a form that is acceptable by machines), and that the results of processing have to be recorded or communicated in some way or another. Between the input and output stages a number of operations may be performed—processing—designed to produce the output reports demanded of the system. One essential feature in the application of the processing operations is that they should be performed in a predetermined logical sequence. The name we give to the command that results in the execution of an operation is *instruction,* and the assembly in a logical pattern of a set of instructions designed to accomplish a defined purpose is a *program.*

By definition, a machine is only able to carry out the finite range of operations it has been designed to perform. These operations, however, can be marshalled together in an almost infinite range of sequences. In the final analysis, a program consists of an arrangement of these operations in the logical sequence that will result in the performance of a predetermined aim, and, of course, can only include operations the machine is capable of performing.

If, for example, we had a machine that would perform instructions such as:

READ, WRITE, ADD, SUBTRACT, MOVE, OPEN, STORE, etc.

then to work out a problem, say $x + y$, all we need do is to take the relevant operation names and put them in the correct sequence, and we have a program that will solve the problem:

READ x, READ y, ADD xy = z, WRITE z

The mechanics of the performance of these operations will vary from machine to machine. In a manually operated machine it may be simply entering x and y through a keyboard and then depressing the + (add) key. In an electromechanical machine the + function may well be performed by the automatic engagement of a 'stop' on a program bar. In a computer the function would be performed by communicating to the machine the binary codes representing the selected operations.

Since, in a computer, as in any other machine, the number of basic operations is finite, it is a quite straightforward procedure to allocate to each operation a code number so that, when this code is communicated to the machine, it will know what to do. For example, ADD = 0001, SUBTRACT = 0010, READ = 0011, WRITE = 0100, etc. This list of codes is permanently stored in the central processor. When a code is presented to the computer as a program instruction, the list is scrutinized until the identical code is located, and this triggers off the performance of the operation represented by that code. The list of codes representing computer functions is known as an *operation code,* an *instruction code* or a *function code.*

However, it is not sufficient just to tell the machine what to do; we must also identify the data element upon which the operation is to be performed. If, for example, we wanted someone to read a specific passage to us from a book, it would be pointless just to tell him or her to 'read'. We would have to qualify this by saying 'read page 45'—that is, we have to quote the location of the passage we wish read. A computer works in much the same way. As we have already seen, each data record is stored in an addressed location in the central processing store and so, to identify the data on which we wish the machine to work, all we have to do is to quote the location in which it is to be found.

This means that there must be two elements contained in a program instruction.

(1) The *operation* quotes the code identifying the operation the machine is to carry out.

(2) The *operand* quotes the address of the location in which the data on which the operation is to be performed are found.

Since the computer will work only with binary expressions, a program instruction could look like this:

$$\begin{matrix} Function \\ 0100 \end{matrix} \text{ (Operation)} \quad \begin{matrix} Address \\ 1110 \end{matrix} \text{ (Operand)}$$

Now, as we shall see later, when a computer program is being written, this binary notation is not used, but instructions are written in ordinary digits and characters and it is left to the computer, through an automatic conversion process, to translate these 'open' instructions into the binary coding the machine can store and operate upon.

Of course, for the computer to execute these instructions it must have access to them. This is gained by storing the program of instructions in the central processor memory along with the data that are to be worked on, but with one reservation. Whereas a data item can be stored in any location available for data storage (the address element of the instruction will tell the computer where to find it), there is no similar method of telling where the instructions are stored. It is, therefore, necessary to store them in a number of sequential locations, so that, the first instruction (the address of this will be known by or can be communicated to the machine) having been executed, the computer control element will know that the next instruction is in the following location. Should it become necessary to break the sequence of locations, then the final location in one sequence must direct control to the location of the first in the next sequence (see Fig. 10.1).

As we saw earlier, another factor that must be present in the processing function is the capacity to carry out arithmetic and logical operations. These, in a computer, are performed through a special unit in the central processor known as an *arithmetic and logic unit* (ALU). This will cope with such functions as carrying out arithmetic; comparing data items with one another, in order to decide upon alternative courses of action; and matching record keys, so that master and movement data items are brought

Address

Storage words

12460	12461	12462	12463	12464	12465
Data	Data	Data	Program	Program	Program
12466	12467	12468	12469 Program (Instruction go to 12479)	12470	12471
Program	Program	Program		Data	Data
12472	12473	12474	12475	12476	12477
Data	Data	Data	Data	Data	Data
12478	12479	12480	12481	12482	12483
Data	Program	Program	Program	Program	Program

Fig. 10.1. Data and program instructions in central processor store. Program instructions are worked sequentially from word 12463. Word 12469 contains a jump instruction directing control to word 12479

together for processing. Data items are transferred from the working area of the CPU store to the ALU, where the logical operations are carried out and the results then transferred back to store.

A highly simplified version of how an instruction is executed in the central processor is as follows (Fig. 10.2):

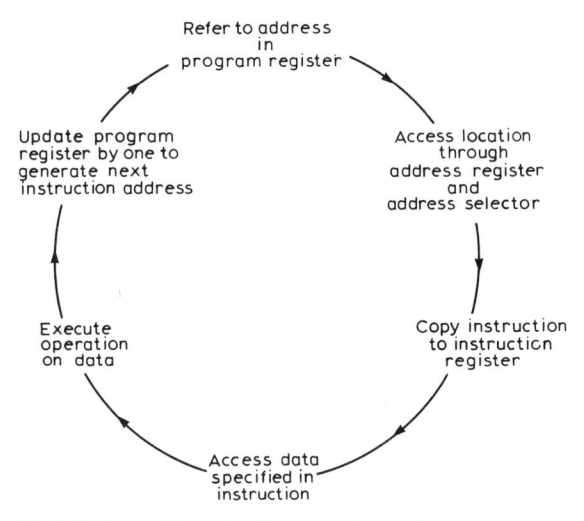

```
                    Refer to address
                           in
                    program register
      Update program                         Access location
      register by one to                        through
      generate next                         address register
      instruction address                         and
                                            address selector

      Execute                               Copy instruction
      operation                             to instruction
      on data                                   register

                     Access data
                     specified in
                      instruction
```

Fig. 10.2. Execution cycle of program instruction

(1) The location address in which the first instruction is held is entered into a program register counter—this is a special register reserved for this purpose that will hold the address in binary notation.

(2) The address is transferred to another special register—an address register.

(3) The address is then circulated through an address selector which switches in the necessary circuitry to gain access to the location in which the instruction is stored.

(4) The instruction is then copied into a program instruction register.

(5) The operation (or function) element of the instruction is then circulated through an instruction decoder which will activate the circuitry necessary to carry out the specified instruction.

(6) Meanwhile, the operand (data address) element of the instruction is communicated to the address register and passed through the address selector, and the location in which the data are stored is accessed.

(7) The data to be worked on are then moved to the ALU—this will incorporate special registers known as *accumulators* in which the data items can be held while processing takes place—and the operation in (5) above will be carried out.

(8) The address contained in the program register counter is now incremented by 1 to give the address of the next instruction.

(9) The results of the processing are moved back from the ALU under control of the address selector to a location in store.

If we look at the computer configuration as a whole and take into account the interaction between the central processor and its input, output and storage peripherals (Figs. 10.3, 10.4), a highly simplified version of what takes place in a processing routine is as follows (it being borne in mind that each stage is under the control of the stored instructions previously referred to):

(1) Prepared data—that is, data in a machine readable form—are passed through a reader (see Chapter 7); read into the central processor, where they are subjected to various accuracy checks (this is a validation procedure that is dealt with in detail in a later chapter); and then written out to backing storage.

(2) When a processing run takes place, a block of data is read from backing storage into the input section of the CPU store.

(3) The record contained in this block which has to be worked on is now selected and moved into the working area of the store.

(4) Elements of this record upon which logical or arithmetic functions are to be performed are then subjected to the routine described above for the execution of a program instruction.

(5) On completion the results are then moved back to the original record in the working area.

(6) From here the record is transferred to the output section of the store.

(7) The record is then either communicated to an output peripheral (for example, a printer) or returned to backing storage for future additional processing or for later communication through an output peripheral.

The above presupposes that all input data are first stored on backing storage for later processing. This is not always the case, as we shall see later when discussing computer operating modes, when, in some cases, input is communicated direct to the processor for immediate processing.

Fig. 10.3. Simplified view of a central processor

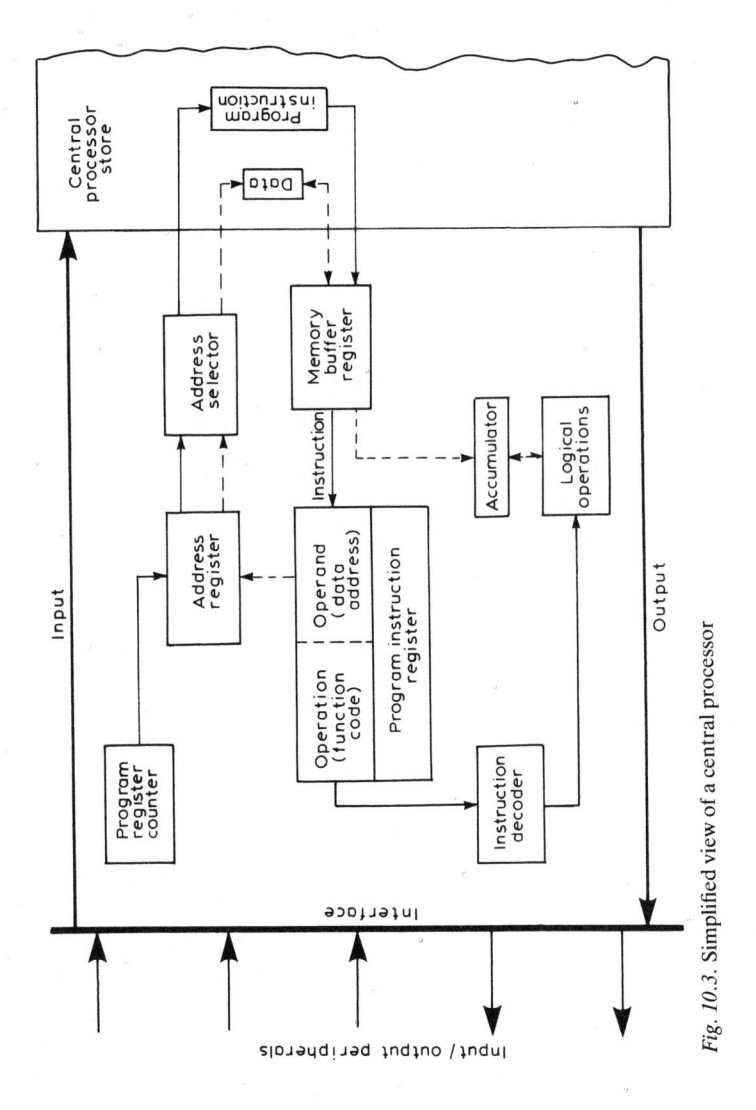

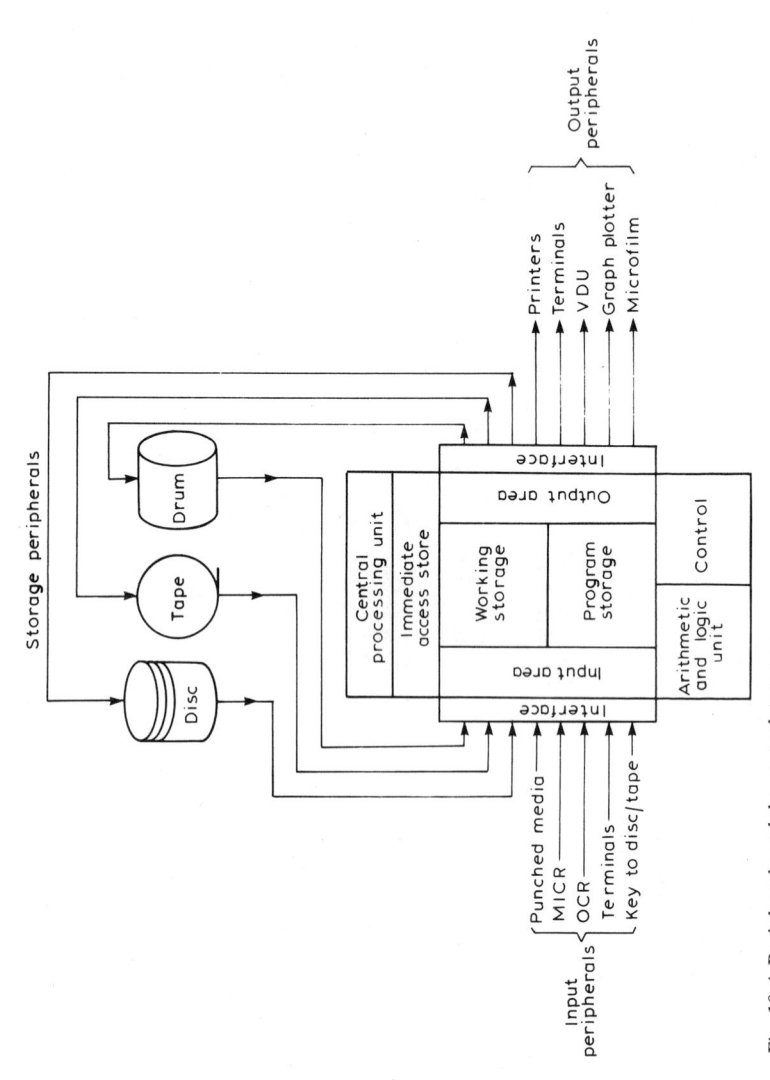

Fig. 10.4. Peripherals and the central processor

Exercises

10.1. What are the two elements in a program instruction? Explain the purpose each of these serves.

10.2. Explain briefly the cycle of operations involved in executing a program instruction in a computer.

10.3. What is an arithmetic and logic unit in a central processor? Suggest three processing operations which this will carry out.

10.4. Explain what happens to an item of handwritten data from the time it originates until it is held in backing storage, mentioning in your answer all of the hardware devices that would be used.

Chapter 11
Processing modes

In terms of time, two alternatives present themselves for processing data records. On the one hand, the demands of the system may require the immediate processing of records as they occur, or, on the other hand, the system may allow for a lapse of time between the record originating and its processing.

In the former case records must be dealt with individually (this is often known as unit record processing and may be real time or time-sharing processing); but in the latter, records are collected over a period of time and processed collectively at predetermined intervals (this is known as batch processing). To illustrate this point, an example of unit record processing is a hotel room booking system when, in response to a client's request for a room, records will (a) be searched immediately to see whether there is a room available and if so (b) records will be updated immediately to show the new booking. An example of a batch processing routine is a sales ledger system in which statements of account are produced only at the end of each month. In these circumstances the source documents holding the movement records can be collected together over a period of time and then processed as a batch.

Batch processing

Batch processing is a form of processing suitable for many of the routine tasks found in most businesses, such as payroll, sales and purchase ledger accounting, stock control, etc., and is ideal for the efficient, accurate and rapid processing of large volumes of similar records. It can be coped with by any basic computer configuration—for example, a central processor with magnetic tape backing storage and line printer output and with data preparation and input equipment that lends itself to high-volume work: punched cards or key-to-tape. Software requirements are also basic. Application programs tend to be fairly standard and no special operating system is required.

The following is an outline of the stages involved in batch processing.

(1) Source documents are collected in the originating department over a specified period of time.

(2) When the batch is due for forwarding to the data processing department, a 'batch slip' is prepared on which all or some of the following control information will appear:
> Date batch prepared.
> Serial number of batch.
> Number of documents in batch and, if numbered serially, the first and last numbers in the sequence.
> Control totals. These may be arrived at by prelisting quantitative data, to give a total.
> Hash totals, obtained by totalling non-quantitative numeric data such as document reference numbers, account number, etc.
> A signature authorising the acceptance of these data into the data processing system.

(3) The batch is then forwarded for processing in time to meet the deadlines set for the receipt of batches by the processing department.

(4) The batch slip is verified by the control section of the data processing department and the details are entered in the batch control register.

(5) The batch is passed to the data preparation section for data preparation—for example, preparation and verification of punched cards.

(6) Batches of cards may be accumulated until a computer run is due.

(7) Input to computer through a card reader, written to magnetic tape and then sorted into the same sequence as master file.

(8) During reading to magnetic tape, a validation check will be applied.

(9) This tape may be built up over a period of time by adding batches of records in sequence as they become available until a movements tape is prepared holding all records up to the time of the master file updating run.

(10) Control and/or hash totals are printed out for each batch for reconciliation with batch control register.

(11) An updating run, when movement records are applied to master records and required reports are printed out.

Advantages are:

(1) Hardware and software costs are relatively low.
(2) Records are processed in a sequential mode which lends itself to fast processing.
(3) Control over accuracy and loss of records is very positive.
(4) Updating involves copying the original record and rewriting the new updated version rather than overwriting. This means that the original records are left intact and can be kept to reconstitute the updated file in the event of destruction or corruption.

Disadvantages are:

(1) Processing is historical and therefore records are never completely up to date. They will only reflect the position as it stands immediately after the last updating run.
(2) In a computer designed for batch processing only, there are no facilities for interrogating records on demand. The only reports available are those produced at the last updating run.
(3) In a batch processing system, work 'peaks' tend to occur both in the computer department, when the periodic runs are made to produce the reports, and in dealing with the reports by the department being serviced.
(4) If reports are designed to satisfy every conceivable need within the organization, a great deal of unnecessary paper work may be churned out, but, on the other hand, if too narrow an approach is made to reporting, reports may be insufficient for some needs. It is often difficult to reach a reasonable compromise between these two extremes.

Factors affecting other operating modes

Before we consider other computer operating modes, there are two factors which first need attention, as they have a bearing on these operations. They are multiprogramming and data transmission.

Multiprogramming

A factor which limits the degree of efficiency at which a central processor will work is the comparatively slow operational speeds of input and output devices. A modern processor works incredibly fast, with operation cycle times measured in thousandths of millionths of a second. However, although it is capable of these speeds, one inhibiting factor from a practical point of view centres around the problem of supplying it with input data fast enough to keep it occupied and, indeed, extracting processed results fast enough to let it get on with the next problem. A name commonly given to this situation, when a central processor is kept waiting for new data to get on with, is 'peripheral bound'.

It is rather like working on a production line where the objects on which you are working arrive at 1-minute intervals but it takes you only 6 seconds to do the work. In these circumstances we may argue that a sensible thing to do would be to start a second production line and alternate between the two rather than wait for 54 seconds in each minute. This would, at any rate, have the effect of doubling your efficiency from a resource point of view from 10 per cent to 20 per cent. We may further argue that by providing ten production lines your efficiency rating could be maximized at 100 per cent. This is theoretically feasible, but hardly possible in practice.

Similarly with a central processor. If while one job is being processed there are, comparatively speaking, lengthy idle periods while one waits for input/output operations to be completed, why not provide another job the processor can be getting on with during these intervals? This can be done by holding two or more programs in the processor simultaneously, so that when it is unable to work on one of them owing to slow peripheral activity, it can switch to another that is demanding processing time. This mode of operating is known as *multiprogramming*.

Multiprogramming can only be carried out on a configuration designed to provide this facility. A sophisticated operating system is necessary and also a sufficient range of on-line peripherals to support the concurrent running of a number of jobs.

Assuming that two programs are loaded into the processor, A and B, then the instructions in one of these will be carried out in the normal way (let us say A) until a statement involving a transfer to or from a peripheral is encountered. At this point the transfer will be initiated, but the operating system will leave the peripheral to carry it out automatically. While this transfer is going on, instead of leaving the processing unit ticking over awaiting its completion, control is switched to program B and its instructions are then got on with. This operation is known as program suspend. When the transfer demanded by A is completed, we could then have a position where both A and B are demanding processing time. A decision on which to operate is reached in the light of priorities previously written into the operating system. This is known as *work scheduling*.

Assuming that A has priority, processing will then be switched back to that program, which interrupts the work being done on B, the intermediate results from B being dumped into registers so that operations can again commence where left off when B is switched back again. This is known as a *program interrupt*.

This example is based on two programs only—a situation referred to as *dual programming*. Multiprogramming occurs when several programs are operating simultaneously, each with its own level of priority.

Data transmission

It is not always the case that data items originate in close proximity to a computer; it may be necessary to convey them by one means or another over considerable distances. This process is known as data transmission. Strictly speaking, this term has been associated with three different methods:

(1) When data items are physically transferred from source to a computer installation. For example, when a punched paper tape is prepared at a remote point and sent by courier to the computer centre.

(2) When communication lines are used to transmit data to an off-line machine at the computer centre. For example, when data items are transmitted to a paper punch which will prepare a paper tape for future entry to the computer.

(3) When data are transmitted over communication lines and entered directly into the computer. In this case we say the transmitting device is on-line (Fig. 11.1).

However, the term 'data transmission' is generally accepted as referring to a situation where telecommunication lines are used between the point of data origin and the computer.

The unit used to define the rate of transmission is a *baud* (by convention a baud represents the transmission of one bit per second). Data transmission usually makes use of the Telecom network, although private dedicated lines are used in some cases and also data may be transmitted over radio links, including communication satellites. There are a number of types of transmission line, each working with a maximum data transfer rate—for example, the telephone network lines are known as Datel 200, 300, 600, 2400 and 4800 services, the numbers indicating the maximum transmission rate in bauds. Wide-band or broad-band lines are available that are much faster than the telephone network, with speeds up to 50 000 baud.

The device originating the data is linked to the network by means of a device called a *modem*, an abbreviation of 'MOdulator–DEModulator'. Modulation is the process of converting the data (that is, data in binary form) into an analogue representation

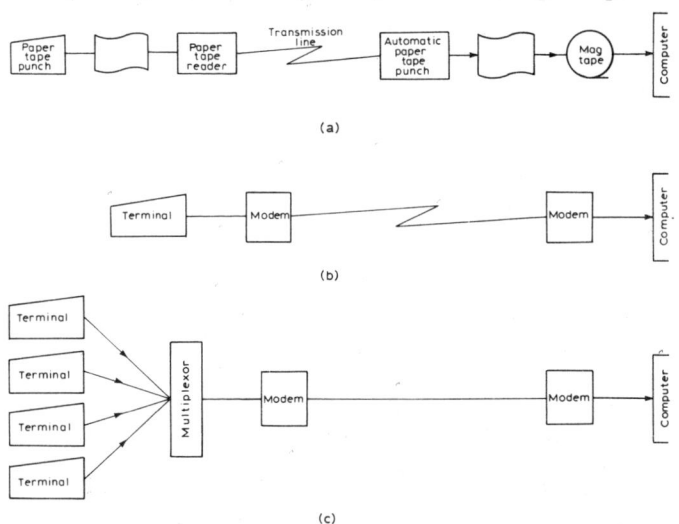

Fig. 11.1. (a) Example of off-line data transmission. (b) On-line data transmission—single terminal. (c) On-line data transmission—multiple terminals

for transmission. Demodulation is the process of reversing the pattern at the other end. In circumstances where a number of terminals are used which transmit and receive data at low speed, a *multiplexor* may be used. This will accept data from a number of 'slow' transmission points and can channel them all into one fast transmission line, which leads to economies in the use of communication links.

Another way of transmitting data, although this works at very slow speeds, is the use of a device known as an *acoustic coupler*. An ordinary telephone instrument is inverted into a cradle designed for this purpose which is an integral part of the terminal. The digital signals are converted into audio signals for transmission. At the other end of the line they are converted back to digital pulses. Transmission by acoustic coupler has two main disadvantages: (1) low transmission rate, with an effective maximum of 200 baud; (2) the danger of data becoming corrupted by extraneous noise picked up on the system. One major advantage is that acoustic coupling can be used with any standard telephone instrument, and thus permits the use of portable terminals.

TRANSMITTING MODES

There are three transmission modes, known as *simplex, half-duplex* and *duplex* (often known as *full-duplex*). Simplex lines transmit in one direction only. This mode is suitable when a terminal is being used solely as an input device to the computer and there is no need for the results of processing to be transmitted back to the terminal. Half-duplex lines enable data to be transmitted in either direction but in only one direction at a time. There is a short pause when the transmitting direction is reversed. Duplex lines permit the transfer of data in both directions simultaneously.

Time sharing

We saw earlier that data may originate at a number of points remote from the computer. This situation gives rise to two alternatives: either to site a number of small machines at the remote points to process the data locally or to transmit the data to a large centralized machine. A time-sharing system provides a situation where a number of users at remote points have access to a central computer virtually simultaneously via terminals linked by communication line to the computer.

In practice, what happens is that each user terminal is allocated a period of time during which it has, in effect, exclusive use of the computer. This period, known as a *time slice*, is quite small, around 10 ms (Fig. 11.2).

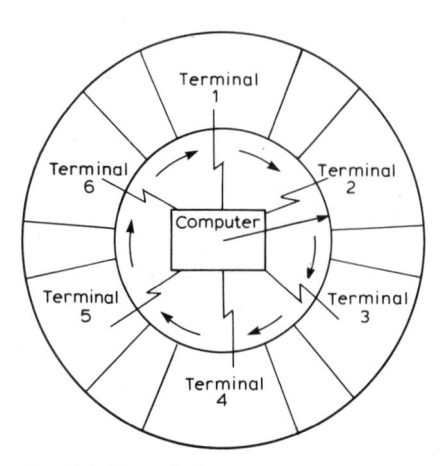

Fig. 11.2. Time-sharing system

The operating system controlling a time-sharing operation will circulate all terminals, allocating a time slice to each in rotation. In 1 second a modern time-sharing system can service many terminals. With a large number of users linked to one machine, all demanding processing facilities, a correspondingly large number of programs may have to be available to meet those needs. It therefore becomes necessary to store users' programs in direct access backing storage from which they can be transformed to the processor on demand, although there is no reason why more than one program should not be stored in the processor at one time. Programs may be 'queued' in the processor awaiting their turn, and as the one at the top is moved out, having finished its processing, another is moved in to the base of the queue.

Time-sharing systems may operate in a unit processing or a batch processing mode. In the former case, individual records may be entered to interrogate and/or update existing records, while in the latter, given the required hardware at the terminal end (say a punched card reader), a batch of records may be transmitted and written to backing storage to await processing in a later updating run.

Real-time systems

The essence of a real-time system is that it is designed to accept data relating to an activity immediately it occurs, to process the data and to output the results quickly enough to have an effect on the activity. This means that:

(1) The files containing records and programs relating to a system must be held in direct access storage, usually magnetic disc, permanently on-line to the computer.

(2) Facilities must exist, also permanently on-line, for the input and output of data, usually Teletype or VDU terminals.

(3) While the computer may not be dedicated to real-time processing (that is, it may work in batch mode as well), there must be an operating system that will instantly interrupt other work in favour of a real-time demand emanating from a terminal.

Features of a real-time system include:

(1) The transaction or enquiries may be entered into the system on demand at any time.

(2) A response is received from the computer in a very short

time. This response time must be short enough to enable any modification to take place in the activity giving rise to the query.

(3) Master files are updated immediately movement data are received and so always show a completely up-to-date situation.

Because of this facility for receiving an enquiry on demand and providing an immediate up-to-date reply, real-time systems are often described as conversational, interrogative and interactive.

The classic example of a real-time system is that handling airline seat reservations, in which entering a request for a seat through a terminal will result in a display of the seats available on a flight. When the seat is booked, this fact must immediately be recorded (that is, the files held in storage updated); otherwise, incorrect information will be shown when the next client comes along.

There are problems associated with the use of real-time systems.

(1) Real-time systems are expensive for both hardware and software. In addition to a central processor with a large immediate access store, hardware costs will include high-volume direct access backing storage, terminals and data transmission links between the computer and terminals. On the software side, a sophisticated operating system is required.

(2) Checks on data accuracy may be less stringent than those imposed in a batch processing situation.

(3) Since a large number of users may have access to master files, data on these may be less secure.

(4) The system is vulnerable in the event of a breakdown. It may be necessary to provide standby facilities for use in the event of a major hardware or software failure.

Distributed processing

Another way of dealing with data processing when data items originate at a number of scattered points is to site a small computer at each point to cope with local processing needs. When these machines work in a 'stand-alone' capacity (that is, are not connected or reliant upon one another), the term 'decentralized processing' is often used. However, this situation is not common, the tendency being either to have terminals at the remote points transmitting data for centralized processing, as we have already seen, or to site small 'satellite' computers or terminals at each point and not only have them linked to a central machine, but also have them interlinked with one another. This is known as *distributed processing*.

Such a system means that hardware applicable to local needs is sited in remote departments, factories, etc. This hardware may range from interactive terminals in a sales office, for ascertaining stock availability or customer credit limits, to machines capable of coping with production planning, stock control, payroll, etc., in individual factories. Access is available, where necessary, to the centralized files on the main computer. Also, when desirable, machines are linked with one another, as could be the case with factory-sited computers in order to co-ordinate production scheduling, maintenance of optimum stock levels, etc. (See Fig. 11.3.)

Decentralized processing

The term 'decentralized processing' refers to a situation where, in preference to a large computer department coping with all the processing needs of an organization, a functional approach is made to the problem. This means siting small machines in individual departments, which will cope with the processing requirements of the functions for which the department is responsible. These machines work in a stand-alone capacity and may well be dedicated to a particular system or sub-system—for example, invoice preparation, stock control, payroll, sales accounting, etc. With microcomputers being used for this purpose, the economics of processing in a decentralized mode can be a marked incentive to its use.

Microcomputer processing

Processing data by microcomputer is rather different from the processing modes discussed earlier. It cannot be described as batch processing or as real-time processing, although it incorporates elements of both these modes. Source documents can be batched and control totals taken out for reconciliation after the entry of a batch, although the procedures explained earlier of creating a movements file for subsequent updating of a master file do not take place. Instead, as is the case in a real-time system, as each movement record is entered, the master record is immediately updated. This form of processing can be described as an on-line direct updating process. With microcomputer processing there is no need for data preparation routines, as data may be keyboard entered direct from source documents.

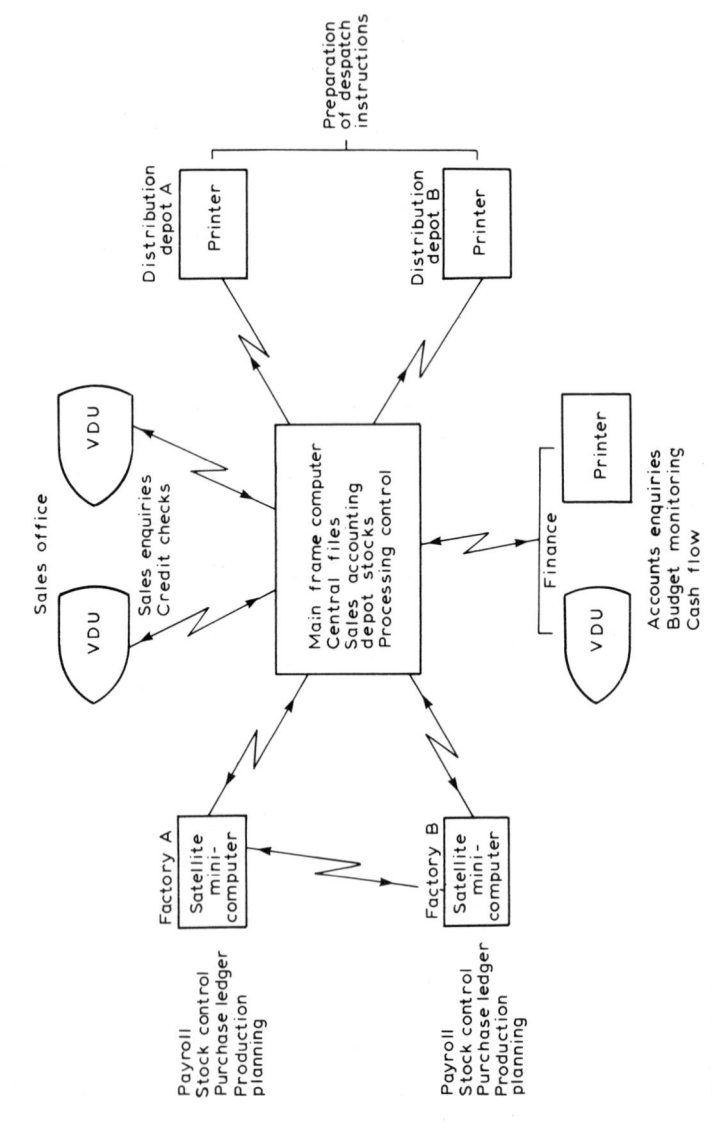

Fig. 11.3. Distributed processing

Programs are usually held on magnetic tape cassette or floppy disc and are read into the processor when the operator depresses a 'load' key. Segments of the program are then displayed on the visual display screen, known as a *menu*. For example, in a sales ledger system:

1. File maintenance
2. File enquiry
3. Invoice posting
4. Cash posting
5. Sales analysis
6. Sales statements

The operator will then type into the keyboard the reference number of the program module to be operated. This will result in the display of further details relating to that section, known as a submenu. If, for example, a 1 is entered for file maintenance, the following may well be displayed:

1. Add customer
2. Delete customer
3. Change customer details

Again the relevant section will be selected by number and this will result in the relevant record format being displayed. Assuming again that 1 is selected, a record format could appear on the screen as follows:

Account number ....
Name ....
Address ....

              ....
Trade discount ....
Credit limit ....

This lists each separate data field making up the record, with spaces for the maximum number of characters each field contains. The operator will then key in the requested details, and as this is done, the characters will appear on the screen against each heading. This enables a sight check for accuracy to be carried out, but the program will also incorporate validation checks as an additional safeguard before the data items are taken on to file. On depression of the relevant command key, the new record will be written to the file.

152 Processing modes

Exercises

11.1. Two computer processing modes are batch processing and real-time processing. Suggest any systems considerations that would have an influence on the choice of either of these two modes.

11.2. What is the purpose of a 'time-sharing' system? Give an account of the hardware needed to operate such a system.

11.3. Explain what is meant by 'real-time' computer system, using in your answer a description of any application of your choice to illustrate how such a system works.

11.4. What do you understand by 'batch processing'? Give an account of the control information you would expect to find on a batch control slip.

11.5. Describe the routine involved in a batch processing system from the moment the data are captured on the source documents until the movement record file is ready to be applied to the master file for updating.

11.6. Distinguish between 'off-line' and 'on-line' data transmission. Describe the process of transmitting data to a computer in each of these situations.

11.7. Give an account of the advantages and disadvantages in using an acoustic coupler as a medium for data transmission.

11.8. Explain the functions of (a) a modem and (b) a multiplexor in the process of data transmission.

11.9. Three commonly used computer processing modes are: (a) time sharing, (b) batch processing, (c) real-time working. Give an account of what is meant by each of these, mentioning, in particular, the computer hardware necessary to operate each mode.

PART 3
Systems and software

Chapter 12
The computer data processing system

We discussed in Chapter 3 some of the general considerations relating to data processing systems; the purpose of this chapter is to review the development of a computer processed system.

Factors influencing structure of computer system

There are a number of factors that will influence the overall structure of such a system, in which any combination of the following could apply.

Physical environment

(1) The organizational structure of the activities giving rise to the data.
    (a) Are these activities concentrated in one location—a single plant manufacturing a product for distribution through independent wholesalers?
    (b) Are the activities dispersed—a number of factories in different locations manufacturing the same product?
    (c) Are the activities diversified—a number of factories distributing the product through a number of their own depots and retail outlets, involving a complex system of intercommunications?

(2) How are the data emanating from the activities generated and how are they to be fed into the processing system? The form of the source data generated in a vehicle records system, with millions of people scattered all over the country filling in forms manually, will call for a totally different systems approach from that employed with a similar number of people operating cash dispensing machines throughout the country.

(3) What response time is demanded from the system to provide the level of control called for? In the case of a hotel booking system this must be very rapid, while a delay of weeks is quite acceptable in a television licensing system.

(4) The form and distribution of output reporting: hard copy for external distribution such as a sales invoice, microfilm for distribution of, say, stock levels to dispersed depots, visual display for internal record interrogation, etc.

In an existing organization systems for the processing of data will already be there in one form or another, probably having grown up over a long period of time as the organization has developed, and tailored to meet its particular requirements. This gives rise to a question we might well ask ourselves at this stage: 'Should the existing data processing structure determine the format of the system or should the system generate its own completely new structure?' In practice, the solution usually falls between the two hypothetical situations. The process of introducing a computer system within an already existing structure does not necessarily sweep away the old completely, nor does it necessarily exclusively fit into the present order of things. It will seek—retaining, where desirable, present procedures and introducing, where desirable, new or revised procedures—to formulate a system, within the framework of available resources, that will provide the best service.

Systems considerations

It is suggested that the factors outlined above will have a bearing on the following:

The methods used to capture, prepare and input data.
The form and circulation of output reports.
Whether processing will take place centrally or be distributed over a number of centres.
The provision of remote input/output points with their associated communications network.
The computer operating mode—that is, batch processing, time sharing, real time, etc.
The structure of systems files—serial or direct access.
The controls imposed upon the system to ensure security and accuracy.
Software requirements, particularly in regard to operating systems.

These factors will, of course, determine not only the structure of the system, but also the hardware and software requirements necessary to operate it.

Economic considerations

The costs associated with computer processing fall under three main headings.

(1) Capital expenditure. The provision of hardware and any software requirements obtained from outside sources.
(2) Revenue costs. Employment of specialist staff, data capture and preparation costs, maintenance, supplies, etc.
(3) Environmental costs. Provision of work areas, heating, lighting, and special computer operating conditions where necessary (humidity, temperature and dust control).

As we shall see later, one of the objects of a feasibility study is to assess these costs as far as possible and to relate them to the costs of existing or alternative processing methods so as to assess what economic benefits may accrue. These are usually classified under two headings: (1) direct benefits—that is, the cost of computer processing compared with that of other approaches; and (2) indirect benefits—those resulting from a general toning up of administrative and operational efficiency.

It cannot be automatically assumed that direct savings will result with the employment of a computer in data processing; indeed, in the past the reverse has often proved to be the case. The advent of low-cost microcomputers, however, brings a new dimension to the problem of cost effectiveness, particularly in small business systems that lend themselves to decentralized processing. On the other hand, indirect savings should result from any computerized system—for example, an improvement in cash flow, reduction in stock levels, more effective production planning and work scheduling, enabling more effective use of production resources.

It will also be recognized that computer systems can lend themselves to procedures that waste time and money. A system should, therefore, incorporate facilities for checking that the system itself is being used to the best advantage. This is known as *systems audit*, and will be concerned with:

(1) Quantitative checks to show the extent to which the system is meeting its objectives.
(2) Monitoring the use of hardware, checking the incidence of 'down' periods arising from machine and systems faults, and, particularly in the case of configurations using remote access devices, monitoring the extent to which these are used.
(3) Ensuring that unnecessary output reports are not produced,

that those that are adequately meet the needs of the user, and that terminals are not used pointlessly.

(4) Monitoring data capture and preparation routines, with the object of recommending changes in procedures, form design, etc., if necessary.

(5) Diagnosing errors in the system which may have escaped all of the checking procedures during the systems and program checking routines.

However, the systems audit itself will use computer time and it is, therefore, a question of balance from a cost point of view as to whether the savings made by a systems audit are greater than the cost of the audit itself.

Social considerations

As we saw in Chapter 1, an increasingly wide range of data relating to our personal lives is being held on computer files. Some of the fears and problems associated with this practice are:

(1) Data may not be accurate and therefore incorrect conclusions may be drawn from their use.

(2) It is possible to sell data from computer files to a third party, for a purpose never originally intended, without the consent or even the knowledge of the person to whom the information relates.

(3) There is no guarantee that a person with access to computer files will not retrieve data, using them to his own advantage and to the disadvantage of the person they concern.

A computer system should, therefore, incorporate safeguards that will restrict access to records to authorized nominated personnel. It is also socially desirable that facilities exist for a personal check of the accuracy of records relating to an individual.

Audit considerations

In a manual system the role of an auditor in protecting the assets of the company and checking for errors and fraud is a fairly straightforward one, his checking procedure taking him from one written record to another. In a computer system, where records cannot be scrutinized in this way, the following points arise:

(1) The auditor must acquire a working knowledge of computer systems and be involved at all stages in the development of a

system—feasibility study, systems design, systems and program testing, systems implementation.

(2) Insurance against collusion can be achieved by insisting on the segregation of the different functions in the overall system and their performance by different individuals.

(3) Checking input against output can be done by manually processing selected input records and checking the answers against the computer output.

(4) The use of standard audit packages will allow sampling of the contents of a file by printing out selected records, will print out control totals on demand and will cause exceptional items to be output.

(5) Special 'test packs' may be created during the systems development stage incorporating deliberate errors. On the test pack passing through the machine, a test can be made that the data have been processed correctly and that the errors have been detected.

(6) In real-time systems, auditors should ensure that there is no unauthorized access to the system and that spot checks are made by logging transactions for a period and then checking back on their authenticity.

(7) Spot checks should be made on all activities in the processing department to ensure that standards are being adhered to.

(8) Copies of all documents, specifications, manuals, logs, input and output documents should be available for scrutiny by the auditor.

Development of a computer system

A great deal of work spread over a fairly lengthy period is necessary for the development of a computer system. This work may be classified into the following areas:

(1) An initial survey to see whether it is worth while to change over to computer methods. This is known as a 'feasibility study' and will form the basis on which the decision is made.

(2) The investigation into and the analysis of existing systems and procedures.

(3) The design and specification of a system in a form suitable for computer processing.

(4) Constructing and encoding the programs required to operate the system.

(5) Implementing the new system.

Feasibility study

In early days of computing it was often not so much a question of assessing whether it was worth while to introduce a computer but rather of seeing whether the computer was, in fact, able to do the job. Nowadays this question rarely arises: it would be safe to say that from a technical point of view computer processing for all commercial systems is feasible.

What is more to the point is to ask whether computer processing is economically and/or organizationally desirable. The criteria upon which the decision is based will, of course, vary from situation to situation. In one case, expense may be the critical factor; in another, time may be of prime importance, even at the expense of cost; while other points of judgement may centre around staff shortages, degree of accuracy, supply of management information. Within the framework of such a study information may well be required on the following points:

(1) The overall objectives that will be attained in terms of the areas of work absorbed and the information that will be generated by the system.

(2) Improvement resulting over the present system in terms of accuracy, timeliness and the availability and control of data.

(3) The provision of adequate and up-to-date information for management control purposes.

(4) An estimate of cost and comparisons with current costs, taking into account direct costs and any indirect savings that may accrue.

(5) The overall effect on the structure of the organization, particularly the changes needed in departmental organization and managerial responsibility.

(6) The effect on staffing, with an estimate of possible redundancies and the need for retraining.

(7) An estimate of the date by which the machine is expected to be installed and become operational. A computer is not necessarily the immediate answer to a current problem.

(8) An estimate of the life expectancy of the equipment. Are there any technical developments around the corner that will make the processing techniques proposed redundant or uneconomic in the near future?

Systems investigation

The next stages are the detailed investigation of existing systems and the design of the new computer systems. This is known as a systems project and covers two main areas of work—systems analysis and systems design. Analysis is concerned with investigation of present systems—fact finding—and the recording of the information acquired so that a clear and precise picture is built up of what is going on. Systems design is concerned with working out how the objectives of the system can be achieved in the most effective way and specifying in detail all of the procedures involved.

FACT FINDING

The systems analyst will be interested in the what, where, why, how, when and who of the situation, and, further, he will be concerned not only with what is actually happening, but also with what should happen according to company practice and policy. There is often an appreciable difference between the two.

A number of techniques are used in the investigation process:

(1) The examination of records, documents, files, organization charts and procedure manuals.
(2) Personal observation of staff as they carry out their work.
(3) Getting staff to complete questionnaires.
(4) Personal interviews and discussion with staff.

The analyst will be looking for the following information:

(1) Objectives. What is the system or procedure trying to achieve?
(2) Output. What form does it take? What are the contents of each? Is it used, and if so, for what purpose and by whom? Is it suitable for the purpose required? Is it necessary at all? Is the same information produced through another system or procedure? Does the output of this procedure become the input of another?
(3) Input. What is the input? What form does it take? Where does it come from? Is it the output of another procedure? What is its detailed content? Are all input records treated in the same way or are there exceptions?
(4) Records and files. What files are kept? How often are they brought up to date? What purposes do they serve? How long are they kept before being disposed of?
(5) Processing. What procedures are followed to convert input data into the required output reports? What is the frequency of each procedure? What special skills are required? Could the job be done more effectively if the input or output was in a different form? Does processing anticipate further processes later on?

(6) Volumes and growth. What are current volumes? Are there any peak periods or seasonal fluctuations? What has been the rate of growth over the past few years? Is continued growth anticipated?

(7) Enviroments. What is the context within which the system operates? This will involve research into the organizational structure of the departments involved, the adequacy of staff in terms of numbers and performances, communications with other departments and the degree of reliance upon other services within the organization.

(8) What is company policy in relation to the particular functions being investigated?

(9) Are there any external constraints to be taken into consideration, such as trade practices, legal requirements, union agreements, etc?

(10) Exceptions. Are there any exceptions to the general processing routine? If so, is it feasible to incorporate these in the overall machine system?

(11) Controls. What controls exist over the accuracy of the data being processed and the timeliness of the output reports?

Four other things, in addition to the above procedural details, will be of interest to the analyst:

(12) The equipment already in use—accounting machines, calculating machines, etc.

(13) An estimate of the cost of running the system under present methods in order to provide a comparison with any proposed new system.

(14) The deadlines that have to be met by the output of the system and why output has to be produced at these times.

(15) Which members of staff are responsible for making decisions, the type of decisions they make and the criteria upon which they are based.

Fact finding, then, is the process of finding out how data are being processed within the organization. It enables the analyst to build up a detailed picture (Fig. 12.1) of requirements and ensures that he is conversant with all the factors that must be taken into consideration in redesigning the system.

FACT RECORDING AND ANALYSIS

All information obtained during the investigation is recorded in a

Development of a computer system 163

systems investigation file in which also are kept copies of all documents relating to the system.

While a number of techniques are used for recording and analysing the facts of the situation, there are two overriding considerations. The first is that the information should be set down in a clear and concise form so that it is readily understood later on, during the design phase. The second is that any documentation standards

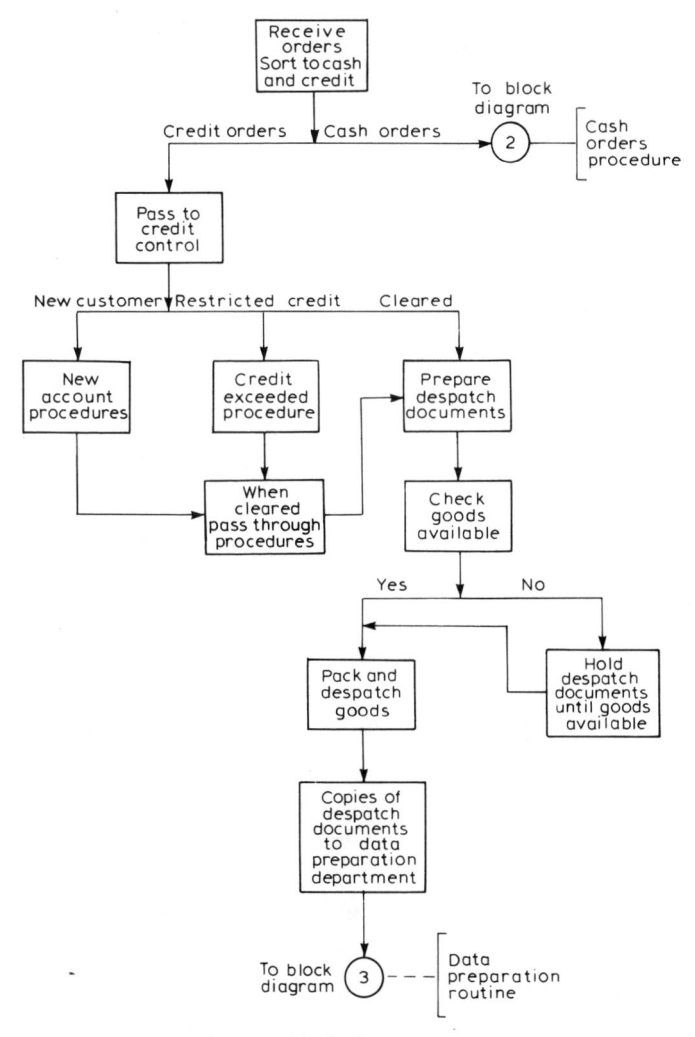

Fig. 12.1. Example of systems block chart

adopted by the organization should be conformed with. Should there be any change of personnel working on the project, this will minimize handing-over problems.

The following summarizes the techniques commonly used in fact recording.

Information flow diagrams
The information flow diagram is a chart to show the logical sequence of the events that take place (Fig. 12.2). Use is made of standard symbols representing activities joined with flow lines and with additional explanatory notes where necessary. Flow charts are considered in more detail in Chapter 15.

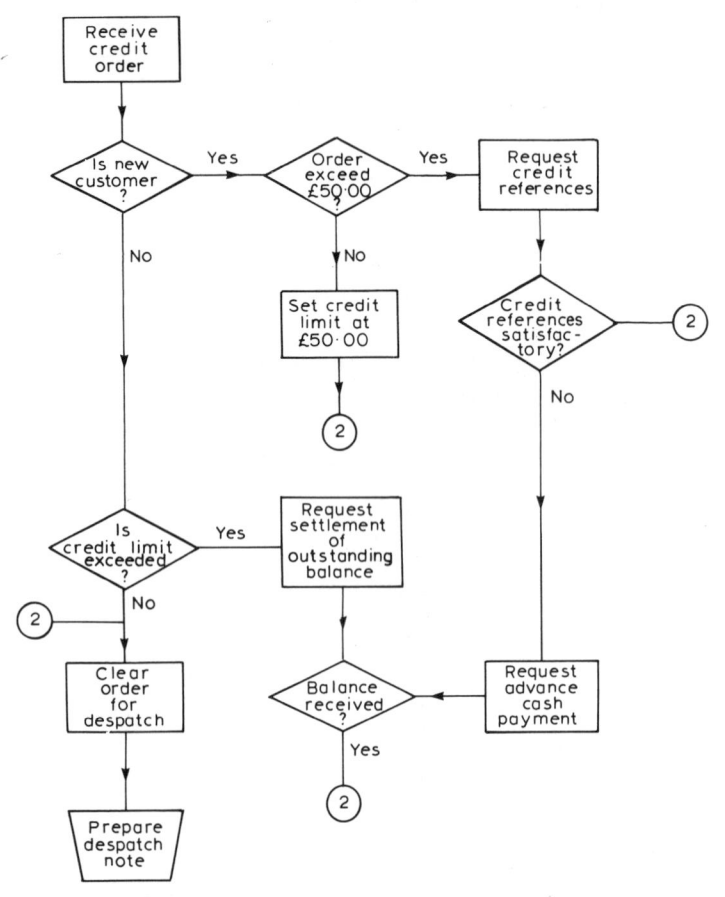

Fig. 12.2. Example of systems flow chart

Procedure narrative
A procedure narrative is an organized descriptive account of procedures in detailed form. Usually it will contain three elements:

Operator	Operation	Operand
Who does it?	What is done?	On what is it done?

Organization chart
The organization chart shows the organizational structure of the departments responsible for the work and defines areas of responsibility. It may also include the number of staff engaged upon each type of activity.

Document flow chart
The document flow chart traces graphically the flow of documents through the system and the procedure to which they are subject from the time they originate until they are eventually filed away. The detail should include the number of copies, where they are sent and what happens to each copy.

Cost tables
In order to give a breakdown of operating costs, tables can be constructed analysing these costs under main headings—staff, supplies, equipment and accommodation. These headings, in turn, can be broken down in terms of procedures within the department or system.

Document description form
The document description form contains a brief description of the document for identification purposes and a detailed record of the data appearing on it, giving minimum and maximum sizes of data fields and records, where applicable. It should indicate how the document originates, the volumes processed during a given period (with any periodic fluctuations) and how often documents are processed (daily, weekly, monthly, etc.). Finally, it should state the use to which the document is put—for example, for updating a master record or for distribution to customers.

Systems design

The following paragraphs break down the system design procedure into a number of areas of work and present them in the order in which they would probably be tackled by the analyst.

OUTPUT SPECIFICATION

The feasibility study and the investigation stage will have determined what, in principle, is required of the system. At this stage we are concerned with designing in detail the contents of each of the output reports.

This means, in the first place, deciding exactly what data fields or records are really needed in the report and then specifying the size and content of each, and the sequence in which they will appear on the report. An estimate will be made of the volume of reports necessary for a particular application. Where appropriate, the principle of exception reporting should be adopted and the criteria upon which the production of the report is based specified.

A further consideration is the frequency with which reports should be prepared, a factor which will depend to an extent on the computer operating mode applicable to the application. In real-time processing, most reports will be required on demand, while others will be output at fixed intervals, whereas in batch processing normally all output records will be periodic. The time interval between periodic reporting needs to be carefully weighed up in the light of need, benefit and cost.

Finally, the output medium needs to be determined in the light of user requirements. As we have already seen in Chapter 8, this may be printed, visual display, microfilm, etc. Bearing in mind that the purpose of output reporting is to provide information that will be used by somebody, it is important that consultation should take place between the analyst and the user before output content and format are finally decided upon.

FILE DESIGN

As in the case of output reports, data field and record sizes and content must be clearly defined, but two other matters need careful consideration. These are: (1) how the records will be organized on file, and, arising from this, (2) the physical file medium that is to be used. An important point in determining these two factors is an assessment of the proportion of the records that will be processed in any one run. This is known as the hit rate.

In a real-time system the hit rate is minimal, since each transaction is processed individually and therefore only one record on the file needs to be accessed. It follows that records can be held in random order and must be held on a direct access file medium, such as magnetic disc, in order to select quickly the appropriate record demanded.

In a batch processing system a different situation arises, in that a number of records are processed in a single computer run. It does not necessarily follow from this that the hit rate is high; this will depend on the ratio between the number of records in the batch and the total number of records on the file being processed. For example, a wages system would give a very high hit rate, since each employee's record would have to be processed periodically—say at the end of each week. Under these circumstances, the most efficient order in which to store the records would be sequentially. The medium on which they are held could well depend on the hardware available. While a magnetic tape will adequately, and possibly more economically, serve the purpose, the records could equally well be held sequentially on magnetic disc.

$$\text{Hit rate} = \frac{\text{master records to be updated} \times 100}{\text{total master record}} \%$$

On the other hand, a particular batch processing system might offer a low hit rate: for example, a firm with 10 000 customers, of whom it sells goods to only 100 each week. Assuming a weekly updating run, this would mean only 1 in every 100 records being processed. In a low hit rate situation like this it could well be more efficient to access file records at random using direct access storage rather than searching through an average of 100 records every time one needed updating, as would be the case with sequential organization.

In some file situations a combination of these two factors arises. For example, we may have a sales ledger file with a high hit rate that is processed in batch mode periodically but, for credit control purposes, requiring the facility of interrogating individual records to determine whether an order is accepted or not. Under these circumstances, we have to combine a random interrogating facility with a sequential batch processing mode.

INPUT SPECIFICATION

The basic considerations here are that (a) input records must be designed so as to keep master file records up to date, and (b) they must be capable of producing or generating, in conjunction with the master file records, the outputs demanded of the system. This means that attention must be given to the following:

(1) Contents. File and record sizes and content must be clearly defined, bearing in mind that the information contained in output reports arises from an interaction of input and master data. This

means that it is unnecessary to quote in the input record some of the information already held on the master file record. For example, there is no point in quoting a customer name and address, since this is already held on file. All that is necessary to identify the customer is the record key. In the interest of economy, particularly at the data preparation stage, it is advisable to keep the volume of data on input records down to the minimum compatible with the accurate recording of the event giving rise to the data.

(2) Frequency. In a batch processing situation the frequency with which updating runs are made must be determined and also their timing in relation to deadlines for output reports. In a real-time situation inputs will occur as and when required.

(3) Input mode. A range of input methods is described in an earlier chapter. Major considerations affecting the choice of mode are: How the source data originate (for example, from a meter reading or from purchase invoice); cost; the degree of accuracy in recording that can be expected; the time lapse between the occurence of an event and its computer entry; and possibly the hardware available.

PROCEDURE SPECIFICATION

Procedure specification is concerned with working out the procedure necessary throughout the whole system—manual and machine operations—in order to produce the required outputs. Although there are recognized methods of recording these procedures (block charts, computer-run charts, flow charts, narrative, etc.), there are no firm rules that can be applied to the actual procedure development process. This relies on the experience and aptitude of the analyst and his ability to bring creative and logical thinking to bear on the solution of the problems inherent in systems design. It is, to a certain extent, a process of trial and error—formulating a possible solution, testing this against known conditions, modifying and adjusting it if requirements are not met, until eventually a satisfactory solution is found.

INPUT AND OUTPUT FORM DESIGN

The analyst will now be concerned with the design of the forms that will contain source data and output reports. Source data are usually recorded on preprinted forms, the design of which should take into account any data preparation routines that may be required, ensuring that fields appear in the most convenient order for transcription to an input medium—for example, the order in which they are to be keyed in to a key-to-tape data recording system. To promote easy and accurate recording at source, source documents may well specify the size, or maximum size, of each data field and the type of field (alphabetic or numeric), and incorporate any notes that will help in the completion of the form. Non-variable data can be included when the form is first printed.

Output forms for external distribution can usually be preprinted, while data for internal use are often produced on ordinary lined paper. In both cases the layout of the data, the position of fields within the output record and the size and content of fields must be clearly defined and communicated to the processor, through the program, so as to control the format of these reports.

Recording the system

The system having been designed, the whole must be recorded formally and in detail. This formal record of the system is known as a *system specification* and should contain the following information:

(1) An overall description of the system, listing the inputs, outputs and files, and outlining the procedures involved and the aims of the system.

(2) A detailed specification of input, output and file records, accompanied by appropriate charts, specimen documents and explanations.

(3) A detailed account of all procedures, again with appropriate charts and notes.

(4) For the guidance of programmers, a specification of each program required to operate the system.

(5) Details of how the system is to be implemented, specifying exactly how the changeover from the previous system should be done.

(6) Specification of the equipment needed to operate the system, not only for the actual computer processing and data preparation, but also for any ancillary operations needed in the course of preparing source data and for dealing with output reports.

(7) Specification of testing procedures and test data for proving both the system and the programs that operate it.

Constructing and encoding programs

Constructing and encoding programs is dealt with in detail in Chapter 14.

Implementing the system

On the assumption that at this point hardware, specialist computer staff requirement and data preparation have been catered for, the following additional considerations apply to the implementation process.

FILE CONVERSION

File conversion is the process of transferring the information required by the system from the old manual to the new computer files. This entails a large volume of work and it may be necessary to divert staff from less pressing jobs or to enlist the aid of a computer bureau.

One complication in file conversion is that records are probably continually changing as transactions take place. To overcome this problem the conversion can be done in two stages: by first transferring the non-variable content of each record and then (a second and much shorter stage) transferring the variable fields. This means that the original files can still be updated while the conversion of the non-variable element is taking place.

As an example, consider a stock inventory record containing the following data:

Stock item number
Description
Minimum stock
Maximum stock
Unit price
Quantity
Value

The first four data fields could well be taken on to the new files during the first stage, since these are not likely to change in the short term, and then in the second stage the last three fields, together with stock item number a second time, in order to marry up the two parts of the record.

CHANGEOVER PROCEDURES

There are these approaches to the changeover to the new computer system:

(1) *Parallel running* means that, for a period, data items are pro-

cessed by both the old and the new methods. Results of the two are compared and the old method is discontinued as soon as the new one is proved.

(2) In *pilot running* the new method is proved with simulated or old data while current data are being processed by the old system. Using old data that have been previously processed manually has the advantage that the results of processing are already known and can be checked against the output of the new system. When the new system has been thoroughly tested and proved, a switch is made, from the old to the new.

There is a second type of pilot running which consists of the gradual adoption of a system, procedure by procedure. This is, of course, only viable with a system that lends itself to this piecemeal absorption. As each procedure is taken over, the output is fed back and used in the old system until progressively the whole system is taken over.

(3) *Direct changeover* means closing down the old system completely and starting up the new as soon as possible afterwards. It does not provide the safeguards of parallel and pilot running, and is normally only used when there is insufficient similarity between old and new methods to provide a comparison. A direct changeover usually has to be implemented during a break in normal business activity—for example, at holiday time or at a weekend.

Decision tables

It is often difficult in the analysis and design of computer systems to appreciate all the aspects of a problem and all the situations that might arise from any combination of these. A decision table sets out in a formal way all the factors that need to be considered and the procedure that any combination of these factors will give rise to. The factors taken into consideration are called *conditions*; the different combinations of these factors are known as *condition rules*; and the procedures the condition rules give rise to are known as *action rules*.

For example, if one were going out, one might say: 'If it is cold, I will take an overcoat—if it is raining, I will take an umbrella.' Within this situation there are two conditions: 'Is it cold?' and 'Is it raining?' This leads to four different combinations of conditions, or condition rules: it is both cold and raining; it is raining but not cold; it is cold but not raining; it is neither cold nor raining. These condition rules give rise to four alternative actions: take overcoat and umbrella; take umbrella; take overcoat; take neither. This problem is set out in the form of a decision table in Fig. 12.3. The conditions are listed on the left-hand side of the top section, and the combinations of conditions are on the right-hand side under the heading 'Rule Number'. If the condition is present, it is indicated by the insertion of a Y, and if not, by an N. The lower half of the table lists the possible actions that could arise from these combinations by inserting an X in the appropriate column.

Conditions	Rule number			
	1	2	3	4
Is it cold?	Y	Y	N	N
Is it raining?	Y	N	Y	N
Actions	Action rules			
Take overcoat	X	X		
Take umbrella	X		X	
Take neither				X

Fig. 12.3. Example of simple decision table

In order to ensure that every possible combination of conditions is taken into account, the number of combinations can be determined as being equal to 2^n, where n is the number of conditions. The possible number of combinations having been found, to ensure that each combination is unique, the following rule, known as the *halve rule*, is applied. In the first row Ys are repeated for one-half of the number of condition rules (that is, 2^{n-1} times), followed by the same number of Ns. In the second row groups of Ys and Ns alternate, the size of the groups being one-half of those in the first row (that is, 2^{n-2} times). This process of halving the group size is repeated for successive rows until the final row contains single Ys and Ns (see Fig. 12.4).

To simplify the table by reducing the number of condition rules, if two rules, different in one row only, result in the same action, these two rules can be combined. This is done by placing a dash (—) in the appropriate row. An example of this is shown in Fig. 12.5, where rules 7 and 8, the same except for row three, result in the same action. That is, the performance of condition 3 is immaterial to the action taken. By combining this pair of rules the total number of rules is reduced by 1. This principle is known as the *dash rule*.

This now means that the number of rules is no longer equal to 2^n. In order to prove that all rules have been considered, a dash count column is added to the right of the condition rules in which the number of rules absorbed is entered. This dash count plus the number of rules will now reconcile to 2^n.

Advantages claimed for the decision table are:

(1) The problem is more easily defined. The decision table helps to identify the problem and the rules associated with it.
(2) It positively determines the number of different conditions and the actions arising from each.
(3) It provides a method of describing the logic of the system.

Table number: 130	Title: Admission	Date: 30 Nov.	Author: B. Jones	Rule number
	Conditions			1 | 2 | 3 | 4 | 5 | 6 | 7 | 8 | 9 | 10 | 11 | 12 | 13 | 14 | 15 | 16
C1	Passed final examination			Y | Y | Y | Y | N | N | N | N
C2	5 year's experience			Y | Y | N | N | Y | Y | N | N
C3	Science graduate			Y | N | Y | N | Y | N | Y | N
	Actions			Action rules
A1	Accept			X | X | X | | X
A2	Special award			X
A3	Reject			| | | X | | X | X | X

Fig. 12.4. Decision table showing rules for acceptance on a training course. Applications are accepted if two conditions are met and a special award is made if all three are met. Otherwise applicants are rejected

Table number: 130	Title: Admission	Date: 30 Nov.	Author: B. Jones	Rule number	Dash count
	Conditions			1 | 2 | 3 | 4 | 5 | 6 | 7 | 8 | 9 | 10 | 11 | 12 | 13 | 14 | 15 | 16	
C1	Passed final examination			Y | Y | Y | Y | N | N | N	
C2	5 year's experience			Y | Y | N | N | Y | Y | N	
C3	Science graduate			Y | N | Y | N | Y | N | —	1
	Actions			Action rules	
A1	Accept			X | X | X | | X	
A2	Special award			X	
A3	Reject			| | | X | | X | X	

Fig. 12.5. Decision table showing use of 'dash' rule

(4) It is a means of communicating the logic of the system to programmers.

(5) Since the logic can be broken down into small natural modules, the decision table facilitates amendment to the system.

Exercises

12.1. What is a feasibility study? Give an account of the main factors on which you would report when carrying out such a study.

12.2. Explain three ways of changing over from a manual to a computer processed system.

12.3. Describe how you would set about converting the files held in a manual system to files for use in a computer system.

12.4. Explain, in a computer system, how you would allow for the demands of your company's auditor.

12.5. Give an account of the methods you would employ and the information you would be looking for in a systems investigation.

12.6. Make a list of the main items of information you would expect to find in a systems specification.

12.7. Draw a systems flow chart to show how purchase invoices would be dealt with from the time they are received by your company until they are forwarded to the data processing department for computer entry.

12.8. Candidates are admitted to College if two of the following three conditions are met: (1) three GCE passes, (2) good school report, (3) satisfactory interview. Draw a decision table showing the actions arising from these rules.

12.9. What do you understand by the 'dash' rule in connection with decision tables. Explain how this rule would be applied in Exercise 12.8.

Chapter 13
Checks and controls

One major difference between a manual processing system and a system processed by computer is that in manual processing records will usually pass through a number of different hands as successive procedures are carried out, whereas with computer processing, once the source data have been entered to the machine, they will usually not be seen again until processing is completed, and even then, probably not in the same form.

At each stage in manual processing the person performing the task will be in a position to scrutinize the data being worked on and to exercise common-sense to query any situation that appears to be incorrect—for example, if a data item is obviously missing or if a quantity appears to be unreasonably large. It should, of course, be borne in mind that the converse of this is also true. In passing data through a number of manual stages performed by different people there is a very real chance of transcription errors being made. Computer processing does not provide opportunities for sight checking, and therefore the following two considerations are important:

(1) Attention must be paid to ensuring that source data are accurately prepared. An error at this stage might well progress through the whole system without coming to light.

(2) The computer will do exactly and only what it is instructed to do through the medium of its program and outside this is unable to exercise discretion or common-sense, as is the case with people working manually. It becomes, therefore, essential that adequate and specific checks and tests be provided in both the program and the hardware operating it, and that the machine be instructed to report any situation arising that does not conform to these checks and tests.

In computer processing the following techniques are commonly used:

Batch controls

176 Checks and controls

Check digit verification
Verification
Parity checks
Validation
Machine checks on reading, writing and transfer of data.

Batch controls

The term 'batch controls' covers the use of batch control totals, hash or nonsense totals, documents sequence checks, etc., which are discussed in detail in the section on 'batch processing' (see Chapter 11).

Check digit verification

Check digit verification is a mathematical method of checking the validity of numeric codes appearing on documents. It involves giving each reference number unique qualities, so that, when the reference number is subjected to a mathematical test, the answer is always constant. It means adding one or two digits to the reference number in order to make it conform with the criteria demanded by the method used. These additional digits are known as *check digits*.

The system basically involves weighting each digit in the reference number by a predetermined amount, the digit being either multiplied by or added to the weight. The sum of the products or the additions is then divided by a predetermined modulus and a test is made of the remainder. To meet the requirements of the test, this must be a constant.

While a number of different bases can be used in check digit verification, it is proposed to explain only one of these in detail to illustrate the system. This is a method commonly used in checking reference numbers in data processing systems, such as account reference numbers or stock code numbers. The object is to generate reference numbers such that, when each digit is multiplied by a weight that increases by 1 for each digit from the right, a sum is given of the products exactly divisible by 11, leaving a remainder every time of zero.

Example: Taking a reference number 86372, find the digit that must be added as the last figure in order to make the resultant number conform with the above principles.

(a) Weight each digit by multiplying from the right by 1, 2, 3, 4, 5, etc.:

```
8     6     3     7     2     ?
                        1           ?
                  2           4
            3           21
      4           12
5           30
6           48
```

(b) Sum of the products (excluding the final check digit) = 115
(c) Divide the total 115 by the modulus 11 = 10 remainder 5.
(d) The check digit now becomes the difference between the modulus and the remainder: $11 - 5 = 6$.

This check digit, 6, now becomes the final digit in the original reference number—863726, which now conforms with these check digit verification principles:

$$(6 \times 1) + (2 \times 2) + (7 \times 3) + (3 \times 4) + (6 \times 5) + (8 \times 6) = 6 + 4 + 21 + 12 + 30 + 48 = 121$$

which on division by 11 leaves a remainder of zero.

One disadvantage results from the use of a modulus 11. On an average, once in every 10 times, when the remainder is 1, the required check figure will be 10, and it may be impossible or undesirable to accommodate two extra digits in the field holding the reference number. In practice, when it is necessary to avoid increasing the number by two digits, the reference numbers to which this applies can be discarded.

TABLE 13.1

Type of error	Example	Percentage of errors revealed
Transposition	Reversing the position of digits: 4782 becomes 7482 or 4728	100
Transcription	Misreading a digit and entering a different one: 4782 becomes 4982	100
Omission	Leaving a digit out completely: 4782 becomes 482	100
Addition	Putting in an extra digit: 4782 becomes 43782	100
Random	A combination of two or more of the above: 4782 becomes 7342	91

Check digit verification is carried out electronically. It is not limited to computer processing as such, but a verifier can be linked to, say, an accounting machine, which will make the check on keyboard entry. The types of error arising in the transcription of numeric data are given in Table 13.1, with the percentage of errors that will be revealed by the verification system described above. The average error finding accuracy is 98.2 per cent. Assuming that an operator makes one error in every 50 entries, this type of verification will give an accuracy of 99.964 per cent.

Verification

Essentially, verification is the practice of double checking the accuracy of data before they are read into the computer. This is standard practice when data are prepared in punched card and punched paper tape and in using key-to-tape or key-to-disc techniques. These procedures are described in Chapter 7.

It is not always practical, however, to impose a verification check by entering the data twice and comparing the results. In some cases the check takes the nature of a 'sight' check, as, for instance, when data are keyed into an on-line terminal. In this case the data may be shown, as they are entered, on a visual display unit or, indeed, printed out as a hard copy that can be visually checked before release to the computer.

Parity check

In principle, a parity check is a technique designed to help safeguard the accuracy of data when they are transferred from one storage medium to another or from one location to another. It is used wherever data are held in 'bit' form in a computer system. It operates by ensuring that the total number of bits set at '1' to represent a unit of data, held, for example, as a frame on magnetic tape or as a word in the CPU, is always odd or is always even, depending on the method used. Odd-parity systems appear to be more commonly used, since a safeguard is offered in the case of a location containing zeros only. One additional 'bit' position must be available in each unit of recording to hold, if necessary, the additional '1' (parity) bit. In an odd-parity system a character represented by an even number of bits, say 010111, would have an additional bit automatically added by the hardware—1010111—to make it conform to this principle.

On the transfer of a group of bits, a test is made to ensure that an odd number are set to '1'. Should this not be the case, the hardware will automatically read the group again, but should, after repeated attempts, the group still not contain an odd number of bits, an error state is signalled.

Validation

The principle underlying validation procedures is to apply tests to data items in order to ascertain that they conform with predetermined criteria specified at the systems design stage and written into the computer program. Failure to so conform results in the data being rejected as invalid. Such checks may be applied at all levels within the construction of a computer file—to individual characters, to fields, to records and, indeed, to the file as a whole. These tests may take a number of forms:

(1) *Format checks* to check that the nature of the characters is as specified. For example, a field containing a statement of quantity could well be specified as containing numeric characters only; a colour, alphabetic characters only. Some data fields may specify a mixed alphanumeric content, in which case the nature, position and number of each character will be specified.

(2) *Size checks* to test that the correct number of characters are present in a field—for example, a stock item code always consisting of six digits.

(3) *Special characters*. In some situations one of a limited range of characters must be present—for example, A for 'administrative', M for 'manual', S for 'supervisory'. The absence of one of these alternatives or the presence of any other character will be reported.

(4) *Limit checks* place a predetermined upper or lower limit on quantitative data. For example, the limit check could be set to reject any overtime claim of more than 40 hours in any one week or to reject any hourly rate less than an agreed minimum.

(5) *Range checks* seek to ensure that data items fall within a specified range. For example, the day of the month must fall within the range 1–31; any number outside this range will be rejected.

(6) *Presence checks* to test that certain data fields, essential to the construction of a record, are always present—for example, the customer account number in a sales ledger record.

(7) *Interrelationship tests* to ensure that the relationship between fields within a record is not illogical—for example, in a personnel record with one field quoting the title 'Mr' and another F for 'female'. Each of these fields in isolation is correct and would pass

other tests but in conjunction with each other they present an illogical situation and will therefore be rejected as invalid.

Although the above tests are applied to source data when they are first entered to the computer, the mechanics of the application will depend upon the mode of operation being used. In batch processing, when a number of movement records are entered in one run with a view to eventually updating master files, the checks are made through a special validation program—known as *data vet*. This program identifies and reports on any invalid data and also prints out control totals relating to the batch so that any errors can be corrected before the batch is finally written, as validated data, to a file for a subsequent updating run. Incorporating validation procedures would be hardly practical in the updating program, as this would mean holding up the updating run while errors shown up by the validation checks were corrected and put back into the system.

Real-time processing presents a different situation, as in this case records are processed and files updated as each individual transaction takes place, and so it is necessary to write validation procedures into the application program rather than using two separate programs, as in batch processing. In this case not only must the incoming data be validated (for example, checking and reporting back if an incorrect personal code is entered in a bank cash dispensing machine), but also checks must be made in relation to the master record to which the source data refer—for example, a demand for cash in excess of a current balance.

Checks on reading, writing and transfer of data

Having applied validation checks listed earlier on source data, we still cannot discount the possibility of an incorrect statement getting through the net and landing up as validated data on a movement file to be used for updating master records. Further checks are, therefore, incorporated into the updating programs, as follows:

(1) *Consistency checks* are made to ensure that there is no conflict between data held on a movement record and the master record to which it relates—for example, to check that the credit limit quoted on a sales ledger master record has not been exceeded, or to check that the discount given to a customer equates with the discount agreed as stated in the master record.

(2) *Matching checks* to prove that movement records are applied to the correct master record—for example, in comparing the record keys of the two and ensuring that they are identical, rejecting as invalid a part number quoted on a movement record for which no corresponding master record exists.

(3) *Trailer record checks*. We saw earlier that at the end of a data-vet run on a batch of movement data, control totals are produced. In addition to this, a count will be made of the number of records in the batch and this information is then written as a final 'trailer' record on the file. During an updating run similar totals and counts will be made for comparison, at the end of the run, with the control information on the batch trailer record.

During the update run, the program will supervise the printing out of any errors coming to light, so that these can be investigated and corrected (Fig. 13.1).

Security of data and program files

Particular attention must be paid to the storage of magnetic media on which are held data files or programs. Although their magnetic state is quite stable, care should be taken to avoid exposure to stray magnetic fields such as those from electric motors or from cables carrying heavy currents. Temperature and humidity should be controlled and the air kept as dust-free as possible. Rigid control should be exercised over the use of files, a formal record being kept of the issues and receipts of each file and a history of its mechanical performance. Magnetic tape files, in particular, should be handled with great care, as a small mishap, such as creasing a portion of the tape, could well result in partial destruction of the magnetizable coating, with the resultant loss of recorded data. It is important that the erasure date of data on magnetic media should be controlled. A *purge date*—that is, the date on or after which data can be overwritten—should be kept and recorded on the header label of each tape file.

Facilities should exist for the reconstruction of all types of file in the event of complete or partial destruction. The method used will be determined by the type of file and the method used to process it. For example, in a magnetic tape system, where master files are updated by movement files, if the previous master and movement files are retained, the current master file edition can be reconstructed if necessary. As an additional safeguard, three generations of file are frequently kept. This is commonly known as a 'grandfather, father, son' technique.

Direct access files can be periodically copied on to magnetic tape and movement files subsequent to copying retained. This again provides sufficient information to reconstruct the current file in the event of its destruction.

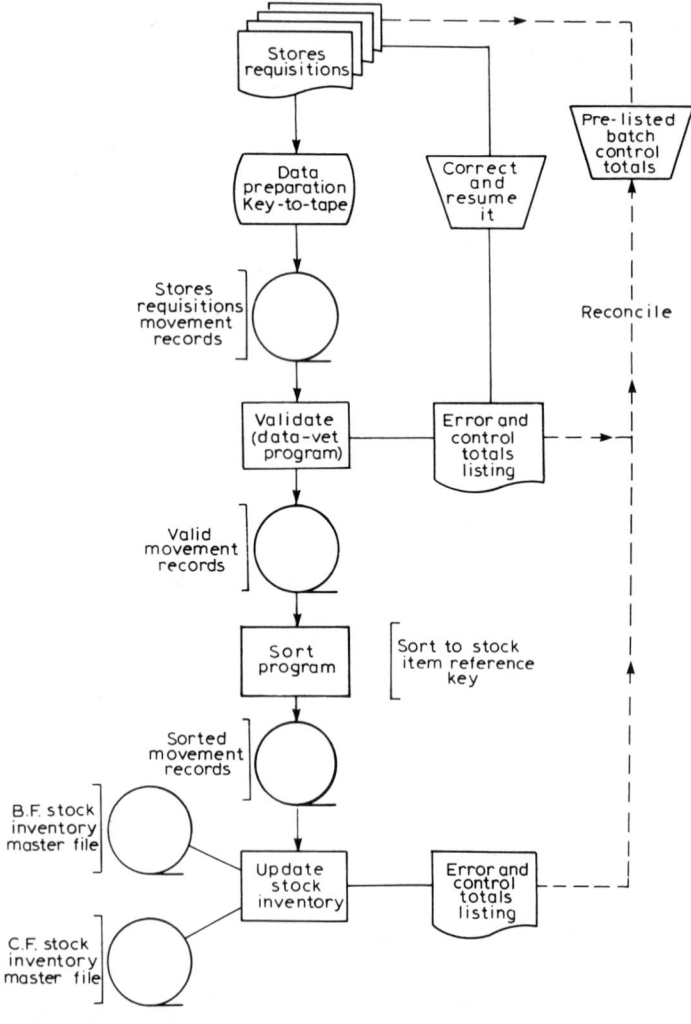

Fig. 13.1. Computer run showing validation and batch control reconciliation

It should, perhaps, be remembered that the complete collection of computer records and programs constitutes a very costly investment. While it is impossible to completely insure an organization against the disruption which would be caused if they were entirely destroyed by a fire or explosion, it would certainly mitigate the situation if copies of all files were stored at a place remote from the computer installation.

Other security measures that may be taken are:

(1) The use of write permit rings on magnetic tapes. The computer will only allow overwriting on the tape when the ring is in position.

(2) Software checks on file labels to ensure that the correct files are loaded and that all records have been processed.

(3) Prevention of unauthorized access to the computer installation.

(4) Particularly in the case of multi-access systems, the use of passwords by computer users that will permit access only to those files relevant to the user's systems.

In addition to the tests and checks described above, there are checks to safeguard against errors arising from machine fault or failure. These are dealt with in Chapters 5–9 concerned with hardware, and are summarized below:

(1) *Double read checks:* data are read for a second time at a checking station incorporated into a reading device and the two readings compared and queried if not identical.

(2) *Read after write checks:* data having been written to an output or storage device, they are read back and compared with the original record.

(3) *Dumping procedures* to safeguard data held in the control processor in the event of machine failure.

Exercises

13.1. Calculate the digit that must be added to the following reference numbers to make them conform with a check digit verification check using a weighting 1, 2, 3, 4, . . . and a modulus 11: 4871; 2963; 6794; 7489.

13.2. Distinguish between (a) verification and (b) validation. A data field may be verified as correct but rejected as invalid. Why?

13.3. Suggest the safeguards you feel should be taken to: (a) prevent damage or corruption to data held on magnetic tape, and (b) make possible the reconstruction of a magnetic tape file in the event of its destruction.

13.4. In the preparation of a source document the reference number 7496 is entered incorrectly as 749G, and the account number 4639 is entered as 4369. The value £96.58 is entered correctly on the source documents but is misread at the data preparation stage and entered as £76.58. Explain how you would expect these errors to be detected.

13.5. Give an account of the checks you would expect to be applied to data records and fields in the process of validation.

13.6. In a batch processing situation describe the checks and controls that would be applied to ensure that the data eventually recorded on a movement file ready for updating a master file are correct.

13.7. Techniques commonly used to safeguard the accuracy of data during processing include: (a) parity check, (b) validation, (c) control totals and (d) verification. Give an explanation of each of these and an example of the type of data on which you think each technique could be usefully employed.

13.8. Explain the significance of a record key. Give an account of the purposes for which this can be used and suggest what precautions could be taken to prevent a key being inaccurately recorded.

13.9. An essential feature of any data processing system is the maintenance of data accuracy. Suggest the ways in which you feel the following errors could be safeguarded against: (a) loss of a source document; (b) misquoting a customer account reference number; (c) posting a transaction to the wrong account; (d) posting an incorrect amount to the right account.

Chapter 14
Computer languages and programs

We saw in Chapter 10 that each operation performed by a computer is in response to an instruction containing two elements—the machine function code to tell it what to do and the address of the data upon which the operation is to be performed. Furthermore, we saw that these instructions are expressed in binary coding and that in the final analysis a computer program consists of an assembly of these instructions brought together in a logical pattern.

However, writing a program in binary notation presents some problems:

(1) Binary codes are difficult to remember.
(2) Writing instructions in a series of zeros and 1s is very prone to error.
(3) If absolute addresses are used, a log must be kept of the data held in each location—a mammoth task when thousands of locations are involved.
(4) The program is not easily read and understood.
(5) Making changes to the program would be difficult.

To overcome these problems, computer *languages* have been devised to enable a programmer to construct a program using, to a greater or lesser degree, the ordinary digits, letters and symbols we use in everyday communications and in ordinary language statements having a greater affinity with the problem definition.

Low-level languages

One way of simplifying program writing is to substitute a mnemonic (an easily remembered group of letters) for the numeric function code and an abbreviated description of the data for the numeric data address. This means that a machine coded instruction to 'add hours':

Function	*Address*
0010	111
(add)	(address in which hours are stored)

can now be written:

ADD	HRS

The use of a mnemonic instead of a function code and a *symbolic address* instead of an *absolute address* gives rise to instructions in this form being known as symbolic language statements.

Of course, writing instructions in this way creates one major problem. The programmer is now using a language, known as an *assembly language*, that the machine is unable to understand. It becomes necessary, therefore, to interpose between the program statements and the computer a translating device that will convert the symbolic statements into the binary numeric statements—the machine code—the computer is designed to act upon. This translation device, supplied by the manufacturers for use on their own machines, is known as an *assembler program*. It contains a list of all permissible symbolic statements and their equivalent in machine code. The translating or assembling process takes place like this:

(1) The program, having been written by a programmer (at this point it is known as a *source program*), is prepared, statement by statement, in a machine readable form—for example, punched into cards.

(2) The manufacturer's assembler program, which may be supplied stored on tape or disc, is then read in its entirety into the central processor.

(3) Under the control of the assembler program, source program statements are then read one by one into the computer, the identical statement is traced in the assembler and its machine code equivalent is written out to a storage medium, usually magnetic tape. At the end of this process the tape will hold the complete program in machine code form—now known as an *object program*—and it is this program that will be used for future computer runs (Fig. 14.1).

(4) If, during the course of assembling, a source program statement is read in that does not conform to the rules of the language (this is known as a *syntax error*), the mistake will be printed out for subsequent correction. For example, a mnemonic code may

have been quoted that is not included in the assembler's list of acceptable codes or a symbolic address may be quoted for which there is no provision.

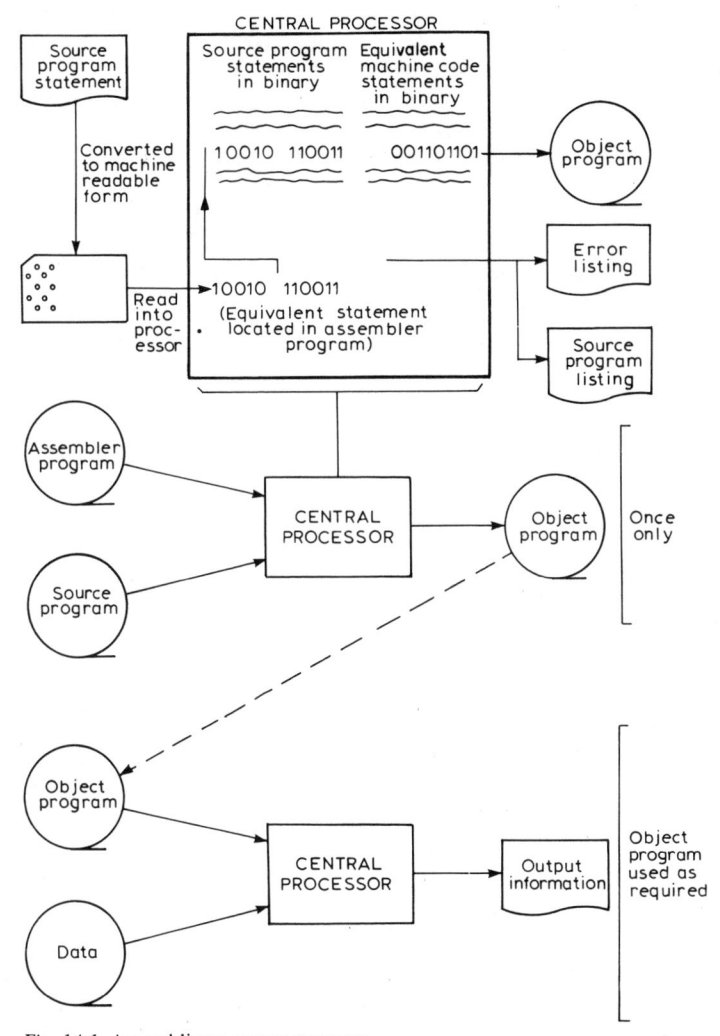

Fig. 14.1. Assembling a source program

(5) In the process of assembling it is usual to print out a complete source program statement listing.

Low-level languages have these important features:

(1) The construction of a statement does not materially depart from the machine instruction format. While mnemonic function codes and symbolic addresses are used, the statement is still basically in the same form, each statement with its operation and operand element. For this reason languages of this type are said to be *computer oriented* or *machine oriented*.

(2) To a great extent every individual machine code statement has to be represented by a corresponding symbolic statement. This one-for-one relationship gives rise to the symbolic statements being known as *micro instructions*. However, in the course of programming experience it was realized that groups of instructions designed to execute an often used procedure were recurring fairly regularly. To save constant rewriting of all the instructions in the group, single instructions were introduced to represent the whole group. This one instruction, on being quoted, would result in the whole range of machine functions within the group being executed. This type of instruction, with a one-to-many relationship, is known as a *macro instruction*. It can be used in low-level languages, the assembler indexing against the macro instruction statement the list of machine code statements it represents and including the whole list in the object program.

(3) The range of permissible symbolic statements is limited to a particular machine's function code. The construction of the function code varies from machine model to model, which means that the program can only be run on a particular type of machine and therefore tends to be *machine dependent*.

High-level languages

These features gave rise to the development of what are known as high-level languages, which:

(1) Enable the construction of program statements having a greater affinity with the problem definition—that is, within the limits of the rules of the language, can be written in ordinary English statements that do not have to conform with the machine instruction format. These are known as *problem oriented languages*.

(2) Make far greater use of macro instructions.

(3) Are not machine dependent—that is, can be used on any machine having the processing power to translate the program into the machine code statements. This means that new programs do not have to be written for new machines.

(4) Can incorporate standard processing routines supplied ready-made by the manufacturer.

As is the case with low-level languages, high-level language statements also have to be translated into machine code before the program can be run by the computer. The program for doing this is known as a *compiler program*. This contains a list of all the permissible statements used in the language and for each statement a list of the machine instructions necessary to perform the statement. Thus, by running the source (high-level language) program with the compiler program, an object (machine instruction) program is produced for future use in processing runs.

The more generally used standard high-level languages are as follows:

FORTRAN (FORmula TRANslator)

FORTRAN is a language used mainly for programming mathematical problems. It is written in simple English statements and permits mathematical expressions to be stated naturally in the form of algebraic notation. Since it is not far removed from the language of normal scientific and mathematical usage, it is easily used by the mathematician and the scientist.

Algol (ALGOrithmic Language)

Algol resulted from efforts to standardize a large number of algebraic languages used on different machines. It is basically a language for processing mathematical problems. An algorithm precisely describes a procedure for solving a particular problem. An Algol program consists of a number of statements defining algorithms.

The following languages are commonly used, although not necessarily exclusively, in commercial data processing. A significant difference between the 'algebraic' type of language and those used in commercial data processing lies in the relationship between data volumes and arithmetic/logical processing requirements. In the first case it is usual for small data input and output volumes to require lengthy processing operations (sometimes referred to as 'number crunching'), while the latter involves very high data input/output, with very limited arithmetic/logical operations. A commercial data processing system is essentially a file processing operation and therefore a language devised for this purpose must contain the following features:

File, record and field definitions
Validation routines
Input/output instructions
Record retrieval routines
Editing routines for output reports
Control of a range of peripherals
Record matching routines
Instruction loops to enable program sectors to be repeated on a series of records

COBOL (COmmon Business Oriented Language)

COBOL is a language specially developed for business use, and can be used on any computer able to compile the source program. It uses statements written in simple English that can be associated with the normal terms used in business applications. A COBOL program contains four divisions. These are:

Identification division
Environment division
Data division
Procedure division

IDENTIFICATION DIVISION

The purpose of the identification division is to identify the program. This will include the program name, the identity of the programmer, the date the program was written and a brief description of its purpose.

ENVIRONMENT DIVISION

The environment division has as its purpose to link the program with the hardware devices that will be used to run it. It consists of three main sections:

(1) The configuration section, specifying the computer to be used for compiling the source program, the computer to be used to run the object program and, possibly, the volume of central processor storage needed to run the program.
(2) An input/output section specifying the names, assigned by the programmer, of the files to be used.
(3) A specification of the peripheral devices allocated.

DATA DIVISION

The data division describes the data to be processed. It is in two sections—a file section and a working-storage section. The file section defines in detail the structure of the data giving the name of the file, the record layout giving the name for each field, and the size and format of each data field. This means that each field is defined by size—that is, the number of characters it contains. The working-storage area is used to define special storage areas to be reserved for the accommodation of totals, constants, counters, etc.

PROCEDURE DIVISION

The procedure division specifies the operations that must be performed on the data. It starts with instructions to open input and output files, followed by instructions to read a record from the input file and place it in the working area of the central processor store. Then come the instructions leading to the execution of arithmetic and logical operations, and instructions to move the results into the output area of store and, finally, to communicate these results to an output peripheral.

BASIC (Beginner's All-purpose Symbolic Instruction Code)

This language was developed in the USA and was originally intended for people who knew nothing about computers but still had to use them. It quickly became adopted for students using remote terminals in a time-sharing mode. Over the years BASIC has become very popular and has now developed into a very powerful language extensively used in commercial data processing. The advent of microcomputers, most of which run BASIC programs, has also very much extended its use.

BASIC is easy to learn and fairly simple to write. It lends itself ideally to use with terminals in a conversational or interrogative mode. Fig. 14.2 shows an example of a small BASIC program. The language can be regarded as a 'general' high-level language in that it will cope with mathematical and scientific problems as well as commercial routines.

PL/1 (Programming Language 1)

PL/1 was intended to be a universal language coping with both commercial and scientific applications and to be a somewhat less cumbersome language than COBOL. It has not, however, received the universal acceptance of COBOL or BASIC.

```
10   LET A = 0
20   LET B = 0
30   FOR I = 1 TO 75
40   READ M
50   IF M >100 THEN 140
60   LET A = A + M
65   PRINT A
70   IF M >39 THEN 90
80   LET B = B + 1
90   NEXT I
100  LET C = A/4
110  PRINT "NUMBER OF FAILURES", B
120  PRINT "AVERAGE MARK", C
130  GOTO  160
140  PRINT "INVALID MARK," M
145  GOTO 90
150  DATA < 75 NUMBERS>
160  END
```

Fig. 14.2. Program statements in BASIC

Types of program

Application programs

Application programs are programs, written individually, to operate specific tailor-made procedures and systems—for example, a sales ledger system, a wages system, a stock inventory system, etc. They are usually written by programmers belonging to a specific computer installation and are designed to meet the particular needs of the organization the computer serves. Stages in the development of these programs are considered in Chapter 15.

Application packages

In commercial data processing a number of elements are found which are common to the needs of many users operating the same system. This is very evident in, for example, a wages system or a stock control system, invoicing, share registration, etc. To save programs having to be written by, or for, each individual user, manufacturers, software houses and computer bureaux offer standard application packages for a range of applications. The package consists of the programs covering the processing requirements of a given system or procedure, and will include input and output formats and file specifications as well as processing routines. The package can be varied within limits to suit a particular user's requirements. Packages are usually supplied stored on magnetic tape.

Advantages in the use of application packages are:

(1) They are economical. Considerably less time need be spent by systems analysts designing the program and by programmers writing it; therefore fewer staff may be required than would otherwise be the case.

(2) Testing is less costly, as the package comes as a well-tested set of programs.

(3) It is probable that a greater degree of expertise can be brought to bear on the initial production of the programs by an organization specializing in this work. This results in a high-quality product, with consequent lower maintenance costs.

(4) Package development costs are shared among a number of users.

(5) Usually packages are well documented, including a statement of objectives, detailed system specification, identification of hardware requirements, input, output and file specifications and systems timing.

(6) They are available at comparatively short notice and therefore the system can be implemented earlier than is the case with programs written 'in house'.

(7) Support and advice services are available from the package supplier.

Disadvantages are:

(1) It would be unusual to find a package that exactly fitted into the user's present system and requirements. Its acceptability will hinge on the extent of the changes that have to be made either to the existing system or to the package itself. This raises two questions: First, is it desirable or practical to make the necessary modifications? Secondly, one of cost effectiveness, would it be cheaper to prepare a tailor-made program?

(2) The user is dependent upon the expertise and the reliability of the supplier, not only for the initial package, but also for subsequent maintenance and support services. Although, in general, software suppliers are highly reliable, it is a fact that exceptions have been found.

(3) Before a package is contracted for, the responsibility for future modifications should be clearly defined, it being borne in

mind that the user's staff will not have been responsible for the systems and program development in the first place.

(4) A program designed for general use will be less efficient than a tailor-made program in terms of computer running time and core store utilization.

(5) The package may call for a minimum hardware configuration which is not available.

Sub-routines

A sub-routine is a set of instructions within a main program designed to perform a standard procedure which may be required in a number of different programs or a number of times within the same program. To avoid rewriting the routine a number of times, one version only is held in store and called in by the main program as and when required. (See Fig. 14.3.)

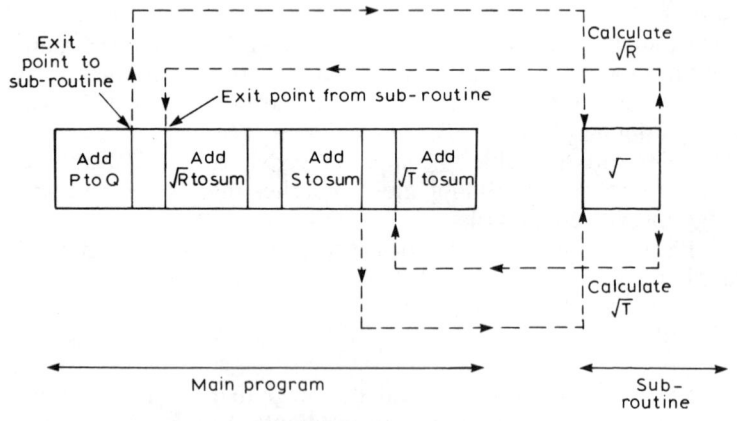

Fig. 14.3. Illustrating the use of a $\sqrt{}$ sub-routine to solve $P + Q + \sqrt{R} + S + \sqrt{T}$

Utility programs

Utility programs are service programs designed to carry out standard routines that are common to most applications. They are usually part of the manufacturer's software library and can be supplied to users as self-contained routines. Examples are:

(1) *Sorting.* As the name implies, a sort program will assemble records into sequence, usually the key-field sequence. As we have seen, this is necessary in data processing situations when move-

ment records are required to be in the same sequence as the master records being updated.

(2) *Merging*. This is the process of merging two files that have been previously sorted into sequence so as to finish up with one sequential file.

(3) *File copying*. These programs transfer or copy a file held on one medium to another—for example, punched card to magnetic tape, magnetic tape to magnetic disc.

(4) *File programs* are available that will initially organize records on the file medium when the file is first created, for subsequently making amendments such as inserting, deleting and amending records, and for controlling routine updating runs.

(5) *File reorganization*. Arising from the practice (discussed in Chapter 9) of using overflow areas on a disc file to accept expanding records no longer fitting their home location, in the course of time organization of records on the file may well become unbalanced, with a high proportion being located in overflow tracks. The consequent redirecting factor then leads to slow retrieval rates. It is, therefore, desirable at times to reorganize the file so that all records once again are located in a primary address. This is known as a *house-keeping* routine.

(6) *Dumping routines* represent an insurance should a machine fault develop during a long processing run. At predetermined intervals during the program, the contents of the processor store are copied to backing storage, after which processing continues normally. In the event of a breakdown, a restart can be made from the last 'dump point' by reading back from backing storage, which obviates the need to start the whole run again.

(7) *Information retrieval* is a utility that allows for the interrogation of individual records and the generation of reports arising from this as required by the user.

(8) *Editing routines*. The purpose here is to convert the output data assembled in store to the format required for visual or printed output. Such things as display, spacing, insertion of currency signs and decimal points, etc., are involved.

(9) *Diagnostic* or *de-bugging routines* are considered in Chapter 15.

Again, as with application packages, the problem of compatability with a given system may arise. In order to overcome this, utility programs may be written in the form of generators. This means that formats can be defined to meet the needs of a specific application and the generator used in conjunction with this format definition to produce a utility unique to the application.

Operating system

An operating system is a supervisory program designed to control the activities of the computer configuration as a whole. In the early days of computing a great deal of operator manual intervention was needed to control these activities. An operating system has, to a great extent, the effect of automating the operator function, carrying out many of the tasks once performed by the operator and organizing the use of processing power in the most efficient way.

Operating systems vary greatly in their degree of sophistication and complexity, depending to a great extent upon the computer operating mode employed. For instance, a system for dealing with batch processing will be far less complex than one to control real-time processing demanding multiprogramming facilities. Like any other program, an operating system consists of a series of instructions that have to be held in the central processor store. This means occupying what could be a substantial amount of space that would otherwise be used to store application programs and data. To mitigate this problem, operating systems are often held in modular form on direct access backing storage with only one part, an executive or supervisor program, held permanently in store. When modules of the operating system are required, they can then be called into store by the executive.

The functions of an operating system are shown diagrammatically in Fig. 14.4. They include:

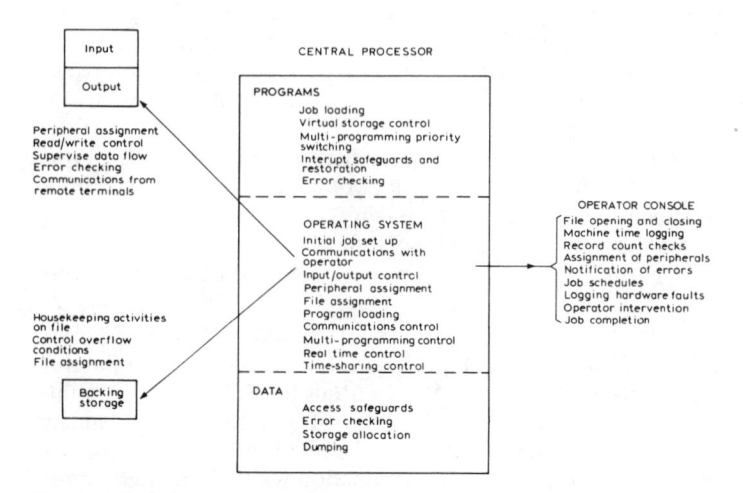

Fig. 14.4. Functions of an operating system

COMMUNICATIONS WITH THE OPERATOR

As we suggested above, with early computers the operator had to instruct the machine. An operating system means that the computer can now tell the operator what to do, when his intervention is needed, and inform the operator of actions the system itself has implemented. The information is usually conveyed to the operator through the medium of a printed message on a control console, through which, also, the operator can pass messages to the computer. Messages generated by the operating system could include:

(1) Automatic logging of machine time utilization.
(2) Notification of opening and closing files and file record check count.
(3) Notification of the assignment of peripheral units to specified files.
(4) Listing of files and programs required for scheduled jobs.
(5) Indication of completion of job.
(6) Notification of error conditions.
(7) Request for operator intervention.

INPUT/OUTPUT CONTROL

(1) Supervise opening and closing of files.
(2) Organize the structure of files into records and blocks of records.
(3) Check header and trailer labels to ensure correct version of correct file, check purge date, reconcile record/block counts.
(4) Superintend writing labels for new files.
(5) Supervise flow of data to and from CPU and input, output and storage peripherals.
(6) Assign peripheral devices to files.
(7) Perform standard accuracy checks such as parity counts, back-spacing and re-read in the event of an error condition.

COMMUNICATIONS SOFTWARE

Communications software is a specialized operating system element that will organize and control communication-line interfaces supervising the transfer of data between remote on-line devices and the CPU. It assembles and checks data flowing between the two, communicates programming requirements to the main operating system and keeps a check for faults in transmission lines and terminals. It will handle time-slice allocation in time-sharing operations.

PROGRAM MANAGEMENT

The operating system will initiate and control the automatic loading of programs—job loading—according to a schedule previously communicated to it. Application programs required for running jobs are 'stacked' on backing storage, and as one is finished, another is called in to take its place, the original program being written back to storage.

In a multiprogramming situation the operating system controls switching from one program to another in the light of established priorities. In the case of a program interrupt, it will safeguard the records being processed by transferring them to temporary locations and then re-establish the position when the program recommences.

With long programs it may be desirable, in the interests of saving space in the CPU store, to call 'pages' (or sections) in as required. This procedure is known as virtual storage.

Other functions controlled by an operating system include:

(1) In the event of a processing breakdown it will dump (that is, transfer to backing storage) the complete contents of store and registers, to enable a restart to be made.

(2) Monitoring storage in direct access backing devices to cope with overflow conditions and guard against unintentional overwrites.

(3) Carrying out initial machine set-up checks to ensure that hardware is properly functioning and ready for processing runs.

Assembler and compiler programs

Assembler and compiler programs are dealt with above (pages 186–189).

Exercises

14.1. Distinguish between an application program and an application package. Discuss any problems that may arise in the use of application packages.

14.2. Explain what is meant by 'utility software'. Suggest some of the procedures that programs falling within this category will perform.

14.3. Give an account of the functions of a compiler program in preparing a program for use on a computer.

14.4. What do you understand by machine code statements? What are the components of such a statement? Give an account of the problems that arise in writing a program using these statements.

14.5. Explain the difference between the source program and an object program. Describe the stages involved in converting a source to an object program.

14.6. Explain the difference between (a) a machine (or computer) oriented language and (b) a problem oriented language.

14.7. Give an account of the divisions found in a COBOL program, briefly listing what you would expect each division to contain.

14.8. Give an account of the advantages that may accrue through the use of application packages.

14.9. What is an 'operating system'? Give an account of the main functions such a system will perform.

14.10. Give an account of what you understand by the following: (a) application program, (b) operating system, (c) utility program. Give, in each case, two examples of the routines these may be designed to perform.

Chapter 15

Program elements and structures: developing a program

We have seen that the purpose of a computer program is to construct a list of instructions which, on automatic execution by a computer, will result in predetermined objectives being realized. Perhaps the important thing to remember is that the program is executed completely automatically—that is, without human intervention—and it must, therefore, be capable of dealing with any situation arising from the data with which it is presented. To this end there are a number of commonly used elements in program construction.

Program elements

(1) *Input and output instructions* are instructions to transfer data between the central processor and peripheral devices, input, output and backing storage.

(2) *Data handling instructions* are instructions to move data items from one element of the central processor to another—for example, to move 'price' from a storage location to an accumulator for arithmetic to be performed.

(3) *Arithmetic instructions* initiate operations by the arithmetic and logic unit of the CPU such as 'add', 'subtract', etc.

(4) The *conditional branch instruction* causes control to be switched from the next sequential instruction in the program to another nominated instruction. It occurs when alternative courses of action present themselves and a decision must be made as to which to follow, the decision being reached by testing the quality of a specific data item. The instruction that will carry out this test is known as a logic instruction.

(5) *Logic instructions* allow tests to be made on or comparisons to be made between data items, the result of the test determining the subsequent series of instruction to be followed. If, for example, in a stock pricing process 15 per cent is to be deducted from all items over £100, then the question 'Is more than £100'? must be asked of each data item, the answer 'Yes' resulting in a different

course of action as compared with 'No'. The next instruction executed is conditional upon the result of the logical test applied and may involve bypassing, by making a jump to a different sequence, the instructions that would otherwise have been carried out. A logic instruction determines the path to be taken in a conditional branch situation, and when this results in control being transferred to a set of instructions out of the main sequence, it is referred to as a *conditional jump*.

(6) *Unconditional branch instructions* divert operations to an instruction out of sequence but do so automatically and without choice. An unconditional branch instruction can, for example, be a means of repeating a sequence of similar operations each requiring the same set of instructions. This means an unconditional jump to the commencement of a routine, providing a *loop* through which processing will continue to circulate until instructed to stop.

Program structures

The simplest computer program routine takes the form of a series of instructions that are operated in sequence without any deviations. This type is known as a 'straight line structure', and examples are given in Fig. 15.1.

Fig. 15.2 shows a program flow chart incorporating a conditional branching structure with a logical test to determine the path operations will take, while an unconditional branching structure is shown in Fig. 15.3. A loop to enable a series of instructions to be repeated is shown in Fig. 15.3, but, of course, an escape from the loop must be provided; otherwise, the computer will keep circulating the loop indefinitely. One way of doing this, particularly when the number of data items to be circulated through the loop is not known, is to insert a 'dummy' record after the last live record. This dummy will incorporate a unique key field—say 99999—which will be tested for on each pass and, when recognized, the program will be diverted away from the loop to another routine. Another way, if the number of records to be circulated is known, is to set up a *count*, reducing this by one every time a pass is made and testing to see whether the count equals zero. When this happens, circulation through the loop is again discontinued. (See Figs. 15.4, 15.5.)

Development of a computer program

The following is an outline of the main stages in the preparation of a computer program.

Program specification

The program specification is prepared by a systems analyst (the work of systems analysts is discussed in Chapter 16), usually in conjunction with a senior programmer. It has as its purpose to

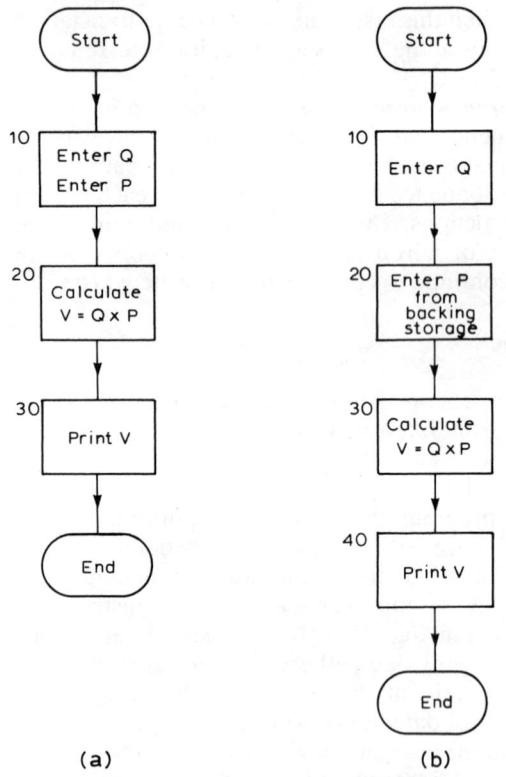

Fig. 15.1. Simple examples of program straight line structures: (a) variables P and Q entered through keyboard device; (b) variable P called in from backing storage. Q = quantity; P = price; V = value

formally set down all of the information required to enable a programmer to write the program. It will include:

(1) An identification.

(2) An explanation of the context within which the program will operate—that is, its place within the system and the place of the system within the organization's overall data processing activities.

(3) An identification of the program's objectives and its main functions.

(4) (a) A detailed specification of input and output records, including precise field and record definitions. These should be accompanied where possible with specimen source documents,

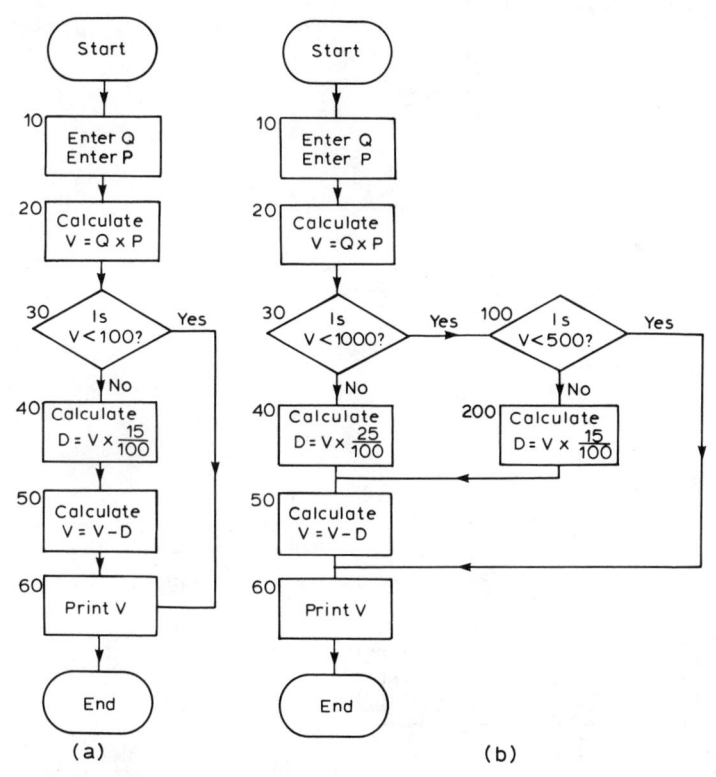

Fig. 15.2. Examples of conditional branching. (a) Discount of 15% given on orders of £100 or more. (b) Discount of 25% given on orders of £1000 or more; discount of 15% given on orders of £500 or more. There is a conditional jump in (a) from 30 to 60 and an unconditional jump in (b) from 200 to 50. Q = quantity; P = price; V = value; D = discount

data preparation documents (for example, punched cards) and output reports. (b) The media on which input/output files will be held and how records will be organized on file.

(5) The precise details of any master files the program will operate in conjunction with, for example, files to be updated.

(6) Specification of the processing the program is to carry out, and the relationship between input, output and master files within the processing routine.

(7) Details of accuracy controls that must be incorporated into the program, such as validity checks, batch controls, etc. (accuracy checks are discussed in detail in Chapter 13).

(8) Details of the testing procedures to be applied to the program.

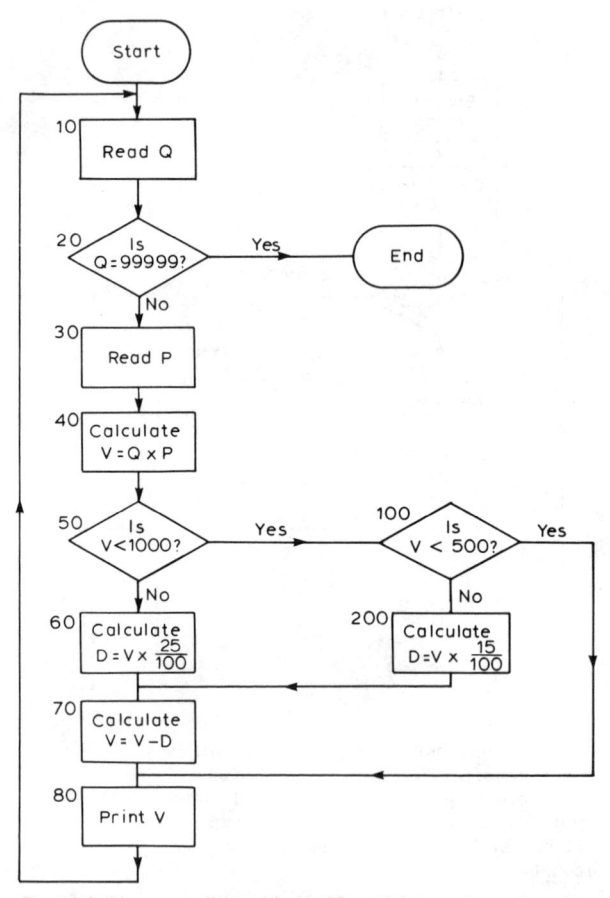

Fig. 15.3. The unconditional jump 80 to 10 forms a loop through which data items will circulate until the test at 20 shows that the last item has been dealt with. Q = quantity; P = price; V = value; D = discount

The preparation of this program specification will involve using both narrative and flow charts. It is important that when the specification is being prepared, the standards adopted by the organization should be strictly adhered to, as a number of programmers will possibly be involved in the initial preparation of the program and its subsequent maintenance.

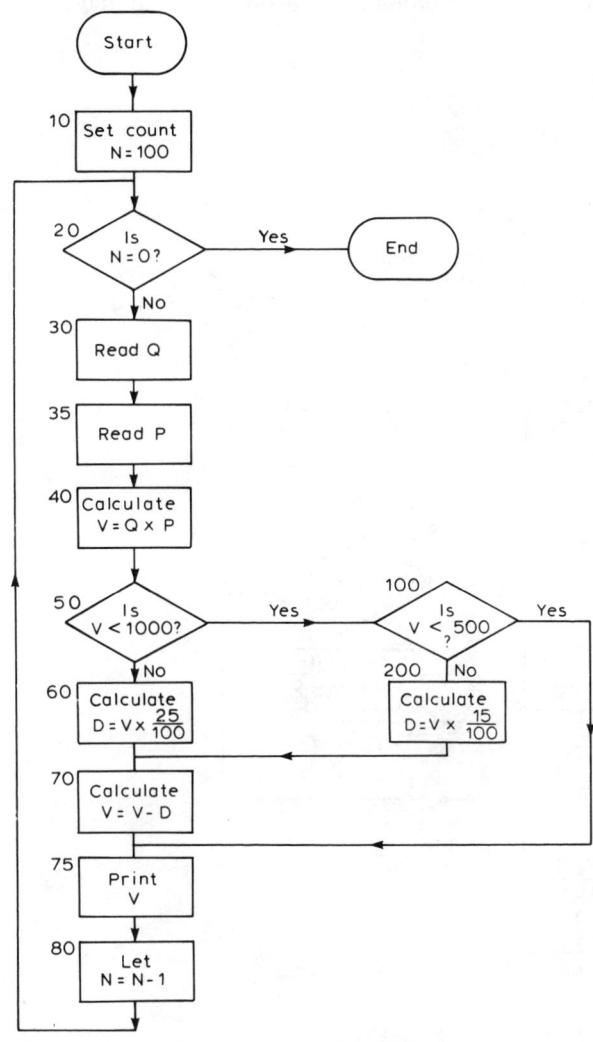

```
         ┌─────────┐
         │  Start  │
         └────┬────┘
              │
   10  ┌──────▼──────┐
       │  Set count  │
       │   N = 100   │
       └──────┬──────┘
              │
    20       ◇
          Is N=0? ──Yes──▶ ( End )
              │No
    30  ┌─────▼─────┐
        │  Read Q   │
        └─────┬─────┘
    35  ┌─────▼─────┐
        │  Read P   │
        └─────┬─────┘
    40  ┌─────▼─────┐
        │ Calculate │
        │ V = Q × P │
        └─────┬─────┘
              │                     100
    50       ◇                       ◇
          Is V<1000? ──Yes──▶    Is V<500? ──Yes──┐
              │No                     │No         │
    60  ┌─────▼─────┐       200 ┌─────▼─────┐     │
        │ Calculate │           │ Calculate │     │
        │D=V×25/100 │           │D=V×15/100 │     │
        └─────┬─────┘           └─────┬─────┘     │
              │◀────────────────────── ┘          │
    70  ┌─────▼─────┐                             │
        │ Calculate │                             │
        │ V = V - D │                             │
        └─────┬─────┘                             │
    75  ┌─────▼─────┐                             │
        │  Print V  │◀────────────────────────────┘
        └─────┬─────┘
    80  ┌─────▼─────┐
        │   Let     │
        │ N = N-1   │
        └─────┬─────┘
              └──────── (back to 20)
```

Fig. 15.4. Showing a 'count' to terminate circulation through the loop 10–80. Q = quantity; P = price; V = value; D = discount

Defining the logic

Defining the logic is probably the most difficult part of programming and the one that entails the greatest amount of creative thinking. A logical sequence of operations must be worked out that will cope with all the combinations of variables that may have

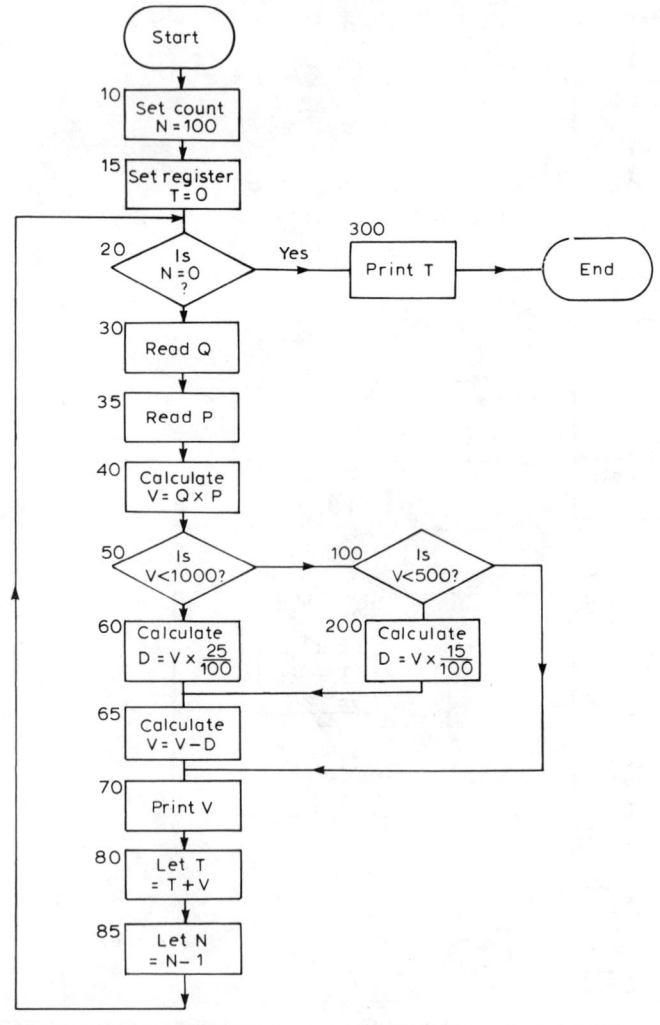

Fig. 15.5. Showing accumulation in register T of the total values of V.
Q = quantity; P = price; V = value; D = discount

to be dealt with to achieve the required results. To induce logical and creative thinking, rough charting can be of help at this stage, to enable the programmer to visualize alternative approaches to the problem, and the use of decision tables will ensure that all combinations of variables have been taken into consideration.

Recording the logic

Recording the logic will usually involve two stages. The first is the preparation of an outline flow chart showing the logical sequence of the main procedures necessary to meet the objectives. This is sometimes known as a macro flow chart (Fig. 15.6). In the case of large programs, it could well be prepared in modular form by a senior programmer so that modules can be distributed to a number of programmers to work on simultaneously. The second stage is the preparation of a detailed flow chart showing step by step sequentially all of the detailed operations necessary. This is sometimes known as a micro flow chart (Fig. 15.7). At this point data records should be traced through the charts to make sure that the correct results are produced for all of the variables that will be encountered in the data. This is known as *dry-running* or a *table check*.

Encoding the program instructions

Encoding is the process of converting the program steps on the flow chart into program language statements within the format and the rules of the particular language being used. These statements are written on special preprinted program sheets.

Preparation for computer input

Preparation involves the conversion of the handwritten encoded statements to a machine readable form—for example, punching into cards or keying in to magnetic tape.

Assembling or compiling the program

The process of converting the source (computer language) program into an object (machine language) program has been discussed earlier. As each source program statement is read in, the assembler or compiler scans for errors in its construction—that is, syntax errors. Any found will be printed out for the attention of the programmer. These error messages are known as *diagnostics*. In practice, the complete source program is usually printed out with appropriate notes against each erroneous statement, with the number of errors shown at the end. When, after correction, the program is free from syntax errors, the compiler controls the output of the program in machine code.

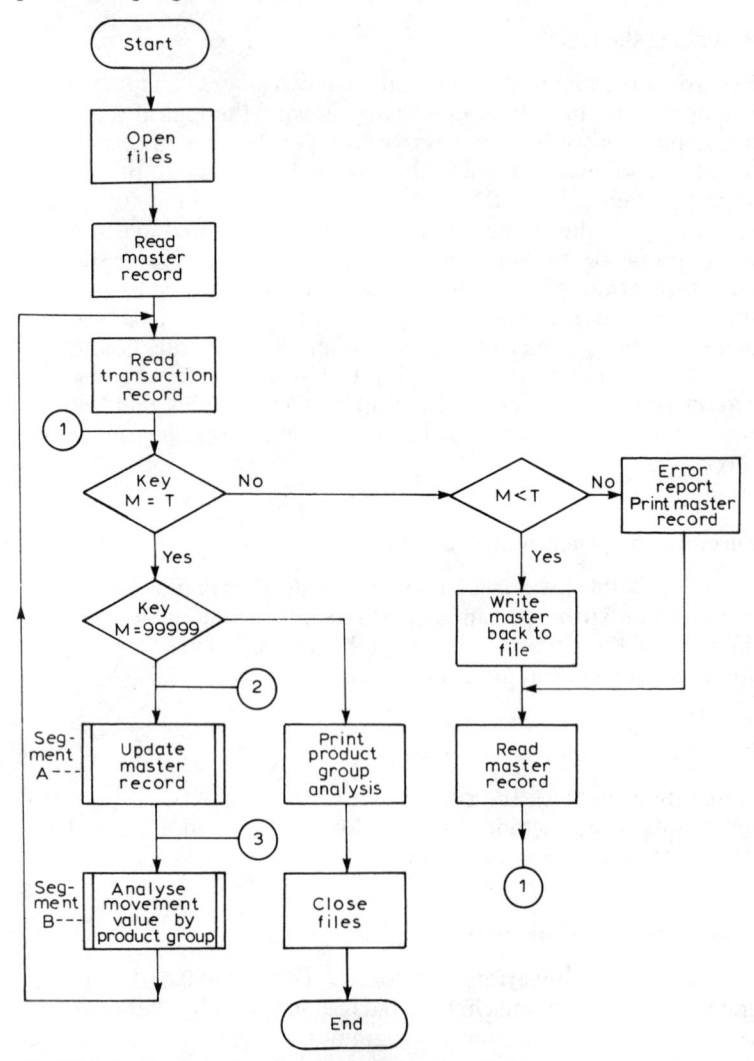

Fig. 15.6. Outline flow chart showing segments A to B

Testing the program

The diagnostic errors found in the compiling process are limited to errors of syntax. Logical errors in the construction of the program will not be revealed, and so it is quite possible for the program to be formally correct in its use of the programming language but still

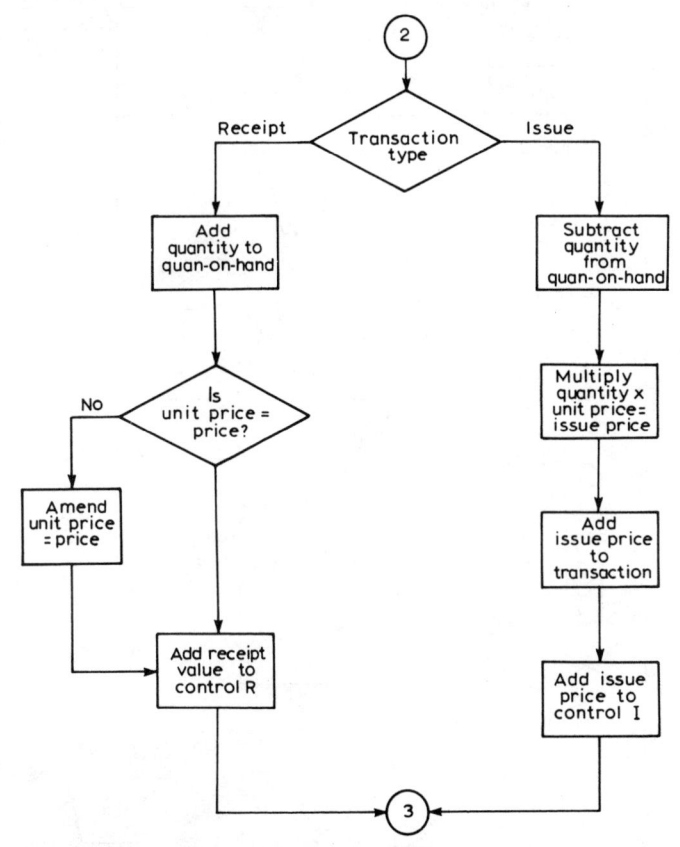

Fig. 15.7. Detailed flow chart of segment A

unable to process all the data correctly because of logical errors. It is, therefore, essential at this point to test it with specimen data of the type it has been designed to process. To this end, the object program is read into store and used to process a comprehensive range of test data specified by the systems analyst, the results having been previously calculated manually. If the correct results are not obtained, amendments will have to be made to the source program. This means carrying out the whole process of compiling again, until, finally, a fully proved object program is produced. It should be borne in mind that there is still a risk of syntax errors

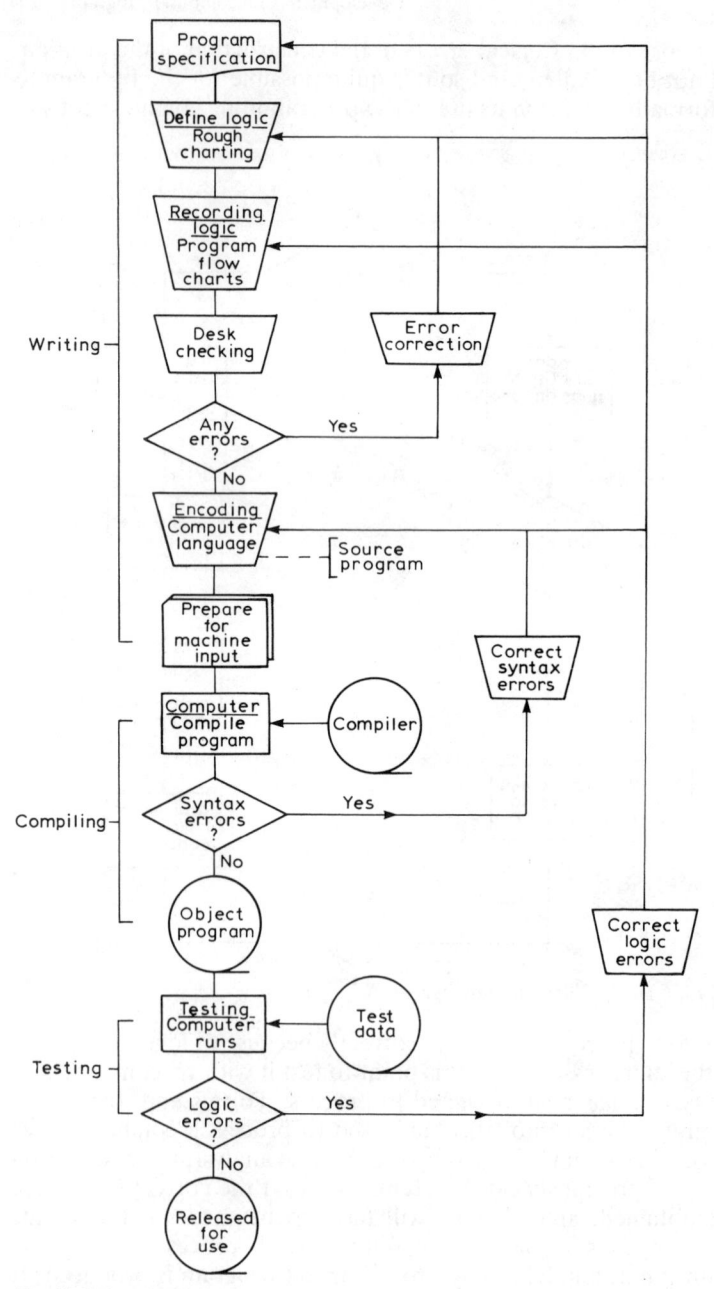

Fig. 15.8. Developing a program

arising from the amendments to the source program. This process of error finding and correction is known as *debugging*. Utility programs are available for helping in this process which will, for example, generate files of test data, organize the print-out of files generated by the program and allow for the print-out of the contents of specified storage locations at stipulated points in the program (Fig. 15.8).

Program documentation

Before the program is handed over to the operations section for live runs, a detailed specification will be prepared for reference in the event of future modifications or updatings. Such a specification will include:

(1) Program identification.
(2) Narrative explanation, logic flow charts and decision tables.
(3) Program coding sheets.
(4) Specimen input, output and file formats.
(5) Test data results, with notes of corrected error conditions.
(6) A glossary of symbolic address names.
(7) A history of program construction and testing.
(8) Operating instructions.

Details of any modifications to the program will be added to the specification as they occur.

Exercises

15.1. Draw flow charts for a procedure that will read in a number of records, and will accumulate and print out the total of the 'quantity' fields in the records: (a) where the number of records is known to be 400, (b) where the number of records is unknown. Explain the peculiarities of each method by reference to your flow charts.

15.2. What do you understand by a 'syntax' error in a computer program? Explain how such an error can be detected.

15.3. On 20 separate occasions an observer records the numbers of men, women and children using a bus route. Each set of observations is punched into a card in this order: (1) men, (2) women, (3) children. Draw a flow chart to read in these records, process them and provide the following information: (a) separate totals of men, women and children; (b) the average number of children per observation.

15.4. Draw a flow chart to read 100 records each containing a positive number that will select and print out the highest.

15.5. Outline the main stages involved in developing and constructing a computer program.

15.6. What information would you expect to find in a program specification?

15.7. XYZ Co. allow discounts when invoicing customers with goods. A bulk discount is given on all orders in excess of £100. Trade customers receive a discount of 10 per cent, irrespective of the value of the order, and trade customers who are also members of the XYZ group qualify for an additional 5 per cent discount. All discounts are calculated on the original value of the order. Show these procedures in flow chart form.

15.8. What is a 'conditional jump' in a computer program? Suggest any application that you are aware of that would incorporate this technique.

15.9. Draw a flow chart for a procedure designed to read in an unknown number of records, each containing 'quantity' and 'unit price', that will multiply these two factors, deduct 15 per cent from the result in those cases where quantity exceeds 75 and then print out the results.

15.10. What do you understand by a 'logic instruction' in a computer program? Illustrate your answer by drawing a flow chart that will list examination passes when the following criteria must be met: (a) 45 per cent or more marks must be gained in each paper; (b) an average of 50 per cent marks must be gained over all papers; (c) there must be an attendance record of at least 60 per cent at lectures.

15.11. Illustrate the use of the following flow charting techniques by constructing a flow chart that will read in 50 records of hours worked and the rates of pay applying to them, calculate the labour cost of each record and print out a total: (a) a conditional jump; (b) an unconditional jump; (c) a loop; (d) a count.

Chapter 16
Organization of a data processing department

While the detailed organizational structure of a data processing department could well depend upon the size of the organization it serves and the range of services it is expected to supply, the following three main areas of work will be present.

(1) The investigation of present systems and the design of systems for computer application. This is done by *systems analysis*.

(2) Writing programs to operate these systems and their subsequent maintenance. This is the work of *programmers*.

(3) The performance of the operations and procedures within the data processing department. This includes such things as the acceptance and control of data, the preparation of data in a machine acceptable form, operating the computer and ancillary machines, the control of work flow, file and program usage, etc. This third area of work is the responsibility of the *operations manager*.

The whole of the department—systems analysts, programmers and operations—is under the control of a *data processing manager*, and its organizational structure could well take the form illustrated in Fig. 16.1. The following are comments on the personnel and the functions involved.

The data processing manager

Inasmuch as the many departments of an organization rely upon the data processing department for their processing needs and for control information, the data processing manager holds a key position in an organization. He should, therefore, have the ability to preserve good relationships between his own and user departments, and have the tact and the drive necessary to cope with the problems and difficulties that are bound to arise in these relationships.

In addition to possessing the general run of management skills—

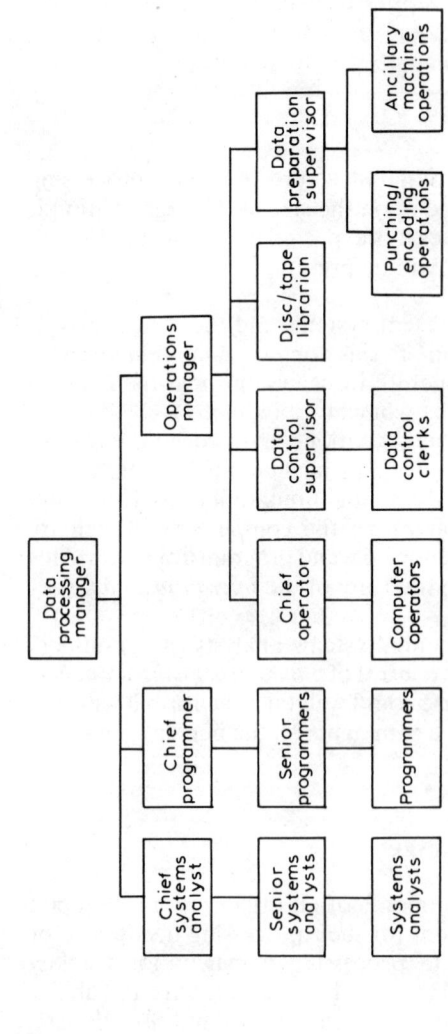

Fig. 16.1. Organization of a data processing department

planning, organizing, motivating, directing, controlling and co-ordinating—he should have a wide practical experience of data processing and a working knowledge of all the activities involved, bearing in mind that he will be responsible for a highly technically specialized staff. He must keep up to date with current developments in the computer field and be able to advise management accordingly. He should have an open mind that is not intolerant of new ideas and be capable of clear, logical and imaginative thinking. The ability to communicate effectively is most important, not only with specialists, but also with laymen, since he will be dealing with his board of directors, the heads of other departments, his own staff, the computer's manufacturer and other suppliers.

The systems analyst

As we saw earlier, data processing is a means to an end. Data are the raw material, consisting to a great extent of a mass of unrelated facts and figures. Processing is the technique of relating all of these, and the required end is the provision of meaningful and useful information. The context within which all of this is carried out is known as a *system*, which comprises all the detailed rules and procedures which must be observed to attain the required end. By usage, the term 'system' applies to a major activity of the business—for example, a sales ledger system or a stock inventory system. In the latter case, we are concerned with relating a mass of data recording stock issues, stock receipts, minimum stock levels, unit prices, etc. When processed, these will provide statements of current stock levels, reorder lists, analysis of materials usage, and so on.

Systems exist in every business but their structure may not be in a form suitable for computer processing. The systems analyst has as his aim the design of a system that can be so processed. This entails three main functions:

(1) Investigation into and analysis of existing systems.
(2) The design of systems for computer application to attain predetermined aims.
(3) The implementing (or putting into action) of the new systems.

The range of work and techniques with which the systems analyst becomes involved is very wide and so a great deal of general experience with commercial systems and a good knowledge of data processing and computers are required. He should also have a detailed knowledge of the policy and organization of the company with which he is working.

It is often the case that systems analysts work in teams, each member contributing specialized knowledge and experience in one or more areas of work. The combined 'know-how' of the team can then be brought to bear on the wide range of problems inherent in systems design. The team is usually led by a senior analyst, who is responsible to the data processing manager.

Success in the investigation and design of a system depends to a large extent on the ability of the analyst to enlist the co-operation of the members of staff involved in the area of work under review (they may not, for one reason or another, welcome the changes brought about by the introduction of a computer). The analyst must, therefore, be a person able to mix easily with people and to communicate effectively. Other qualities required by an analyst are a capacity for logical thinking, a high standard of accuracy, patience, tact and the ability to record his work clearly and concisely and to work to target dates.

Systems analysts have three main tasks:

(1) Forward planning—that is, the investigation of systems that are planned for the fairly distant future.

(2) Current development—that is, the detailed specification of systems planned for implementation in the near future.

(3) Implementation—that is, supervising the testing and taking over of the programs used by the computer operations staff to run the system.

The programmer

Programmers usually take over when the analysts have completed the design of a new computer system and have documented the design in the form of a *systems specification*. Their task is to prepare the program that will operate the systems. The stages involved in this have been detailed in Chapter 15. The programmer will then usually work with the analysts in testing and implementing the system. Two qualities required by the programmer are the ability to reason logically and to pay very careful attention to detail. Also, the need to document programs with complete accuracy and to conform with recognized standards imposes additional disciplines on the programmer.

Data processing operations

Analysts and programmers are concerned largely with work of a 'once only' nature, with perhaps the exception that it is their responsibility to make such amendments and alterations to the system as may be necessary from time to time. However, once the system has been designed, documented and programmed and goes into use for routine processing operations, it becomes the responsibility of the operations section. While the structural organization of this section may vary from company to company, the following basic functions fall within its area of responsibility (see Fig. 16.2).

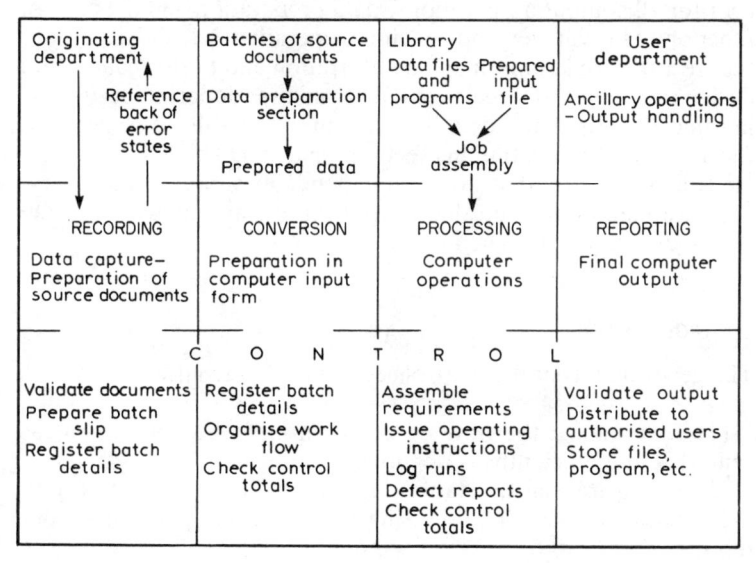

Originating department ↑ Reference back of error states	Batches of source documents ↓ Data preparation section ↓ Prepared data	Library Data files Prepared and input programs file ↘ ↙ Job assembly ↓	User department Ancillary operations – Output handling
RECORDING Data capture – Preparation of source documents	CONVERSION Preparation in computer input form	PROCESSING Computer operations	REPORTING Final computer output
	C O N T R O L		
Validate documents Prepare batch slip Register batch details	Register batch details Organise work flow Check control totals	Assemble requirements Issue operating instructions Log runs Defect reports Check control totals	Validate output Distribute to authorised users Store files, program, etc.

Fig. 16.2. Basic functions of data processing (batch processing)

Recording, conversion, processing, reporting

Because it provides a service for user departments, the operations section has a continuous two-way flow of work: source data flow in and reports to departments flow out. In addition, there is a considerable movement of data within the section itself—source documents to data preparation, input documents to the computer machine room, output reports from the machine room, and so on. Also, the operations section must work to a quite rigid timetable to ensure that reports are available when required by users, that input data are available for processing when needed and that machine time is used efficiently. To co-ordinate all these activities, to meet specified deadlines and to ensure the accuracy and security of processing generally, an effective control must be imposed on the work of the operations department. This is usually done through a *control section* which is responsible for organizing the flow of work through the department, co-ordinating activities and imposing standards to control accuracy and security.

The operations manager

The operations manager is responsible to the data processing manager for all computer operations, data preparation and the control function. He will develop machine operating schedules, ensure that records are kept of machine utilization and performance, and design timetables for receipt of data from user departments, ensuring that the stipulated deadlines are met. He will be responsible for deploying staff within his section, arranging shifts if necessary. He will also ensure that stocks of expendable supplies, stationery, etc., are maintained and that output reports are circulated to the designated recipients when due.

CONTROL SECTION

The general aims of the control section of the department are:

(1) To organize the flow of work through the department as smoothly and efficiently as possible.

(2) To ensure that timetables are adhered to in respect of both the receipt of data for processing and the production of output reports.

(3) To ensure as far as possible the detection and correction of errors, thus saving time and money otherwise wasted in reprocessing.

(4) To keep control records and to ensure that procedures satisfy legal and auditing requirements.

(5) To prevent any deliberate malpractices.

(6) To provide a link, in the course of routine operations, between the computer and user departments. In practice, this is usually done through a receptionist.

The mechanics of control techniques are mentioned in the following discussion on recording, conversion, processing and reporting.

RECORDING

Although it is not the province of the data processing department to orginate source data (this is done in the functional departments of the organization), it is the responsibility of the control section to check that data originate in a way that conforms with the systems specification.

As a basic principle, all source data coming into the installation are handed to a reception clerk. The staff of the department originating the data should not have unrestricted access to the rest of the computer staff. The control section will check that the documents contained in a batch conform with the details on the control slip (the detail of this is discussed in Chapter 11) and check as far as possible that they have been accurately completed and are legible. Registers are maintained in which batch details (date, sequence numbers and control totals) are recorded.

So that queries may be quickly resolved, there should be a defined procedure for reference back to the originating department when they arise on checking source documents. The aim should be to ensure that source data are correct before they are passed on to the data preparation section, on the argument that the sooner an error is detected the less trouble is caused in correcting it.

The principle of batching source documents is discussed in Chapter 11; the following advantages are mentioned in connection with their conversion to a machine readable form:

(1) Batching presents operators with jobs of reasonable size.
(2) It facilitates the tracing of errors. The reason for a failure to reconcile control totals is more easily found when the error occurs in a fairly small batch.
(3) It allows errors to be traced in one batch while processing continues with those batches that have been proved correct.

CONVERSION

The principles and practice of converting source information for machine entry have been discussed in Chapter 7. The control section is responsible for the flow of work through the data preparation stage and for ensuring that prepared data are available for computer runs by the scheduled time. Batches of source documents are handed to the data preparation supervisor, who allocates work to operators and supervises, for example, keyboard entry and verifying. Punch operators must be supplied with clear written instructions for the preparation of each card form and a specimen of the card format.

Once source documents have been dealt with, they should be cancelled, to prevent their re-entry to the system. This is often done by requiring operators to stamp the documents with a numbered stamp. This serves the purpose of both cancelling the documents and identifying the operator.

Control totals taken from the prepared data are compared by the control section with totals previously noted from the source department batch control slips. The general process of controlling the accuracy of punching and verifying is given in Chapter 7 (see Fig. 16.3).

PROCESSING

Before a processing run takes place, the computer operators must be supplied with all the materials necessary for the run. Getting all of these requirements together, another function of the control section, is known as *job assembly*. It is usual to specify the requirements for individual runs in procedure manuals, prepared when the system is first designed. While, of course, these will vary from run to run, the following is a typical list:

(1) Operating instructions stating exactly what processing is to take place.
(2) The program(s) necessary for the run.
(3) The job input data.
(4) Any preprinted stationery for output.
(5) Files required—for example, master files for updating—and, if magnetic tape is used, blank tapes for receiving updated records.

Staffing arrangements for the computer room will depend on the size of the installation and on work volumes, but will consist basically of a computer room supervisor and a number of operators. Shift working may be involved, with a number of operator teams, each under the control of a shift leader.

Operators are expected to keep a log recording the utilization of machine time, with reports of any defects resulting in the loss of machine time, whether through mechanical failure or defects in data or programs.

One function vitally important to smooth processing is the control of the storage and use of data files and programs. A large installation could well be concerned with the storage and use of hundreds of magnetic tapes and/or a large number of

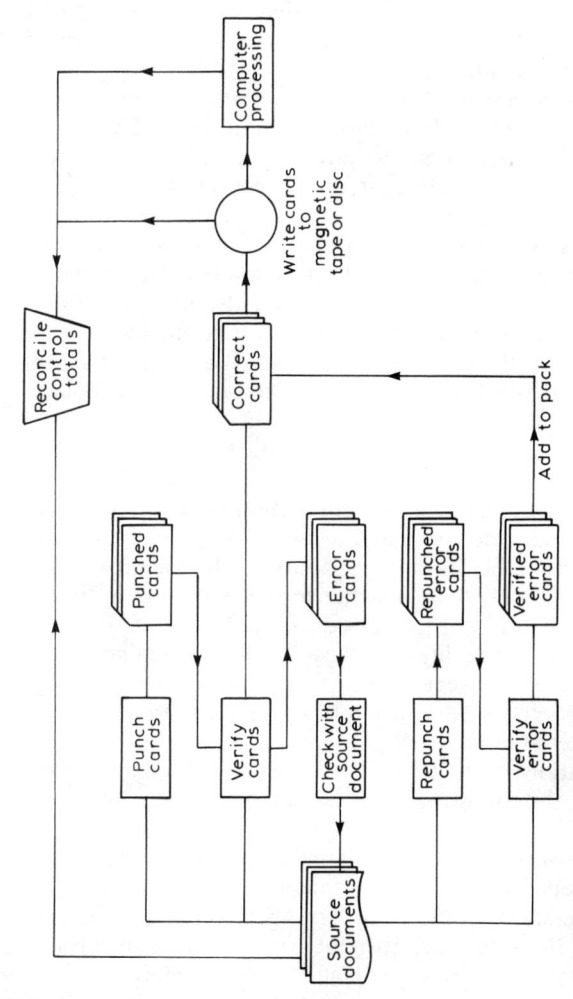

Fig. 16.3. A punched card routine

exchangeable disc packs. These contain programs and master data representing the information requirements, not only of the processing department, but also of the whole organization. It is essential, therefore, that suitable physical conditions be available for maintaining these in good order and that controls be imposed to ensure the use of the right files in processing and the security of the information they contain.

The conditions necessary for storing magnetic file media are basically those required in the computer room itself. Therefore, from both an environmental and a convenience point of view, it is desirable for the library to be situated in a section of the machine room fitted with storage racks on which the media can be stored in dust-proof containers. The control of the files centres around the upkeep of records designed to identify the contents of each and to record their issue to and their receipt from the machine room. Notes should be kept on their physical condition and, where applicable, a note of the earliest date on which data recorded on the files can be destroyed or overwritten. This is known as a purge date.

REPORTING

Another of the functions of the control section is to accept output reports from the machine room and arrange for their distribution to authorized personnel. Before distribution, the validity of the reports should be checked against the format specified in procedure manuals and any control tables should be noted in the appropriate register. In addition to this, ancillary machine operations may be called for, such as bursting continuous stationery, collating, folding, etc. A description of these ancillary operations is given in Chapter 8.

Finally, in relation to the general organization of a data processing department, the following points should be noted:

(1) Staff duties should be clearly defined in writing and an organization chart prepared for the department.

(2) The organization should be so arranged as to guard against the possibility of the whole department grinding to a halt through the absence or irregular conduct of one member of staff.

(3) Allowance must be made for the observance of any legal requirements, such as auditing, and also for any special constraints imposed by management.

(4) Computer department staff should not be allowed to take part in the preparation of source documents or, other than the control and data preparation staff, have access to them.

(5) For security purposes the various sections of the department should, as far as possible, be physically separated, access to records controlled by each section being strictly limited to those people responsible for them.

(6) Strict control must be imposed over important documents such as blank cheque forms and wage payment slips.

(7) Access to the computer machine room and to library files should be strictly limited.

Data processing standards

It is important, in an organization as complex as a data processing (DP) department, that work should be carried out in accordance with predetermined rules and procedures, that all personnel should be familiar with the framework of the department in which they are working, the relationships within the department and the requirements of the users the department serves.

To help achieve these aims, a set of uniform practices and techniques are set out (in other words, standard working practices), and these, together with information relating to departmental structure and relations, are compiled into a *standards manual*. Standards may be of two kinds: (1) those laying down rules and guides as to the *method* by which work in the department should be carried out; (2) those stipulating targets against which the actual *performance* of the department can be measured.

Why standards?

A number of advantages are claimed for the use of standards:

(1) They promote efficiency within the department.

(2) They ensure a reasonable return on the very high capital and revenue costs of running a DP department.

(3) They ensure an effective induction of new members of staff by adhering to common documented work routines, thus preserving continuity.

(4) They provide a comprehensive reference document for all members of staff.

(5) They safeguard the interests of both the DP staff and the organization as a whole.

(6) If standards are observed, the control of activities is that much easier.

(7) Budgeting for departmental costs and planning for future

developments become more objective and more easily formulated.

(8) They safeguard agencies outside the organization against errors (for example, suppliers and customers) and also safeguard the company against non-payment of accounts.

(9) They protect against the criminal use of information and fraudulent practices by members of the DP staff.

(10) They meet auditing requirements.

(11) They comply with current legislation.

The standards manual

While a standards manual will be compiled to meet the requirements of a specific data processing department and the contents will, therefore, vary from situation to situation, the following sections would normally be found:

(1) Details of machine resources available, with notes on their purpose, their capacities and their throughput speeds.

(2) An outline of the organization of the department, its aims and responsibilities, and job descriptions of departmental staff.

(3) Details of departmental records, training facilities, support services (secretarial, clerical, etc.) and the maintenance of discipline.

(4) Details of departmental staff (systems analysts, programmers, data preparation staff, control staff, computer operators, librarian) and also specification of methods of work; the standard documentation involved in each task; procedures for testing and maintaining systems and programs; and specification of control procedures and accuracy checks.

(5) Performance standards for departmental staff and for machine and equipment resources.

All in all, the standards manual should represent a detailed and complete picture of what is required by and from each member of the department's staff and from the department as a whole.

The working environment

Apart from the organizational structure of a DP department, another important consideration is the environment within which processing activities take place. Whether the department is housed in modified existing accommodation or in completely new premises, there are a number of factors worthy of consideration in providing the environmental conditions that will help promote an efficient working unit.

Some of these considerations will be self-evident—adequate lighting, heating, noise control, minimum working areas, fire precautions, etc.—and are mandatory within the framework of legislation. More specific considerations affecting the design of the accommodation in which a DP department will work are as follows:

(1) An arrangement of units within the department to facilitate a logical flow of work and at the same time minimize the distance over which work has to be carried.
(2) The provision of pleasing working conditions and rest area, bearing in mind the repetitive and often boring nature of the work in data preparation procedures.
(3) Provision of support services to ensure conditions essential to the efficient working of the machines—air conditioning, and temperature, humidity and dust control.
(4) Adequate facilities for supervision and control of machines, programs and data.
(5) Security of access to machine rooms and stores and also to confidential records and potentially valuable documents such as blank cheques.
(6) Provision for machine maintenance staff.
(7) The provision of adequate communications network for peripheral–computer interface.
(8) Controlled environment facilities for off-linc storage of files held on magnetic media.
(9) Provision of adequate office accommodation for management, systems design, programming control and operating staff.

Computer bureaux

Up until now we have assumed a situation where the processing requirements of an organization are met by its own DP department. This, however, is not always the case, and an organization may make use of an outside agency to provide all, or some, of its requirements. The main type of agency, known as a computer bureau, is usually an independent company aiming to provide services within the range listed below. Some of these services, however, can be obtained from software houses, computer manufacturers or even some computer users with spare capacity to sell.

A computer bureau will provide services from the following range:

(1) *A complete processing service* in which the bureau does the same range of work for a client as would be done if the client had his own installation. Source data arising in the course of the client's business activities are sent to the bureau, where the programs and files relating to the client's systems are held. Processing is carried out and the output reports sent to the client.

(2) *Software services*: writing application programs to a client's specification; writing and supplying standard application package programs—for example, sales ledger, purchase ledger, stock control, etc.; providing sub-routine and utility packages.

(3) *Hardware services*: a 'do it yourself' service where machines are made available for use by the client's own staff; or a processing service operated by the bureau's own staff on behalf of the client.

(4) *Systems analysis and design*.

(5) *Data preparation*—for example, conversion of source documents to a machine acceptable medium such as punched cards.

(6) *Consultancy*—for example, advice on buying, installing and running a computer.

(7) *Specialized activities*—for example, microfilming, MICR and OCR services.

Current bureaux trends

While the above outlines the traditional role of a computer bureau, the widespread use of microcomputers means that the bureaux must now review the role they are to play in the overall provision of computer services. This means, by and large, a shift of emphasis away from hardware provision towards software, advisory and specialist services. The position is now that the bureau that invested £2m 5 years ago in a computer now finds that their clients are able to install their own machine for around, say, £5000, which means that the economics of using a bureau for hardware services has dramatically changed.

It is expected that bureaux will continue to play perhaps an increasingly important part in the provision of program packages and in systems development, and in addition to these services, it is suggested that the following services could well assume a greater significance:

(1) Advice on the selection of first-time users' hardware and software and in supervising systems implementation.

(2) Handling peak work loads: even a company having its own machine may periodically encounter very busy times when it cannot cope and wishes to off-load some of its work to a bureau.

(3) To train and give experience to users before the installation of their own machine.

(4) To provide stand-by facilities in the event of failure of a user's machine.

(5) To help with the problems and work volumes associated with a manual-to-computer changeover—for example, converting manual files to computer files.

(6) To provide a 'hybrid' service by siting microcomputers in users' premises that will cope with routine processing—payroll, invoicing, ledger updating—but using their own central more powerful machine for the periodic jobs demanding large volume record processing—for example, management information and sales statements. Such a system may operate by users sending files on floppy discs to the bureau for further processing or it could operate on an 'on-line' basis with users' microcomputers connected to the central machine over transmission lines.

(7) Bureaux could well provide a central clearing service for clients' electronic mail communications by establishing a network of on-line terminals in clients' premises. Such a project could well be economically feasible with the ending of the Telecom monopoly.

Of recent years, some computer bureaux have introduced a time-sharing service for their clients by siting terminals in clients' premises connected with the bureau's computer by transmission line. Programs and systems files are held at the bureau and data are transmitted direct for processing. This means that the client has, in effect, processing power on demand and, of course, obviates the need for conveying data and reports to and from the bureau. It is questionable whether such a system is economic in a high-volume data input/output situation, but nevertheless it is possible to install small satellite computers—miniprocessor, card or tape reader and line printer—to cope with remote batch processing should this be desirable. Such a system is probably more likely to be used for file interrogation procedures, for record updating when movement data records are relatively few, or for special activities—for example, performing complex calculations, running simulation models to determine the effect on a situation of the application of a number of variables such as sales forecasting, production planning, price/demand mechanisms, etc. Also, the system can be used for maintaining master reference files such as catalogues, price lists and distribution lists.

A time-sharing system can be a useful way for a company to acquire experience in the use of a computer without committing itself to the purchase and operation of its own machine.

Problems associated with the use of bureaux

(1) The client will want to be assured of the bureau's reliability—past experience has proved that some bureaux have been unreliable. Word-of-mouth recommendation from the bureau's other clients can be a useful guide. Having decided on and specified the work to be done, the client should obtain quotations from a number of bureaux either direct or through a broker. It will be necessary to ascertain that the bureau selected has adequate hardware and software facilities to cope with the client's requirements and that processing deadlines conform with the demands of the systems. The contract should clearly define the basis of payment, fixed price per job or hourly rate, responsibility for machine breakdowns, errors, late delivery of input data and output reports, and stand-by facilities available in the event of a major machine breakdown. The client will probably appoint and train a member of staff to liaise with the bureau to negotiate prices and contracts and to generally monitor the bureau's performance.

(2) There may be problems of security and privacy when using facilities shared by other clients (possibly competitors).

(3) To an extent, control over processing activities is lost, with a consequent loss of flexibility.

(4) Control over accuracy may be a problem, particularly if queries have to be referred back over a long distance.

(5) Generally speaking, the bureau staff may not be as motivated or interested as the client's own staff, a situation possibly leading to a lower quality of work.

(6) With a number of clients 'queueing' for processing requirements, a client may have to wait for an unacceptable period of time to receive information.

(7) Strict attention should be paid to adherence to standards, to preserve continuity should the client later decide to install his own computer.

(8) Building up of experience and 'know-how' by the client's own staff may be inhibited by reliance on an outside organization.

(9) Careful consideration should be given to cost comparisons between bureau and 'in house' processing.

Exercises

16.1. Draw an organization chart showing the various areas of responsibility and work in a large data processing department.

16.2. Give an account of the work a senior systems analyst would be expected to do.

16.3. What duties would you expect the control section of a large data processing department to be responsible for?

16.4. Describe the flow of any processing job of your choice through a data processing department from the time the source documents are handed in at reception until the distribution of the final reports.

16.5. Give an account of the work you would expect to see carried out in the data preparation section of a data processing department.

16.6. Suggest eight reasons why it is desirable to formulate standard procedures in a data processing department.

16.7. Give a list of the main items of information you would expect a standards manual relating to a data processing department to contain.

16.8. Suggest circumstances that would lead to an organization relying on a computer bureau for its processing requirements.

16.9. Give an account of the services you would expect a computer bureau to provide.

16.10. What qualities would you look for in a person applying for the job of data processing manager.

16.11. Explain what is meant by: (a) job assembly, (b) control totals, (c) a library in a data processing department.

16.12. You are investigating the possibility of using a computer bureau for your processing needs. Outline what you consider to be the main advantages and disadvantages in the use of a bureau.

Chapter 17
Examples

Batch processing: sales ledger
Output requirements

(1) The preparation at the end of each month of sales statements for distribution to customers, with copies as sales ledger accounts for internal use. These will contain the balance outstanding at the start of the month, a list of movements (transactions) during the month in date order and, finally, the balance outstanding at the end of the month.
(2) A list of overdue accounts.
(3) Sales analysis by areas.

Input source documentation

Sales:	copies of sales invoices
Returns and allowances:	copies of sales credit notes
Cash receipts:	cash book listing
Discounts allowed:	cash book listing

Data preparation

Documents are batched daily with controls listed on batch slip.
Source document movement data are keyboard entered and written to magnetic tape cassette daily.
Verification is by a second operator.

Storage

All files are held on magnetic tape in record key sequence. The record key is the customer account number. The first digit common to all transactions denotes 'sales ledger'; the second, a transaction code (sales, returns, etc.), and the third, the sales area code.

Files

The Sales Ledger Master File holds the master record for each customer, quoting customer account number, customer name and address, opening balance and date. After updating, it will also contain a list of transactions for the month in date order.

The Movements (transactions) File contains all movement records to date arising from the source documents listed above. It is updated daily with each day's batches of movements, so that at the end of a period it contains all movements for the month.

Processing

DAILY

Cassette tapes from data preparation routine are written to computer tape. Validation procedures are carried out and any errors listed and referred back for correction. Control totals are printed at the end of the run and reconciled with batch control totals. The tape is then sorted into customer account number sequence, giving a daily sorted movements tape. This tape is then merged each day with movements to date tape. (See Fig. 17.1.)

MONTHLY

The master customer accounts file is run with the month's movements file, and the transactions are added to the customer's master record, to give an updated customer account file. This file is then processed (Fig. 17.2):

(1) The updated customer account is printed out in duplicate to give a top copy as a sales statement for distribution to customers and a duplicate as a file copy for internal use.

(2) Movement items for sales, returns and allowances are accumulated under the sales area code to give a sales analysis.

(3) The opening debit balance is compared with the month's total credits for cash receipts, returns, allowances and discounts. Any resultant debit balance will be listed with customer identification in an overdue accounts listing.

(4) A carry-forward master file is prepared on magnetic tape ready to receive the following month's transactions.

(5) Control totals under transaction type are listed for control account reconciliation.

Stock inventory and job materials costing

In the following application it is intended to deal only with issues of stock, although, of course, in a practical situation other factors

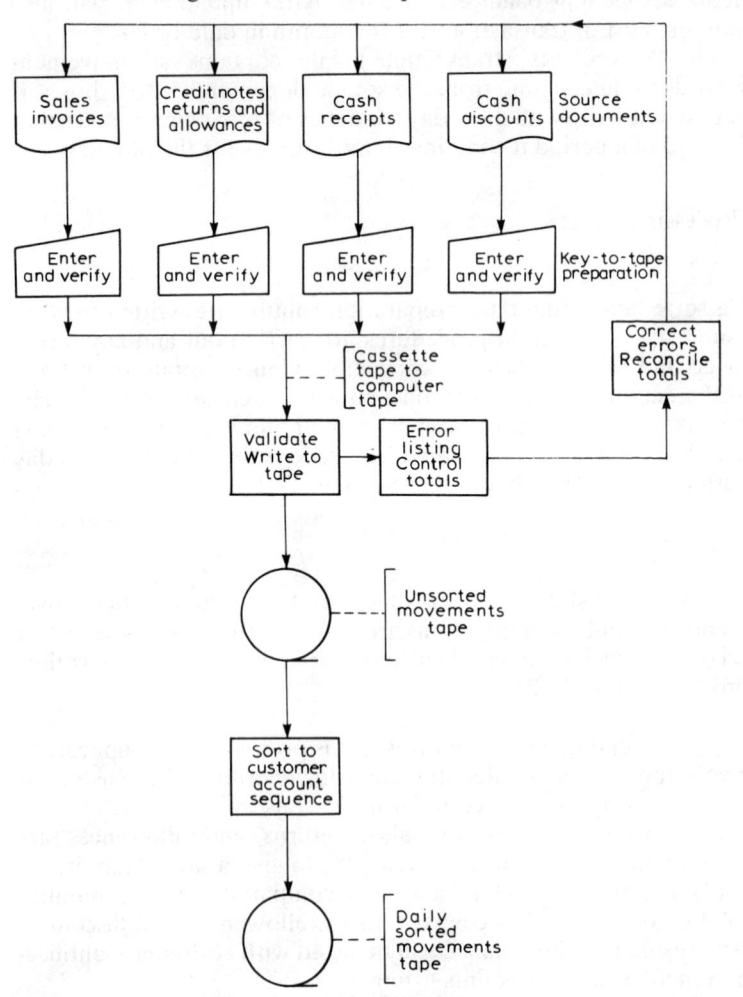

Fig. 17.1. Daily preparation of movements tape

would be present, including the receipt of stock purchased, stock returns, adjustments for stock shortages and price changes, etc.

We will assume the source document to be a hand-prepared stores requisition quoting: requisition number, data, the works order number of the job on which the materials are to be used, and for each item the stock code number, description and quantity. Each requisition could well contain a number of stock items for the

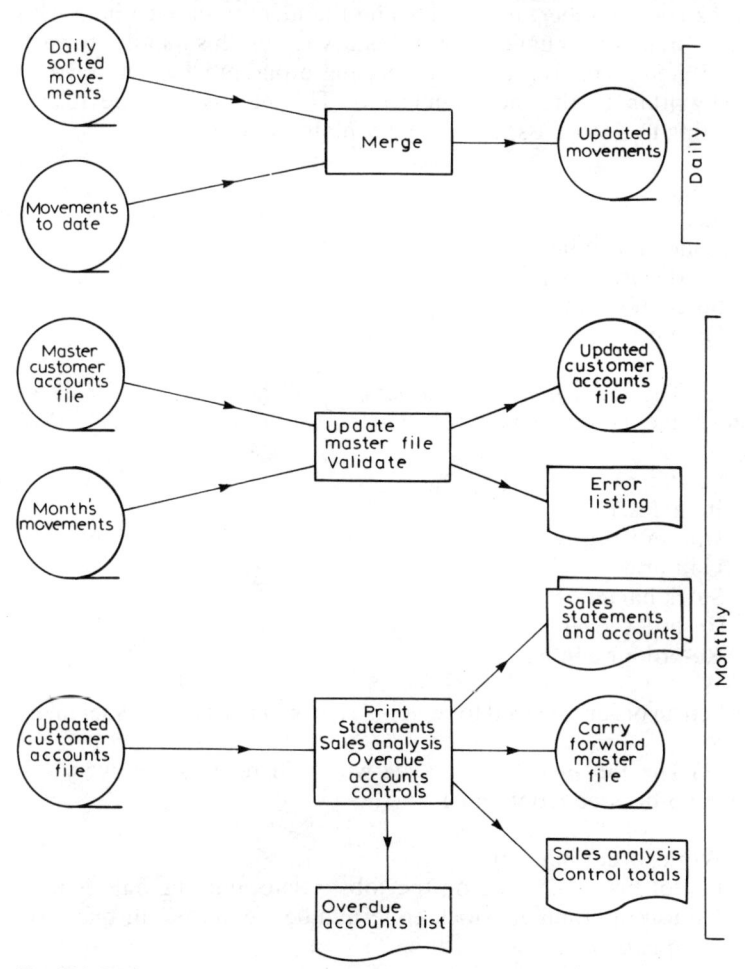

Fig. 17.2. Updating runs

same job but will not contain items for different jobs.

Requisitions are batched daily and forwarded to the DP department, where daily computer runs are made to provide these outputs: (a) list of stock items to be re-ordered; (b) schedule of materials used on each completed job. Files are held on magnetic disc as follows:

(1) The *movements file* holds daily movement items read in from the data preparation stage. Initially the records will be in no particular sequence. Since it will be necessary later to sort records by stock code number, to avoid losing the identity of each item with the works order number it is necessary to add this number to each stock item. This is done by an editing program when the records are written to the movements file. This means that the record relating to a stock issue will now contain these fields:

Date
Requistion number
Code indicating 'issue'
Works order number
Stock item code
Quantity

(2) The *stock inventory master file* will hold records for every stock line, containing fields for:

Stock item code
Item description
Unit of issue
Unit price
Stock balance
Re-order level
Re-order quantity

When an order is placed to replenish stock, a marker 'R' is set in the record.

(3) The *job materials cost file* will hold records for every job being processed, containing:

Works order number
List of materials used on the job to date, quoting date issued, requisition number, stock code number, description, quantity, unit price and value

It is proposed to examine the routines involved in having the data records organized sequentially on the disc. From many points of view, processing in this mode is very similar to magnetic tape file processing. Master records are held on disc in key sequence order in a continuous set of addresses and, before an updating run, movement records must be sorted into the same sequence. From the point of view of the mechanics of storage, this means that there

Stock inventory and job materials costing 235

are two alternatives: (1) completely rewriting the file during updating to a completely separate disc or file area and (2) updating records and writing them back to the original disc file area. As we saw in Chapter 9, this latter method will probably involve the use of overflow areas to accommodate records that have expanded and outgrown their original location. The hit rate will probably determine whether (1) or (2) above is used, with (1) being more suitable in a high hit rate situation and (2) in a low. Figs. 17.3 and 17.4 illustrate these two approaches.

The following routines will be carried out:

(1) Data records from the source documents are prepared for machine entry—this may be by punched card, key-to-tape, key-to-disc, etc. (methods that have already been considered in detail in Chapter 7)—and written in random order to disc D1, with the works order number edited into each record. At this stage also,

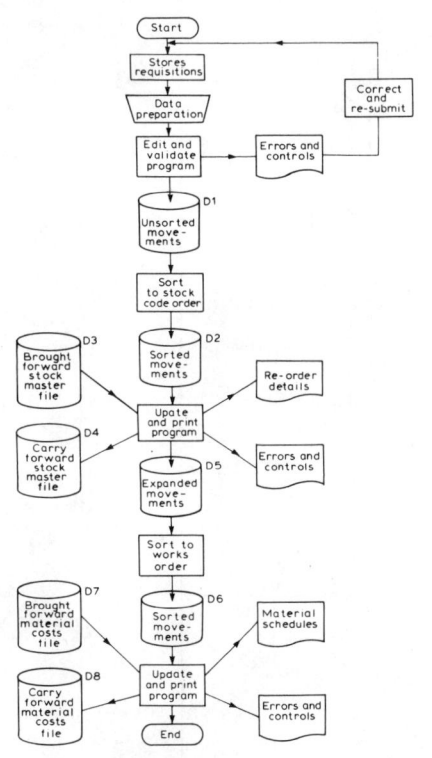

Fig. 17.3. Sequential disc records: rewriting file during updating

validation procedures will be carried out, errors referred back for correction and any control totals reconciled.

(2) Movement records are now sorted into stock code sequence and written to D2.

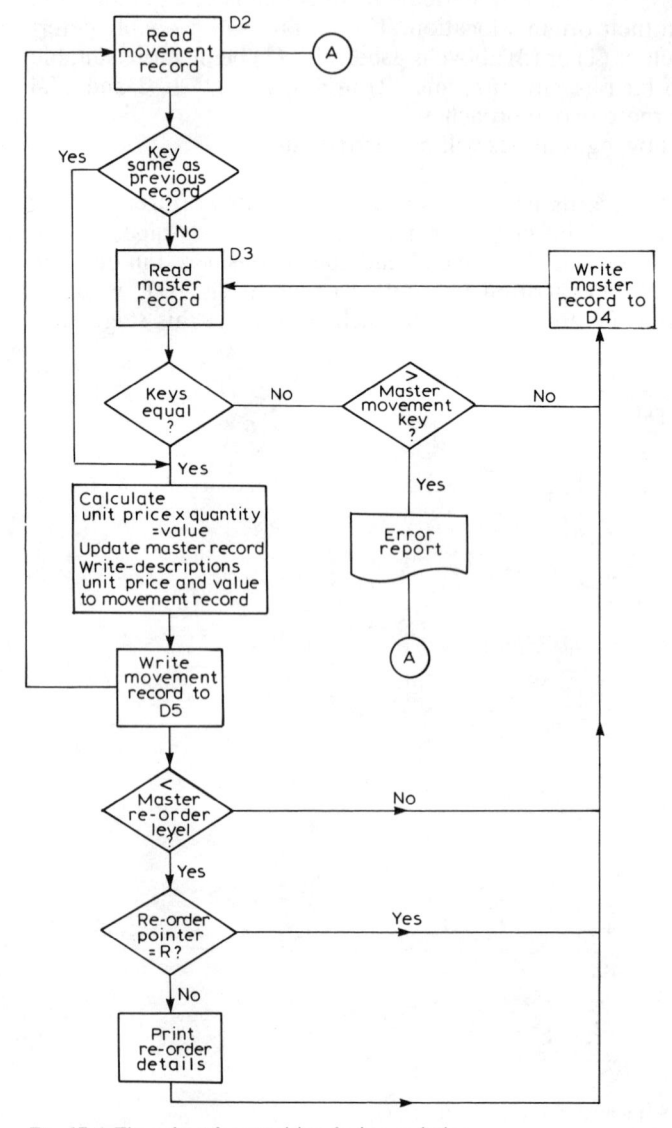

Fig. 17.4. Flow chart for rewriting during updating

Stock inventory and job materials costing 237

(3) This is a run to update the stock master file (D3), writing a new updated version to D4 and printing out the re-order list (see Fig. 17.5). Additional details will be written from the stock master file to the movements file, giving an expanded movements file D5.

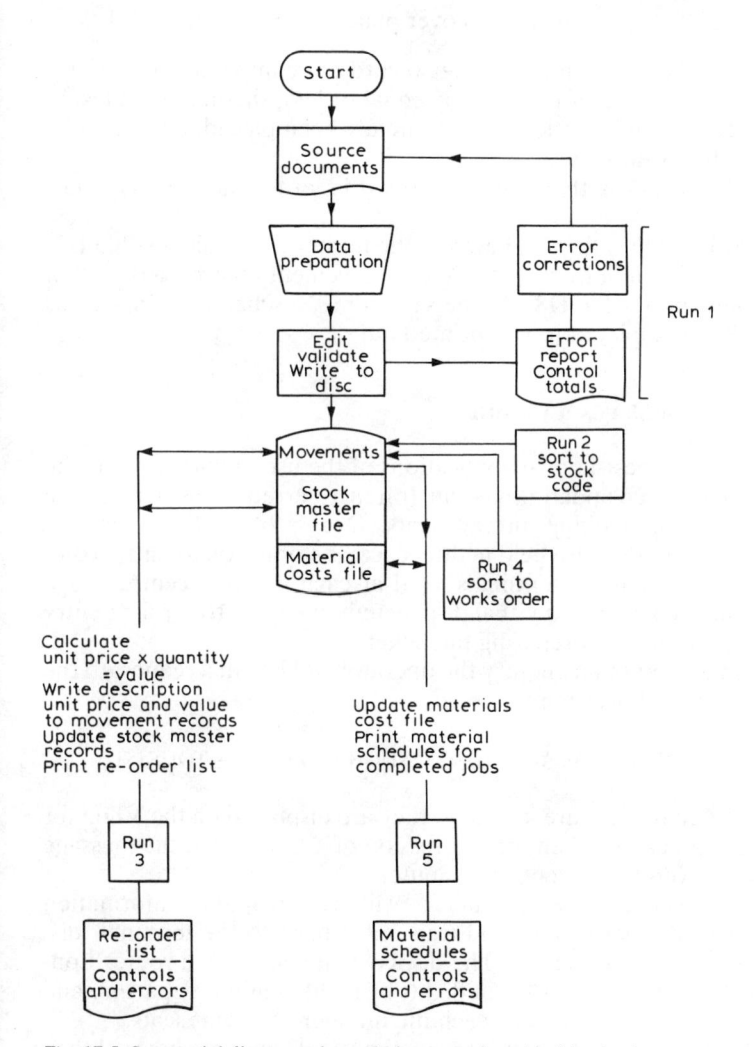

Fig. 17.5. Sequential disc records: updating records and writing back to original file

Examples

                Original Movement Record
 Works order number   Stock item code   Quantity
        2345   6789   18

                Expanded Movement Record
 Works order Stock item Description Quantity Unit   Value
   number   code   price
    2345   6789   cover plate   18   £4.50   £81.00

Revised balances in the master record are compared with the re-order levels and, if found to be equal or less, the marker is tested for 'R', and if an order has not already been placed, a request for re-order printed out.

(4) File D5 is then sorted into works order number sequence D6.

(5) File D6 is then run against the master materials cost file D7, records updated by the addition of movement records and written to new master file D8. At the same time, a schedule of materials used on completed jobs is printed out.

Airline seat reservation

One of the best-known applications of the use of computers is the on-line direct updating system (often referred to as a real-time system) for booking aircraft seats. Details of all flights and all bookings to date are held in direct access storage on a central computer with on-line terminals sited at each booking centre. Each terminal consists of a visual display unit, a keyboard for data entry and a printer for preparing the ticket.

On receipt of an enquiry the operator will key in a request to the computer—for example,

    DISPLAY ALL VACANCIES   LONDON—OTTAWA—TOURIST 31.3.83

As the characters are keyed in, they are displayed on the VDU for visual check and then, on depression of a 'send' key, the message is conveyed to the central computer.

In response the computer will retrieve the information requested from its files and transmit it back to the terminal, displaying it on the screen. The display will confirm the route, London to Ottawa, give a list of flights by flight number, departure and arrival times, and against each the number of vacant seats.

On receipt of a firm order from the client, the operator will then key in a request to book a seat on the appropriate flight number and in response the computer will display a request for details of the client (name and address), whether a return booking is required, how payment is to be made, etc. On receipt of this information from the operator, the computer will then display a confirmation of the booking (flight number, name and address), the amount to be paid and the ticket reference number. Meanwhile the printer will have produced a hard copy of this information—the ticket—which is handed over to the client on payment.

It then remains for the computer to immediately update its own records, reducing by one the number of available seats recorded on its file and also recording the customer's personal details.

Word processing

Whereas data processing seeks to organize and process raw data into meaningful information, word processing seeks to organize textual matter into meaningful typewritten letters, documents and reports. It seeks, in effect, to automate the typewriting function in a more efficient and cost-effective way. There is today a vast selection of word processing equipment on the market, and the following comments can, at best, be of a general nature only.

The essential features of manual typewriting must be present in a word processing system:

Transcription
Error correction
Editing
Copying
Final production of the typed copy

The main additional features of a word processing system are its capacity to store and retrieve text on demand and its capacity to carry out repetitive routines automatically under program control.

Basically, a word processor consists of:

A microcomputer
A keyboard
A visual display unit
A printer
Storage devices—usually floppy discs
Program and control software

Text is initially entered manually through the keyboard, when it is displayed on a VDU for visual scrutiny. Errors may be corrected simply by overtyping, and words and phrases may be moved around or amended for editing purposes. On completion of a block of text, letter, report, etc., it can be automatically typed back and/or transferred to storage for future use and held there permanently until deliberately erased.

One way in which word processors come into their own is in personalizing standard letters which would otherwise be printed or duplicated in mass. A collection of standard paragraphs and phrases, each with its own unique reference key, can be held in store. On communicating to the machine a series of keys to identify the component parts of the letter, they are recalled from storage and the letter is automatically typed. Where appropriate, gaps can be left in recorded standard paragraphs for the manual insertion of variable data. The machine will automatically stop when these insertions are required.

The automatic typing speed is much faster than is the case with conventional typing, being up to about 900 words a minute, compared with a theoretical maximum manual typing speed of around 70 words per minute, although, in practice, error correction, paper insertion, etc., will reduce this manual speed to, effectively, only about 15–20 words per minute. The word processor not only is very much faster, but also eliminates this need to make corrections, to keep feeding paper into the machine and to counter the demands of fatigue and interruptions.

One other very useful function of a word processor is in the production of high-quality text. Reports of this nature usually require a lot of editing, revision and retyping before a word-perfect version is finally produced. The display of text visually, the ease of error correction and the text amendment and rearrangement facilities obviate the need to type a number of hard copy drafts and amended drafts. Recent developments include the networking of word processors so that they can intercommunicate with one another. Text can be automatically transferred from one station to another and facilities are also provided for editing at one station text that has been machine entered at another.

All in all, a word processor offers:

(1) Output of higher quality.
(2) Increased output speed.
(3) Output of higher volume in a given period of time.
(4) Lower unit cost (that is, per letter).
(5) Once only compilation of standard paragraphs, saving dictation time.

(6) Automatic hard copy transfer to remote points.
(7) Personalization of otherwise standard letters and documents.

Point of sales recording

Traditionally the recording of sales in retail outlets has been through the medium of cash registers serving a number of purposes but also having a number of limitations:

(1) The price of an article is read manually—a source of error.
(2) The price is entered through a manual keyboard—also a source of error.
(3) A printed tally roll is produced for handing to the customer as a receipt.
(4) A very limited degree of product analysis is achieved by entering the product group code through the keyboard.
(5) A copy of the tally roll with product group code entered is used for sales analysis purposes, or registers inside the machine accumulate totals under product group codes.
(6) Tally roll totals are used to reconcile cash takings and also to reconcile total stock balances on stocktaking.

The use of computers in point of sales recording has simplified much of this procedure and also reduced the probability of errors. One method is the use of OCR on tally rolls. This means that the data can be automatically read into a computer through an optical reader for subsequent processing, although this technique does not reduce the problems associated with sight reading and manual keyboard entry. Further developments lead to the cash register becoming a terminal of the computer, either on-line, in which case data items from the register are transferred direct to the computer, or off-line, when the data items are recorded on magnetic tape inside the register for subsequent computer entry.

The advent of microprocessors has led to the development of techniques which overcome some of the problems of keyboard entry and provide a medium for more detailed product analysis and more effective stock control. This is achieved by printing on each article a product code, known as a *bar code*, which can be read automatically by a scanner pen. The code consists of an array of lines of varying thickness and spacing representing the numeric code identifying the product (an example of a bar code is shown in Chapter 7). It is scanned by a hand-held optical wand which senses the pattern of alternating black lines and their intervening white spaces, passing the data to a microcomputer in binary coding. Product prices are held in the computer in read-only memory units, from where the relevant price can be retrieved and passed back to the cash register for printout. Accuracy checks are performed through a validation program held in the microcomputer and by check digit verification—the last digit of the code being a check digit. A translation of the coding in ordinary readable characters (an OCR fount) is printed along the base of the bar code.

Bar coding eliminates the need to price every item: the price need only be indicated once on a label attached to the shelf containing the product. If the bar coding is also printed on this label, stocktaking and re-ordering procedures can be simplified. A portable data entry device is carried around the store, the product identification is recorded by passing an optical wand over the label, and stock levels and re-order details are entered through a keyboard. This portable device may be on-line to the computer through a series of 'plug-in' points scattered around the store or may be self-contained, recording the data on magnetic tape cassette for subsequent computer entry.

Non-commercial computer applications

Today the range of activities in which computers play their part in capturing and processing data has been very much extended by the widespread use of microcomputers, and the list is now virtually endless. Some examples of these applications are briefly described below.

Traffic control

The computer has enabled traffic control systems to be developed through the medium of traffic lights that are volume related rather than time related. Instead of having fixed intervals between traffic light changes, monitoring devices set in the road at the approach to traffic signals monitor vehicle flow and transmit this information back to a computer in which control data have been stored in relation to each control point. Traffic signals can then, by computer control, be operated to provide optimum vehicle flow.

Aviation

Both for individual aircraft and for the flow of air traffic generally, computers have been of material use in enhancing the safety of air travel. The development of microcomputers and their installation in aircraft have provided a medium for the continuous monitoring of flying conditions and mechanical performance, and the facility to relate these two factors. This provides the aircraft crew with the information needed for navigational purposes, gives warning of malfunction, and indicates and sometimes initiates corrective action. The very rapid increase in air travel over the past few years has led to the use of computers to process data relating to aircraft movements in order to compute flight paths, take-off and landing schedules, etc., to maximize safety and reliability.

Medicine

Computers are used in a data processing mode for patient and clinical records, and microcomputers are increasingly finding a place in the practice of medicine itself. Scanning devices linked on-line to the computer can be attached to the patient to monitor medical conditions. Any change in condition demanding treatment can be immediately signalled.

Process control

As the name implies, process control involves the use of computers to control actual production and industrial processes. It is an area that lends itself to real-time computer processing. In a continuous production flow situation, data relating to the process must be assessed by the computer and the conclusions it draws fed back in time to modify, if necessary, factors controlling the flow.

One example of this is in the production of paper, where strict control must be exercised over its thickness as it comes off the mill in one continuous length. An on-line monitoring device will constantly measure the thickness, transmitting this information back to the computer. Should the thickness stray outside predetermined tolerances, the computer will immediately flash a message back to the machine, triggering off the action to correct the fault.

Computer in education

A great deal of attention has been paid over the past few years to the use of computers in the learning process. The advent of microcomputers has brought this within the range of most schools and colleges, involving, as it does, comparatively small capital cost. Microcomputers also have the advantage that they are small enough to be portable and so can be used in any learning or teaching situation.

A microcomputer can be used purely as a teaching aid by getting it to drive a large VDU for classroom display, or, what is more often the case, used by individual students as a learning aid—computer assisted learning (CAL). Programs are available covering a wide range of subject matter—languages, maths, sciences, etc. Microcomputers are used in a range of different learning modes:

(1) By presenting the user with a series of tests or problems, the answers to which are keyboard entered by the user with the computer, then evaluating the responses. The sequence of tests can be modified by the responses so that weak areas can be reinforced by further practice.

(2) In a tutorial mode—that is, presenting the student with pages of text on a given subject and then checking to see whether it has been understood, by asking a series of questions. If the answers given are wrong, the program will redirect back to the relevant section of text for a further attempt or call up a different presentation that will help to understand it.

(3) By simulation—that is, making models of a situation on which students can experiment by plotting in variables and assessing the results.

Exercises

17.1. You are concerned with introducing computer data processing systems in the following three situations: (1) the sales ledger system of a small company with some 500 credit customers; (2) the sales ledger system of a large firm with some 3000 credit customers; (3) a holiday booking system from a number of scattered agent's offices. Suggest: (a) the hardware you would recommend to operate each system, mentioning in each case the type of data storage you would use; (b) the way in which data could be entered into the system and how, in each case, information would be retrieved from the system.

17.2. In any computer data processing system the following four functions will be present: (1) the capture or recording of data relating to an event as it occurs; (2) the conversion of these data into a machine acceptable form; (3) the processing of the data; (4) the output of information in the form of usable reports. Describe how these four functions might be carried out in a stock control system.

17.3. Your company deals in spares for domestic appliances, holding stocks of some 8000 different items in store. Sales are made for cash over the counter or on credit from orders received through the post or over the telephone. The system to control the receipts and sales of stock demands the following factors:

(1) The stock level of any item must be available at very short notice so as to inform personal and telephone customers.

(2) The cost of any stock item must be similiarly available.

(3) A receipt must be prepared for cash customers and invoices for post and telephone customers.

(4) A list of stock items needing replenishment must be available to the stores buyer daily.

Outline a computer system that will meet the above requirements, mentioning specifically in your answer: (a) the computer hardware you would use; (b) the contents of the data records you would hold in storage; (c) the documents necessary to operate the system.

17.4. In a sales ledger system a customer's personal account appears as follows:

Date		Ref	Dr	Cr	Balance
1.11.82	Balance b/f				250.00
7.11.82	Sales	1234	125.00		375.00
14.11.82	Cash	789		237.50	
	Disc. allowed	789		12.50	125.00
21.11.82	Sales	1298	160.00		285.00
24.11.82	Returns	2761		50.00	235.00

Assuming your sales ledger is computerized:

(1) Identify the source documents from which you will make the above postings.

(2) Describe a method by which these data could be entered into a computer.

(3) Suggest a suitable computer storage medium on which this account could be held and updated as and when transactions occur.

(4) How would you ensure that each posting finds its way to the correct personal account within your sales ledger?

(5) Suggest the reports and information you would expect the computer to supply you with on completion of the month's postings to the sales ledger.

17.5. Issues from your factory stores are made on receipt of handwritten requisitions listing quantity, part number and description of the material required and also quoting the works order number of the job on which the material is to be used. Your stores ledger is held on a computer and updated once a week in a batch processing mode. Computer files are held on magnetic tape. You are required to:

(1) Outline the controls you think are necessary to ensure that all items on all requisitions are processed.

(2) Describe a data preparation routine that would enable the stores issues to be read into a computer.

(3) Outline computer runs that would: (a) update your stores ledger; (b) give a summary of material costs for the week under works order numbers for costing purposes; (c) produce a list of materials to be re-ordered from your suppliers.

17.6. Your company is engaged in manufacturing, and purchases its raw materials and parts from suppliers on a monthly credit basis. Trading with one of your suppliers during the month of May included the purchase of goods on 7 May, of which some were subsequently returned on 14 May. Cash settlement, less cash discount received, was made on 30 May to clear the balance outstanding on 1 May. You are required to:

(1) Identify the source documents from which you will obtain the data to make the above postings to your purchase ledger.

(2) Give an account of the stages involved in posting the data relating to purchases from the source documents to your supplier accounts.

(3) Make a list of the items of information you would expect to find on a supplier's master file record in your purchase ledger file on completion of the above postings.

(4) Suggest any control information you would expect from your purchases ledger at the end of a month's trading.

Index

Absolute address, 180, 185, 186
Accounting machines, 44, 133
Accumulator, 136
Accuracy controls, 175–180
Acoustic coupler, 145
Acoustic input, 88
Acoustic output, 99
Action rules, 172
Address, absolute, 180, 185, 186
Address, CPU, 107, 134, 135
Address, instruction format, 133
Air-line seat reservation, 238
Algol, 189
Analogue computer, 51
Ancillary output machines, 95, 96
Analysing data, 10
Application package, 192
Application program, 192–194
Applications
   aviation, 242
   education, 243
   job costing, 232
   medicine, 243
   point of sales, 241
   process control, 243
   sales ledger, 230
   stock inventory, 232
   traffic control, 242
Arithmetic and logic unit, 110, 134, 135
Assembler program, 186–188, 207
Assembly language, 186
Audit, systems, 157, 158

Backing storage, 54, 61, 111–130
Badges, 83
Band printer, 92
Bar coding, 23, 83
Barrel printer, 92
BASIC, 191
Batch processing, 140–142, 182, 219
   advantages, 141
   controls, 141, 176, 182
   control slip, 141
   disadvantages, 142
Baud, 144
Binary, 52, 64–69
   alphabetic characters, 71
   arithmetic, 64–68
   coded decimal, 68, 108, 109
   coded hexadecimal, 71
   coded octal, 70
   complementation, 68
Bit, 101, 106, 107
Block chart, 163
Block code, 20
Blocking, 123, 124
Block, magnetic disc, 120, 123
Block, magnetic tape, 114, 115
Branch, conditional, 200
Branch, unconditional, 201
Bucket, magnetic disc, 122
Bureaux, computer, 225–228
Burster, 95
Byte, 108, 109

Calculators, electronic, 46
Card punch, 76
Central processor
   ALU, 110, 134
   capacities, 109
   control function, 110
   data storage, 110
   operating system, 110
   with peripherals, 138
   program storage, 110
   storage, 101–109
   working diagram, 136, 137
Chain printer, 92
Changeover procedures, 170
Changes file, 17
Check digit verification, 176
Checks and controls, 175–180
Chip, silicon, 59
COBOL, 190

Index

Codes, 19–22
  block, 20
  non-significant, 20
  significant, 21
Coding principles, 19
Collating, 10
Communicating data, 11
Communications software, 197
Comparing, 10
Compiler program, 189, 207
Computer
  ALU, 110, 134
  analogue, 51
  backing storage, 54, 55, 111–130
  basic elements, 53
  configuration, 55
  control, 110, 134
  central processor, 53–55, 101–111, 136, 137
  digital, 52, 63
  hardware, 56
  input, 55, 60, 73
  instruction, 132
  interface, 56
  languages, 185, 193–197
  mainframe, 57
  memory, 56, 59, 60
  micro, 57, 59, 60, 61
  mini, 56, 58
  output, 55–60, 91–100
  peripherals, 55, 136, 138
  programs, 110, 132, 185–189
  software, 56
  storage, 101–131
  terminals, 86, 96
  word, 57, 106–108
Computer-assisted learning (CAL), 244
Computer bureaux, 225–229
  problems, 225
  services, 226
  trends, 226
Computer-oriented language, 188
Conditional jump, 200
Configuration, computer, 55
Control data, 19
Control function, CPU, 110
Controls, data processing, 175–180
Control slip, batch processing, 141
Cost table, 165
Count, program, 201
Cylinder, 123, 127

Daisy Wheel printer, 96

Data
  block, 114–115
  business and trading, 7
  capture, 22, 24, 31, 73
  changes, 17
  characteristics, 15–18
  control, 19–32
  conversion, 77, 132, 219
  descriptive, 16, 17
  dynamic, 17
  explanation, 4
  field, 16, 76, 104, 111
  file, 16, 25
  identification, 18–20
  input, 31, 73–90
  legislative, 8
  master file, 17, 111
  master record, 17
  movements file, 17, 111
  movements record, 17
  origination, 22
  output, 31
  personal, 7
  preparation, 23–24, 73
  quantitative, 17
  recording, 10, 23, 219
  recording and processing, example, 11–13
  record key, 19, 25
  retrieval, 11, 31, 41
  static, 16
  storage, 25, 31
  structure of, 15
  technical and scientific, 8
  types of, 9, 16–18
  updating, 11, 17, 18, 31, 118, 124, 233, 235–237
Data processing
  cycle, 6
  electronic, 13
  explanation, 5
  frequency, 40
  manual, 13, 23, 28, 43, 53, 175
  mechanical, 13
  objectives, 37–40
  operations, 10, 217–223
  reporting, 222
  resources, 35–37
  security, 222
  standards, 223, 224
  updating, 11, 17, 18, 31, 118, 124, 233, 235–237
Data processing department, 213–225
  basic functions, 217

Index

control section, 218
manager, 213, 214
operations, 217
operations manager, 218
organization, 214
programmer, 216
systems analyst, 215, 216
Data processing systems
analysis, 162, 213–215
audit, 157–159
considerations, 156–159
design, 165–169
development, 159
economics, 157
elements of, 31
environment, 27, 155
explanation, 5, 27
feasibility, 160
implementation, 170, 171
interface, 28
investigation, 160–162
objectives, 37, 38
operations, 30
procedures, 30
recording, 169
relationships, 27
resources, 35–37
response time, 155
social considerations, 158
specification, 166, 168, 169, 216
structure, 29, 30
sub-systems, 29
working environment, 224
Data records, 8–16, 104
Data security, 181–183
Data transmission, 144–146
Data vet, 180
Datel, 144
Debugging, 211
Decentralized processing, 149
Decision tables, 171–174
Decollator, 96
Descriptive data, 16, 17
Diagnostics, 207
Digital computer, 52
Digital increment plotter, 99
Direct access processing, 127, 128
Direct access storage, 119–130
Direct changeover, 171
Disc, magnetic, 61, 119–130
Distributed processing, 148, 150
Document description form, 165
Document flow chart, 165
Domesday Book, 7

Dry running, 207
Dumping, 182, 183
Duplex, 146

Economic considerations, 157
Education, use of computers in, 243
Electrographic printer, 97
Electrolytic printer, 97
Electronic calculators, 46
Electronic mail, 227
Electrostatic printer, 97
Errors, types of, 177
External storage, 111–130

Fact
analysis, 162–164
finding, 161
recording, 162–164
Feasibility, 41, 160, 161
Ferrite core store, 102
File
conversion, 170
design, 166, 167
maintenance, 11
master, 17, 111
movement, 17, 111
organization, 114–116, 123–128
reconstruction, 181
security, 181, 222
Filing, 11
Floppy disc, 61, 129
Flow charts, 163, 164, 182, 187, 202–210, 232–237
Form design, 168–169
FORTRAN, 189
Frame
punched paper tape, 77
magnetic tape, 113
Function code, 133

Graph plotter, 99
Guillotine, 95

Hardware, computer, 56
Header label, 116
Hexadecimal number system, 70
Hit rate, 125, 167

Immediate access store, 101, 105
Impact printers, 91–97
Implementation, systems, 170–171
Indexed sequential organization, 126–127

Information
  control, 38
  explanation, 6
  management, 7, 38, 39
  operating, 6, 38
Input devices, 73–89
Input/output control, 197
Input specification, 167–168
Instruction
  code, 133
  computer, 132, 133, 134
  execution, 135
  register, 135
Integrated circuits, 57
Inter-block gap, 114
Interface, 56

Job assembly, 220
Jump, program, 201

Keyboard input, 60
Key-to-disc, 85
Key, record, 19, 121, 124, 127
Key-to-tape, 84

Labels, magnetic tape, 116, 183
Languages, computer
  Algol, 189
  BASIC, 191
  COBOL, 190
  FORTRAN, 189
  high-level, 188–192
  low-level, 185–188
  main features, 188
  PL/1, 191
Line printers, 92, 93
Logical errors, 209
Logic instructions, 200
Logic, program, 205
Loop, 201

Machine-dependent language, 188
Machine-oriented language, 188
Macro instruction, 188
Magnetic discs, 119–130
  addressing, 120, 126, 127
  block, 120
  bucket, 122
  characteristics, 119–121
  cylinder, 123
  direct access, 127
  exchangeable, 120, 121
  file organization, 123, 128
  floppy, 61, 129
  indexed sequential, 126
  organization of data, 121, 123
  overflow, 122, 124
  sector, 120
  self-indexing, 125
  tag, 122
  track, 120
  tracking arm, 121
  Winchester, 61, 129
Magnetic ink characters, 78–80
Magnetic ink encoding, 78
Magnetic tape, 112–119
  capacity, 113, 117
  cassettes, 61, 119
  characteristics, 112
  data block, 114, 115
  frame, 113
  inter-block gap, 114
  labels, 116
  markers, 115, 116
  operating speeds, 117
  organization of data, 114
  packing density, 113
  processing, 117–119
Mail handling machine, 96
Mainframe computer, 57
Management information, 7, 38, 39
Marker, magnetic tape, 115, 116
Master data record, 17, 118, 141
Master file, 17, 234
Matching check, 181
Matching data, 11, 124
Matrix printer, 92, 97
Medicine, application, 243
Memory, computer
  RAM, 59, 60
  ROM, 59, 60
Menu, 151
Merging data, 10
Metal oxide semiconductor
   (MOSFET), 103, 104
Method standards, 223
Microcomputer, 57, 59, 60, 61
  input, 85
  processing, 149, 151
Microfiche, 98
Microfilm, 98
Micro instruction, 188
Minicomputer, 56, 58
Modem, 145
Modulus, 176
Movement data record, 17, 118, 141
Movements file, 17, 234
Multiplexor, 145
Multiprogramming, 142

Non-impact printers, 97–99

Index   251

Object program, 186
Octal number system, 69
Operand, 133, 135
Operating information, 6, 38, 39
Operating system, 110, 196, 197
Operation code, 133
Operations, computer, 133–137
Operations manager, 213–217
Operator/machine communication, 197
Optical characters, 80
Optical mark reading, 80, 81
Organization chart, 165
Output devices, 91–100
Output specification, 166
Overflow, magnetic disc, 122, 124

Packing, 108, 113
Parallel running, 170
Parity, 77, 109, 113, 178
Performance standards, 223
'Peripheral bound', 143
Peripherals, computer, 55, 136, 138
Pilot running, 171
PL/1, 191
Point of sales recording, 241
Printer
  band, 92
  barrel, 92, 93
  chain, 92
  Daisy Wheel, 61, 96
  electrographic, 97
  electrolytic, 97
  electrostatic, 97
  impact, 91–97
  line, 92–96
  matrix, 61, 97
  non-impact, 97–99
  serial, 96, 97
  Teletype, 61, 96
  xerographic, 97
Problem-oriented language, 188
Procedure narrative, 165
Procedure specification, 168
Process control, 243
Processing by computer, 132
Program, computer, 60, 185–198
  absolute address, 186
  assembling, 187
  branch instruction, 200
  compiling, 207
  count, 201
  debugging, 210
  development of, 201
  diagnostics, 207
  documentation, 210, 211
  dry running, 207
  elements of, 200–201
  encoding, 207
  flow charts, 202, 206
  instruction execution, 135
  interrupt, 144
  jumps, 201
  logic, 205, 207
  loop, 201
  macro instruction, 188
  micro instruction, 188
  straight line, 202
  structures, 201
  sub-routines, 194
  symbolic address, 186
  storage, 134
  syntax errors, 186
  table check, 207
  testing, 209, 210
Program management, 198
Programmer, 213, 216
Program register, 136
Programs
  application, 192
  application packages, 192
  assembler, 186
  assembly, 186
  communications, 197
  compiler, 189
  computer-oriented, 188
  machine, 188
  machine-dependent, 188
  object, 186
  operating system, 196
  problem-oriented, 188
  source, 186
  utility, 195
Program specification, 202
Punched card machines, 45
Punched card reader, 77
Punched cards, 45, 74
Punched paper tape, 77, 78
Punched tags, 82
Purge date, 181

Quantitative data, 17

Random access memory (RAM), 59, 110
Read only memory (ROM), 59, 111
Read and write checks, 116, 180, 183
Read and write memory (RAM), 59, 110
Real-time system, 147, 148
Rearranging, 11

Index

Record
  changes, 17
  data, 6–18, 104
  master, 17
  movement, 17
  types of, 8, 9
Recording data, 10, 23
Record key, 19, 121, 124, 127
Resources, data processing, 35, 36
Response time, 148
Retrieval, data, 11, 31–41

Search mode, 124
Sector, magnetic disc, 120
Security
  data, 181–183
  data processing, 222
  files, 116, 181, 222
Self-indexing, 125, 126
Semiconductor storage, 102–105, 110
Sequential processing, 117, 118, 124
Sequential storage, 118
Serial file organization, 123, 124
Serial storage, 111–119
Silicon chip, 59
Simplex transmission, 146
Simulation, 244
Social considerations, 158
Software, 56
Sorting, data, 10
Source document, 24
Source program, 186
Standards, data processing, 223, 224
Standards Manual, 224
Storage
  backing, 54, 61, 111–130
  back-up, 130
  central processor, 101–111
  computer, 101–131
  direct access, 119–130
  floppy disc, 129
  magnetic disc, 119–130
  magnetic tape, 112–119
  magnetic tape cassettes, 119
  sequential, 118
  serial, 111–119
  streamer tape, 130
  Winchester disc, 129
Sub-routines, 194
Symbolic address, 186
Syntax errors, 186, 209
Systems
  analysis, 162, 213–215
  analyst, 215, 216
  audit, 158
  block chart, 163
  considerations, 156
  design, 165–169
  development, 159
  environment, 155
  fact finding, 161
  feasibility, 160
  flow diagram, 164
  implementation, 170–171
  investigation, 160
  objectives, 37, 38
  recording, 169
  resources, 35, 36
  response time, 155
  specification, 166, 168, 169, 216

Table check, 207
Tag, magnetic disc, 122, 124
Tags, punched, 81
Teletype terminal, 86, 147
Terminals, computer, 86, 96
Time sharing, 146, 147, 227
Time slice, 146
Tracking arm, 121
Track, magnetic disc, 120
Traffic control, 242
Trailer label, 181
Transactions file, 17
Transmitting modes, 146
Turn-around-document, 82

Unconditional jump, 201
Updating, 11, 17, 18, 31, 118, 124, 233, 235–237
Utility program, 194, 195

Validation, 86, 141, 179, 182
Verification, 76, 83, 84, 178
Verifying data, 11
Visual display unit, 60, 61, 87, 99, 147
Voice input, 88

Winchester disc, 61, 129
Word, computer, 106, 107, 108, 134
Word processing, 239
Work scheduling, 143
Write permit ring, 183

Xerographic printer, 97

Zone/numeric code, 108